MAGIC MINERALS

Key to Better Health

Carlson Wade

ARC BOOKS, INC.
New York

DEDICATED TO MY MOTHER

who put health back into my life by super-charging my body and mind with a mineral-natural foods program.

This edition published by ARC BOOKS, Inc.
219 Park Avenue South, New York, N.Y. 10003
By arrangement with Parker Publishing Company, Inc.
Copyright © 1967, by Parker Publishing Company, Inc.
All Rights Reserved
Standard Book Number 668-02135-7
Printed in U.S.A.

A Medical Doctor's Foreword

This book realistically deals with one of the most important but generally little-known factors of healthful nutrition for persons of all ages. This factor is sufficient minerals of all types in the diet to help secure and maintain excellent health. You will learn in this book about the extremely vital role that minerals in your diet play regarding your physical health and appearance, as well as influencing your personality. Also, you will be well-informed as to the consequences of the lack of adequate minerals in your diet, how to recognize this lack, and what you can do to help yourself in taking corrective steps.

The science of nutrition today is firmly established as one of the chief branches of preventive medicine—building resistance to disease and breakdowns of body structures and organs. The function of minerals, even in minute, or "trace" quantities in the diet, wields a great influence in the conversion of foods you eat for your use and maximum benefit for your well-being, physically and mentally. If people would only avail themselves of the information and health programs that the author, Carlson Wade, has presented between the covers of this book, they could add years to their lives, and healthy life to their years. These healthful and vital years can be inserted into your life now with the help of adequate mineralization of your diet as set down in this book.

To attain and keep a good measure of excellent health requires study and application of such books as this one. I commend Carlson Wade's book for your use.

JONATHAN FORMAN, M.D.

What This Book Will Do for You

How often have you longed for just *one* "magic" food that would have the natural power to provide bountiful energy, relieve high blood pressure, stimulate hormonal power to give you a youthful zest as well as mind and body rejuvenation? You, along with countless others throughout the centuries, have come close to the discovery of such a "magic" food, yet may have passed right by it. For many years as a nutrition writer, I have searched for such a "magic" food and am happy to announce its discovery.

It is more than just one item. It is scores of items that we group together to call MINERALS. The health-building power of minerals is so astonishing, its successes continue to amaze me.

Speaking for myself, I can say that my personal ill health urged me to intensify my search for a special "magic" food. A victim of bronchial disorders such as hay fever, asthma, unusual dust-sensitivity, ever since early boyhood, that was just the start. I was a victim also of chronic tiredness (I used to fall asleep in classrooms), suffered premature aging to the point where my hair started to turn gray when I was about 18. Astonishing? But, it was true. Today, my hair is not completely gray because after I discovered "magic" minerals, I embarked upon a self-mineralization program that helped stem the process. Also, my bronchial disorders have been overcome and I'm now so super-charged with energy, I can happily work six or seven days a week and feel wonderful and anxious to start a new work-filled week!

If minerals could do such amazing things, what else could they do to help relieve more ailments? This started me on a research quest that resulted in the creation of this book. It is this book that takes you by the hand on a "treasure hunt" for minerals and shows you where to find these golden nuggets of health. What are some of the benefits? Consider the following sample cases:

1. A 33-year old secretary wins the arthritis battle. She was young, pretty and otherwise healthy. But her fingers became stiff and difficult to manage. To hold a pencil was painful. To take dictation was embarrassing. As for typing, it was sheer agony. She embarked upon a special mineralization program via special food supplements and natural foods (you'll find them described in this book) and was able to overcome a condition known as osteoporosis (fragile and porous skeletal structure), easing the ravages of the so-called inevitable arthritis. She continues on with her mineral-rich program and is astonished at its anti-arthritis powers.

2. "I'm so nervous, I could scream," lamented a 53-year old sales manager. His actions were upsetting everyone to the point where his job was in jeopardy. He was introduced to minerals and food sources (listed in this book) designed to stabilize rising

pressure and reduce hypertension. Did it work? He told me, "I'm so calm now, even the loudest screech doesn't bother me." You, too, may be able to enjoy a tension-free life with proper mineral intake.

3. When she was 65, this pretty senior citizen started forgetting things. She had memory lapses. Her words became fumbled. She would look off into space, her eyes and mind an apparent blank. She was said to be feeble, senile—an unpleasant and often feared condition. When she was given food supplements and certain fruits and vegetables (listed in this book) rich in specific minerals, she experienced a remarkable rejuvenation. Minerals have an anti-senility factor that may do away with premature aging, and help restore mental vigor to those who have memory lapses. It helped this woman so that she was able to return to the working world and became a receptionist at a large bank.

4. A lawyer, at the age of only 45, complained of prostate disorders. It was embarrassing nightly. It was uncomfortable during days in the courtroom. He found that certain types of foods (described in this book as based upon their use by experts) actually eased and eventually ended some of his prostate gland disorders! He told me, "There must be something 'magic' in those minerals if they could do that for me!"

Then there were the teen-agers bothered with acne, the pale-looking young mother, the perpetual "cold catchers" and those who have cold hands and cold feet. They were introduced to minerals and soon were rewarded with bountiful health and spirit.

This book is written for the young and adult. Youngsters who want to be the life of the party, who seek more of a natural energetic spirit, will benefit from the chapters on a healthy bloodstream, and how to improve personality. They will be overjoyed after taking the special "Cheer Tonic" and "Personality Punch" which are chock full of the "Magic" Minerals that put spark into their young, vibrant lives.

Adults, of course, will be grateful to know of the special minerals that combat wrinkles, gray hair; even falling hair may be controlled when certain minerals go to work. If you're constipated or troubled with headaches, you'll find that certain minerals may help you avoid laxatives and medicines. Return to Nature and return to health!

This book is unique because it explores the fascinating world of minerals for health and puts the spotlight on their youth-building powers. It provides you with endless easy-to-make beverages, mixtures, special blends and foods that are brimming with "magic" minerals for dynamic health.

CARLSON WADE

Contents

Adrenal glands • The mineral magic of goat's milk • Pancreas • An unusual mineral tonic for those insulin-poor • Parathyroids • Female ovaries • Male sex glands • Thymus • Diet can help make you a popular leader • Diet and glands • Personality and glands • Simple diet plan

Diet and longevity • Arteries and age • How cholesterol can affect your health • What minerals reduce cholesterol • Avocado — the miracle "youth" food • How avocados work with minerals • How to use avocados • How to buy avocados • Sauna bath magic • Think yourself young • "Security killed" executives • Nine-step anti-senility plan

Low blood sugar • Muscles need "MDA" action • Coffee breaks are anti-MDA • What is carob? • Grape juice energizer • Reasons for avoiding coffee • Personality defects for low blood sugar • Tensions due to low blood sugar • How to make a hot "MDA" drink • Your mineral rich energy diet

What is the brain? • How the brain rules the body • Mineral feeding your 15 million brain cells • Where to find phosphorus • Tension starves the brain • How to feed iron to your brain • Benefits of a mineral-rich breakfast • Three miracle brain foods • Lecithin • Kelp • Desiccated liver • Special brain tonic

Value of mineral-rich bloodstream • What is blood? • Power of white cells • Signs of mineral-poor blood health • Power of minerals in the blood • Mineral-deficient dangers • Avoid "fluff" foods • Sweets cause fatigue • What causes anemia? • Benefits of blackstrap molasses • Barbados molasses • Other mineral sources • Germinated wheat • 7 ways to build healthy mineral-rich blood • Your blood building diet

*He who has health has hope, and he who has hope has
everything.*

Ancient proverb

ONE

How Minerals
Can Improve Your
Health and Personality

You are about to discover a secret treasure!

This book is your road map. It will take you on a journey into a quest for the greatest treasure that awaits your discovery. Like most treasures, this one has been known about for many decades; it has been described and written about, yet has still remained undiscovered because few people know where and how to find this treasure. That is the prime purpose of this book — to describe the treasure in all its details, to show you where it exists, and then to tell you how you can obtain all the benefits of its discovery.

This treasure consists of minerals, those little known food elements that have the power to help rejuvenate your system, strengthen your nervous system, grow new hair, normalize your heart beat, give you a powerhouse of energy, improve your thinking power, overcome fatigue, and build a dynamic memory.

These same magic minerals have the ability to so supercharge your emotional system that you can become transformed into a brand new person! These magic minerals can, in a manner of speaking, replace a grouchy personality with a pleasant one, turn a frown into a smile, and a harsh word into a gentle one. They have the magic power of changing a lonely person into a popular leader. The magic minerals, when properly used, can possibly make you the business, social and financial success you have always dreamed about.

A fascinating thing about this secret treasure is that whenever someone discovers it, that person is actually swept on to success and power. The person who possesses this secret treasure will not part with it for anything in the world. Fortunately, there is enough of this treasure to supply every man, woman and child, and it is waiting for *you*.

As you read this book (your road map), the discovery will leap from the page. The lid of the treasure chest will spring open and the contents within will await your possession. When this happens, you will know that you have made the discovery that will change your health and entire personality. At this point, stop for a moment. Sit back, close your eyes, and smile. You have every good reason to feel joy and contentment. The discovery of this secret treasure will mark the most vital turning point of your life.

Please remember, too, as we start on this treasure hunt to discover the magic minerals, that this book deals with facts, not legends, or fiction. Its whole purpose is to convey a little known truth through which all who are sincere and hopeful may learn *what* to do to improve their health and personality, and exactly *how* to do it! All this is possible through the treasure of magic minerals.

What Are Minerals?

Often we hear considerably about vitamins, proteins, fats, amino acids, enzymes, calories, etc., but very little about minerals. Other types of nutrients have stolen the spotlight in the exciting quest for the treasure of health and personality improvement. Yet without minerals, without their mind and body building powers, all other nutrients would be useless!

Minerals, or trace elements as they are sometimes called because they exist in such tiny, yet powerful, amounts in the body, are needed for overall mental and physical functioning. They are important factors in maintaining proper physiological conditions and processes, such as the acid-base balance, osmotic action, elasticity, and soft tissues — muscles. Your skeletal structure's strength depends upon these magic minerals. The nerves must have them to be tranquil, strong, and vibrant. Digestion and healthful assimilation of foods depend upon adequate "mineralization" in your system. From 4 to 5 per cent of the body's weight is mineral matter. It is found in *all* tissues and fluids, but especially in the bones, teeth, and cartilage.

Minerals Help Keep You Young

There are close to 30 such minerals, all of which will help prevent premature aging by helping to preserve in youthful vigor your nerves, muscles, heart, hair, blood, brain, etc.

D. T. Quigley, M.D., in *The National Malnutrition,* declares,

> We do know that the person who has a sufficient intake of calcium, iron and iodine…(plus vitamins) will have a resistance against ordinary disease in excess of the average person. Such persons will have more freedom from fatigue and greater ability to work; will live with the retention of all physical faculties to a greater age, and will have a better mind than the person who suffers from some single or multiple vitamin or mineral deficiency. The various vitamins and minerals are ALL necessary. No one can be omitted if an individual would retain good health.

Recently, more official spokesmen including doctors, governmental authorities, and nutritionists are pointing to the magic power of minerals. Professor Kenneth J. Monty of Johns Hopkins University stated in *Food* (Yearbook of Agriculture):

> All living things contain a variety of minerals. Some occur in such small amounts that early chemical analyses could barely detect them. They, therefore, became known as the trace minerals, metals, or elements…At the present stage of our biological knowledge, however, we cannot ignore the possibility that some of the trace elements, we now think of as non-essential do have as yet unrecognized functions in the body's processes.
>
> People found out about the need for trace elements when they saw that some deficiency diseases in livestock, and sometimes in

human beings, could be treated by large doses of a specific mineral.

11 Magical Functions of Minerals in Your Body

There are endless ways in which minerals work in the body, but the prime magical functions that they perform are as follows:

1. Protein — the building blocks of your body — cannot be formed without the presence of calcium, nitrogen, and sulfur.

2. The entire digestive system relies upon the vagus nerve; this nerve cannot function properly without potassium.

3. Vitamins cannot work unless minerals are present. For example, vitamin B12, needed for a strong bloodflow, requires the presence of the cobalt mineral.

4. Minerals are needed to combine with some vitamins to remove internal gaseous waste products. It is known that victims of multiple sclerosis suffer from damage to the nerve covering, caused by an excess of a carbon-nitrogen substance. It is believed that prevention of this diseased condition or removal of the detrimental substance can be achieved if the body is properly fed with minerals, especially cobalt.

5. Since the insulin molecule contains zinc, and since diabetes results from an insulin shortage, there is the possibility that a deficiency of the zinc mineral may be involved with the ailment.

6. Minerals influence muscular contraction and also dominate the making of nerve response.

7. Minerals have the power to control body liquids and to permit other nutrients to pass into the bloodstream. Without minerals, these other nutrients cannot do their proper jobs.

8. Blood coagulation is controlled by a mineral action. This means that bruises, cuts, scratches, wounds, etc., must have minerals for the healing processes.

9. Your alertness, youthful zest, energy, and thought power, all require such minerals as manganese, copper, cobalt, iodine, zinc, magnesium and phosphorous for maximum efficiency.

10. Minerals in your bloodstream act to create a germ-killing action. Therefore, minerals have the power to help create antibiotics directly within your body's system, provided that other essential raw materials are present.

11. Minerals are essential for strong bones and teeth, which are about 95 per cent composed of calcium and phosphorous. There are close to eighteen other minerals involved, too, that act in combination with certain others for glorious health.

Small wonder that a prominent physician said that "nations or individuals, human or animal, we are what we *eat and assimilate into our body*. A properly fed, mineral-rich diet helps condition us to health and normal functioning of the body and mind. The healthier we are, it follows, the better we resist disease."

How Minerals Improve Your Health and Personality

Minerals have the unique power of maintaining a delicate internal water balance that is needed for all mental and physical processes. Minerals draw substances into and out of your cells. Minerals aid in keeping blood and tissue fluid from becoming either too acid or too alkaline. Minerals stimulate the hormonal secretion of glands and cause the nervous system to send commands, mentally communicated, to all parts of your body.

When minerals are ingested in combination with foods, they create what is known as an *ash* which then enters into the composition of every single body tissue and fluid — from your brain to your toe tips. Your body must have minerals to serve as detoxifying (purifying) agents by combining with the acid wastes from your cells. Minerals neutralize these wastes and prepare them for elimination. Otherwise, waste products decompose and make you sluggish, sleepy, ache, nervous, grouchy and an unpleasant person to live or work with.

Osmotic equilibrium

This term refers to the most dynamic power of minerals and here is how it works. Your blood and lymph are liquids in which solids are kept in solution. Your cells are always being bathed in lymph fluids. Your cells, too, are semi-fluid containing dissolved matter.

Now, if the lymph outside your cells contain as much dissolved solid as found within the cells, you run the risk of having your body's cells shrink and dissolve!

Conversely, if you have more dissolved solid inside your cells than dissolved solid outside, your cells may bloat up and burst! This condition turns a calm person into a nervous one; leads to short tempers, irritation, tension, and premature aging. A happy, healthy, and even-tempered person is one who has a balance of the internal fluids. How is this possible? *By minerals!*

Minerals go to work to equalize the amount of dissolved solids both inside and outside the cells. Therefore, internal and external pressures are equalized and the body cells remain normal. This is known as *osmotic equilibrium* — a condition of superb youthful health that must have adequate mineral supply.

Minerals and Personality

A mineral-rich person is a happy, successful person, radiating a personality so vibrant, different, and unusual that you instinctively admire him. But, exactly what is this substance known as personality?

The word personality is taken from the Latin: *persona* meaning "mask" and *sonus* meaning "sound." Originally, it referred to an outer covering such as a mask through which sounds were made. The mask is your entire outer covering of your body and the sounds are *you*. Psychologists define personality as *the group of emotional trends and behavior patterns that distinguishes a person.*

Since minerals strengthen your nerves, give you a keen mind, banish jitters, put a glow in your skin, a sparkle in your eyes, and produce a *look-and-feel-alive* reaction, you can see how they can create a new personality for you. As we progress in this treasure hunt, you will see how this can be done for yourself and others around you.

Minerals are the catalysts that make possible the function of enzymes; they form the structure on which the body is built. Supplied adequately, minerals make possible a healthy, strong body. When deficient in the diet, their absence may result in disturbances of a serious nature.

Many minerals of different types are needed by the human body to provide health and enjoyment of life. Minerals are certainly as important to us as vitamins, yet it is unexplainable why minerals are overlooked, neglected, and their value grossly underestimated. We cannot afford to take minerals for granted.

You may have heard it said that climate does much to improve one's personality. It is true that on a nice sunshiny day, you feel better. Yet, in a talk made by Dr. Harry Warren, Professor of Geology at the University of British Columbia, it was pointed out that minerals in soil and water can influence your personality and health far greater than climate! Also a mineral deficiency can lead to a retarded birth rate, goiter, anemia and poor digestion — even if there is a healthy climate and, assumedly, other proper nutrient nourishment.

The Government Warns of Effects of Mineral Deficiency

This talk about minerals is novel and quite startling. In fact, a realization of the importance of minerals in food *is so new that the textbooks on nutritional dietetics contain very little about it.* Nevertheless, it is something that concerns all of us, and the further we delve into it, the more startling it becomes.

So states a spokesman in a talk presented to the U.S. Congress in Washington, D.C.

Senate Document No. 264, the official publication, then continues on:

It is bad news to learn from our leading authorities that 99 per cent of the American people are deficient in these minerals, and that a marked deficiency in any one of the more important minerals actually results in disease. Any upset of the balance, any considerable lack of one or another element, however microscopic the body requirement may be, and we sicken, suffer, shorten our lives.

This discovery is one of the latest and most important contributions of science to the problem of human health.

The government publication then cites the work of Charles Northen, M.D., an Alabama physician, who went to live in Orlando, Florida. This doctor was the pioneer in the search for the secret treasures of magic minerals.

Dr. Northen is quoted as saying,

> Bear in mind that minerals are vital to human metabolism and
> health — and that no plant or animal can appropriate to itself
> any mineral which is not present in the soil upon which it feeds.
>
> We know that vitamins are complex chemical substances
> which are indispensable to nutrition, and that each of them is of
> importance for the normal function of some special structure in
> the body. Disorder and disease result from any vitamin
> deficiency.

Vitamins are useless without minerals

Dr. Northen adds, "It is not commonly realized, however, that
vitamins control the body's appropriation of minerals, and in the
absence of minerals they have no function to perform. Lacking
vitamins, the human system can make some use of minerals, *but
lacking minerals, vitamins are useless.*"

The official document tells of a test with animals in which a
diseased condition could be created or cured "by controlling only
the minerals in their food."

It tells of one test in which a group of mineral-deficient animals
were put inside a maze. They could not find their way out; were
confused and upset. Another group of mineral-rich animals were
put in the same maze and were able to get out quite easily.

Listen to these golden nuggets of wisdom in *Senate Document
No. 264:*

> The dispositions can be altered by mineral feeding. The
> animals can be made quarrelsome and belligerent; they can even
> be turned into cannibals and be made to devour each other.
>
> A cage full of normal animals will live in amity. Restrict their
> calcium, and they will become irritable and draw apart from one
> another. Then they will begin to fight. Restore their calcium
> balance and they will grow more friendly, and in time, they will
> begin to sleep in a pile as before.
>
> Many backward children are "stupid" merely because they are
> deficient in magnesium. We punish them for our failure to feed
> them properly. Certainly our physical well-being is more directly
> dependent upon the minerals we take into our systems than upon

calories, vitamins, or upon the precise proportions of starch, protein, or carbohydrates we consume.

Where to Find Minerals

As we go along, you will be told of food sources for each of the valuable minerals. As a little advance tip, here is a thumb-nail source list of the major minerals: milk, green vegetables, legumes, fresh fruits, fish, poultry, and meat, such as liver, heart, kidney, or other organs.

A little-known dynamic source of minerals is that of *dried fruit.* Before I tell you how a certain dried fruit completely changed the life of a glamorous film and TV personality, I want to refer to a classic statement made by Robert G. Jackson, M.D.:

> Dried fruits, when properly prepared, by simply evaporating the water from them by the rays of the sun, are natural foods. When they happen to be the sweet dried fruits, as raisins, dates, figs, prunes, they are truly wonderful foods. Like almost all natural foods, they are rich in minerals. Like all natural foods, they are also rich in vitalizing elements that the chemist cannot find.

Dr. Jackson then points out:

> In dried fruits there is not only an abundance of minerals, undisturbed by cooking other than as Nature cooks in her great solar oven, but there is also an abundance of potential energy in the plentiful supply of fruit sugar.
>
> The best dried fruits are those that are dried in the sun, since all such foods are vitalized by absorption of the radiant energy vibrations from the sun.

The Simple Fruit That Spelled Success for a Film Actress

To preserve her identity, she will be called Lillian. A lovely blonde young woman in her middle 20's, she was married and the mother of a pink-cheeked baby boy. She had achieved stardom in Hollywood and came to New York to act in a comedy series on television as the lead role of a family type situation. At first, everything went along smoothly. TV ratings were high; fan mail poured in; the sponsor was going to pick up Lillian's option at an increase in salary.

"Then it happened," she told me, as we sat opposite each other in her dressing room at the network studio. "The director, a wonderful person to work with, started complaining. He said that I wasn't putting forth my best efforts; he said that I looked tired and thin, not at all the picture of an American wife and mother."

"I'll admit," was my gentle comment, "That you *do* look a little under the weather. You have crow's feet beneath your eyes, dark shadows, and there's a feeling of tiredness that is 'felt' by the viewer of your performance."

She said that she was not always this way. "I watch my diet. I eat plenty of protein foods and lots of vitamin-rich vegetables and salads." She also took supplementation. "I just don't feel up to it. Imagine—an Academy Award nominee being floored by a simple TV series."

We had lunch during which I noticed she went heavy on protein foods—these included lean meats, egg souffle, green peas and soya bread. "Shouldn't this be doing the trick?" she asked.

I shook my head. "Not quite. *No* food element can work by itself. *You must have an overall balance.* I think you're suffering from a *mineral deficiency*. That's why you're nervous, jumpy, irritable — and you look it, too. Your fans are noticing it." It was known, backstage, that Lillian had developed a temper and was difficult to work with. "When you first came to New York, you were charming and lovely. Mineral deficiency may be causing this complete reversal of health and personality."

Lillian looked at me with tired eyes. "But I thought if I eat lots of vitamin and protein foods, I'll get my minerals."

I shook my head. "Not quite. Just as you take efforts to have special vitamin and protein rich foods, you should also take time to select mineral rich foods. Without minerals, your other nutrients can't do a good enough job."

Then I outlined a very simple program for Lillian. She was to continue on her diet plan of lean meats, lots of fresh fruits and raw vegetables, whole grain breads, but she was to add the following simple foods.

1. *Mid-morning, eat one ounce of Monukka raisins.* There are no other grapes like the giant Black Monukka Seedless Grapes — just as there are no other raisins as sweet, delicious, or rich in precious minerals as these raisins. They are different; made from the Black Monukka Grape which originated in Pakistan, India, near the Russian border around 500 A.D. For five centuries, a special wine was made from this grape to be used in religious services and weddings of the Greek Orthodox Church. The Monukka is treasured because there are no other grapes like it in the whole world.

In the 1930's, the Monukka Grape Vines were brought to California from India. They were planted here because the mountains send down mineral-rich waters which feed the roots and vines. Sunshine and air further add more minerals. From these grapes, the precious mineral-rich Monukka raisins are prepared. It means that farmers have to wait for a few weeks of hot and rainless weather for the grapes to dry in the sun. (Remember Dr. Jackson's plea for sun-dried fruits as mineral treasures a few pages back?)

These sun-dried Monukka raisins are rich in *potassium* which influences muscular contraction and also glycogen deposition which is a form of energy metabolism. Potassium in these Monukka raisins works to send oxygen to your brain and give you a wonderful memory and "thinking power."

Monukka raisins contain sulfur, the "youth" mineral that nourishes the hair, improves complexion, puts a sparkle in your eyes. Also, the famed Monukka raisins are rich in calcium for heart normalization, strengthening of the nervous system and calming of the entire mental processes. Monukka raisins also have blood-building iron as well as the valuable vitamins A, B-complex, and C which you need for skin and nerve health, among other things.

2. The second mineral tip to Lillian was to prepare a beverage known as "clabbered milk." Here is how she was told to make it. Put one teaspoon of sour cream to each glass of freshly made soya milk. Mix well, pour in separate glasses, and let stand in a warm place for 24 hours. Mix once again during this time. Do not cover

glasses tightly. When milk has thickened, place in refrigerator, and keep there until ready to use.

Lillian was told to eat four glasses of this "clabbered milk" throughout the day. This milk is a powerhouse of mineral energy because the soybean is one of our most treasured sources of calcium, phosphorus, as well as iron. These three minerals are dynamic in building nerve, muscle, skin, and brain power, not to mention a healthy bloodstream. Soya milk, prepared in the "clabbered" form, will provide a complete mental and physical rejuvenation, that a new personality can be thusly created.

After three weeks of this Monukka raisin and "clabbered milk" plan, in addition to a balanced meal plan consisting of a variety of meats, seafood, fresh fruits and vegetables, whole grain products, Lillian had changed so much for the better that everyone begged her for the secret.

"It comes from within — from Nature," was her reply as the two of us winked at each other during a special backstage party celebrating renewal of her contract at a double increase in salary. Lillian *had* changed. Gone were her wrinkles, straggly hair, insomnia, nervousness, and grouchy disposition because of which three makeup artists had quit.

What or who deserves credit for this miraculous change? In a word — *Minerals!*

You, too, can avail yourself of the wonderful power of health in both Monukka raisins and "clabbered milk" made with soya powder. Most special diet shops and, especially, health food stores will sell you these mineral-rich items. Some stores stock canned soya milk, ready to use. Others have a powder which you mix with water and make your own. It depends upon your own individual preference.

Are You Really Healthy?

Health is a word taken from the Anglo-Saxon *haelth,* meaning "whole." Can you say you are healthy as a whole? Just what is good health? According to H. Curtis Wood, Jr., M.D., author of *Overfed But Undernourished:*

Health has been defined as the absence of disease or the freedom from bodily pain. Many people are willing to accept such a limited and negative definition, and think they are healthy if they manage to stay out of hospital beds and can get along without the services of a physician.

Such individuals do not consider themselves sick, but they admit that they do suffer now and then from a bit of sinusitis, bursitis, neuritis, arthritis, indigestion, constipation, flutterings of the heart, high blood pressure, athlete's foot, fatigue, anemia, obesity, skin disorders, baldness, colds, decayed teeth, poor eyesight, assorted allergies, brittle fingernails, nervousness, and even occasional mental depressions! So many of us may not be really sick; but how many are every really well, in the full sense of the word, exuding physical well-being like a small, energetic child or a boisterous puppy?

Most people just accept many of these conditions as the inevitable accompaniment of old age and comfort themselves with the thought that if things get too bad, a few shots of some new miracle drug will take care of the situation. So we continue to overeat, oversmoke, overdrink, get insufficient rest and exercise and try not to worry too much about the future.

This is not a happy way to live. If you can honestly admit that you have just *one* of these ailments, then you must face the facts that you do not have the picture of complete mental and physical health.

Warning Signs of Mineral Deficiencies

Because minerals so dominate the picture of health, the early warning signs are frequently unnoticed. But mineral deficiency can be serious if neglected. Writing in the *Handbook of Nutrition,* James S. McLester, M.D., tells us:

Scrutiny of the life histories of patients and *studies of their personality* have shown that the earliest effects of nutritive deficiencies are *not* to be found in the polyneuritis or beri-beri or in the bleeding gums of scurvy or in the dermatitis of pellagra, but rather in the mental depression, nervous instability and other forms of *vague ill health* which almost always come first!

Indeed, the severer, more outspoken manifestations, may remain indefinitely in abeyance; the patient is simply called a neurasthenic, or such terms as inadequate personality and constitutional inferiority are applied. After watching these patients, one is impressed by the truth of the statement that no greater catastrophe comes to man than the loss of efficiency, the lack of initiative and the mental depression which accompany nutritive failure!

Can you recognize yourself in the above mineral-deficient pi ture? Efficiency is slumping. You lost your urge for initiative. Y shuffle around. Yes, you may be getting things done but yo attitude is, "I want to get them done with." Instead, you shou tackle a task with vim, vigor, pep and youthful zest.

Another doctor who refers to nutrition and personality health Herbert Lawrence, M.D., in *Life and Health:*

Chronic substandard nutrition leaves the body unable to cope with the stress and strain of everyday activities and their physical and emotional energy requirements. Fatigue, unrecognized or unheeded, is often a consequence of this inadequate diet; and emotional tension, although not the direct result, certainly may be aggravated thereby.

An exciting example of the magical power of minerals presented by Drs. Pottenger, Allison and Albrecht in *Report* medical periodical issued by the Merck Corp.):

Such varied symptoms (in human patients) were initially present as to be too baffling for accurate diagnoses. Yet they disappeared after consumption of *trace element minerals* and carefully regulated, high-protein, low sugar diets during some 12 weeks or more.

Relief occurred from this vast array of symptoms, which included aches of the back, shoulders and joints, allergies, arthritis, anorexia, hyperhidrosis, fever, constipation, enlarged spleen, mental depression and others amounting to a list reportedly as large as 200.

So we can see that as many as 200 different types of ailments, physical and mental, were relieved by the magical power of minerals.

Now do you see how important it is for you to discover the treasure of minerals? It can save your life and health. These golden nuggets may be invisible but they are indispensable. But let us continue on our treasure hunt.

CHAPTER ONE SUMMARIZED

1. Minerals are nutrients which have the power to influence your mind and your body. Nearly all bodily processes depend upon the action of minerals.

2. Minerals maintain "osmotic equilibrium," that internal water balance that enables your muscles and nerves to contract, your blood to coagulate, your wounds to heal, and also helps keep you alert and youthful.

3. Some minerals can make you happy, cheerful, ambitious, energetic and a dynamic thinker. Minerals can so change you that you can actually change the whole world, let alone your own environment, by their internal magic power.

4. An alarming 99 per cent of our American people are mineral-poor and this may account for the high rising rate of mental and physical illness.

5. All other nutrients such as vitamins, proteins, enzymes, amino acids, carbohydrates, etc., require minerals for action.

6. Minerals are found in milk, green vegetables, legumes, fresh fruits, seafoods, poultry, and meat, such as liver, heart, kidney and other organs.

7. Daily, eat one ounce of mineral-treasure Monukka raisins, prime sources of potassium, sulfur, calcium, iron, and other nutrients.

8. Daily, eat four glasses of "clabbered milk" made with mineral-rich soya milk.

9. You are not as healthy as you may assume if you have just one of the "vague" ailments described herein. Take the hint. Nature is trying to warn you about your mineral shortage.

The first wealth is health.

Emerson

TWO

The Magic 14 Star Minerals
and
How They Can Work for You

There is no escaping the truth that *all* elements work together. This means that *if you have a shortage of just one mineral,* the entire body machinery can "go out of kilter." Although the amounts may vary, the need is consistent. Professor Kenneth J. Monty in *Food,* explains, "A diet must supply a proper balance of essential nutrients to insure overall physiological perfection." And you *do* want to have a perfect condition of health and a perfect personality, don't you? Then, let's continue on our treasure hunt for the secret nuggets.

You need all nutrients

Dr. William Halden states in *Health Secrets From Foreign Lands:*

> About 35 years have elapsed since these milestones and many new discoveries have been made in the field of nutrition research, to the great benefit of mankind. Now we know that about 50 "essentials" must be present in our daily food in order to keep us healthy and full of pep.

Is it our duty to know by heart all those nutrients that help out in the assimilation of carbohydrates, fat and protein? It is, of course, not necessary to know all that, just as it is not necessary to enumerate all the single parts of an automobile. But you must know something about the most essential parts of the car engine you drive and you should be familiar with the qualities of the food that keeps your own human motor running.

It is not difficult to remember what really counts in nutrition. Is it one vitamin or two or three that make the difference between illness and health? Not at all. Rather it is the wisdom of the relationship of all parts of naturally whole foods, grown on soils equipped with all the indispensable organic, mineral and trace elements.

While there are close to 30 "essential" minerals, all of which are vital, we shall take up the "Magic 14" because they rule and dominate over all the others. If you eat the proper foods containing these minerals, you will also be feeding yourself the lesser known trace elements. Let's see how these minerals work to control your health and shape your personality.

1. Calcium

An excellent example of how all nutrients work together. Calcium must have vitamin D, phosphorus, Vitamins A and C in order to function — these other nutrients must have calcium to do their work, too. About 99 per cent of your calcium is found in your bones and teeth. A tiny 1 per cent circulates in your body fluids and tissues. Calcium is needed for blood clotting, to activate enzymes (digestive juices), and to regulate fluid passages throughout cellular walls.

Calcium works to normalize the contraction and relaxation of the heart muscles. If your blood calcium level drops, you become nervous and irritated. An adequate calcium intake means that some is stored in the ends of the bones in long, needle-like crystals called trabeculae. This reserve storage is used when you face a stress situation. If you do not have it, your body seizes calcium from your bone structure, usually the spinal and pelvic bones.

Calcium and phosphorus must exist in a certain proportion if they are to be used properly. The ratio is two to one, or, twice as much calcium as a given amount of phosphorus. The presence of vitamin D helps to normalize this ratio and maintain a good balance. So get enough of vitamin D from sources, such as cod liver oil, irradiated milk, and sunshine, too.

A deficiency may cause height reduction because of fractures of the vertebrae which results from pressure. Osteoporosis, or brittle bones, is one symptom. Osteomalacia is another calcium-deficiency disease: the adult version of rickets.

Calcium is vital for your nerves; this mineral helps transport impulses of your nerves from one part of your body to another. Without calcium, you wouldn't be able to pull your hand away from a hot flame, move out of the way if someone is going to bump into you, or even be able to taste your food. Cramps or convulsions may occur. Heart palpitations and slow pulse are also traced to low calcium intake. Calcium, too, helps in maintaining the delicate acid-alkaline body balance.

Prime sources of calcium are all dairy and milk products (cheeses) and green vegetables (broccoli, kale, collards, string beans, mustard greens). The *best* calcium source is bone meal, a supplement made from cattle bones and dried in a vacuum process so the minerals are not depleted. Bone meal is excellent because the calcium-phosphorus balance is built in; other minerals exist in bone meal to facilitate proper calcium absorption.

Bone meal is available in tablet, powder, and flour forms at special diet shops and health food stores. Take about six tablets a day; try using bone meal flour in recipes for a taste thrill that will improve your health and personality. Sprinkle bone meal powder over fresh raw salads, in soups, in yogurt, or mix with any freshly squeezed green vegetable drink.

2. Phosphorus

You will find this mineral in all of your body cells. About 66 per cent of body phosphorus is in the bones in a form known as calcium phosphate; 33 per cent is in soft tissue as organic and inorganic phosphate. This mineral converts oxidative energy to cell work.

High energy phosphate influences protein, carbohydrate and fat synthesis, and also stimulates muscular contraction, secretion of glandular hormones, nerve impulses, and kidney functioning.

Phosphorus sparks internal energy. It works to neutralize excess blood acidity; it also helps create lecithin and cerebrin, ingredients needed for mental power; it metabolizes fats and starches. Overweight may be traced to insufficient phosphorus.

A deficiency of this mineral may cause appetite and weight loss, nervous disorder, mental sluggishness, general fatigue. In extreme difficulties, there is irregular breathing and a pale, wan appearance.

Avoid white sugar foods. The delicate calcium-phosphorus balance is interfered with in the presence of white sugar in your body.

Your brain power (which also determines personality strength) needs phosphorus. Although 85 per cent of your brain consists of water, the solid matter is made up of phosphorized fats. These fats should increase in proportion as your nervous system matures — and your brain should grow wiser.

To be sure you have a good phosphorus supply, take the special food supplements sold in most pharmaceutical houses and in health stores. Bone meal (particularly from veal bone) is excellent. Try calcium from eggshells, known as *chalaza*. This food supplement, available in capsule or powder in health stores, is a treasure of phosphorus. Take about one or two tablets daily or as indicated on the container.

3. Iron

Billions of your body cells and tissues need iron for life-giving oxygen. Without iron, about 300 quarts of blood, rather than the present six or so, would be necessary to handle oxygen needs. Iron is found in the red blood cells and is needed to form the red colored substance called hemoglobin. Iron influences proteins. On the other hand, iron must have calcium and the other nutrients in order to properly function.

A shortage of iron may lead to anemia, a sickish skin pallor, poor memory. Iron carries oxygen to your brain so it can work properly. A sore mouth with cracks around the lips is also traceable to an iron deficiency. The same iron-weak person has a poor memory and unable to think clearly because the brain is starved for valuable oxygen.

Since you have five million red cells in just one cubic millimeter of blood, and since iron is needed for every single cell, you see how valuable this mineral can be. Iron also works with other nutrients to influence respiratory action.

Good food sources for iron include egg yolks, green leafy vegetables, molasses, plums, cherries, and especially *sun-dried raisins*. One prime powerhouse of iron is found in a food supplement called desiccated liver. Available in tablet form or powder at almost all health food stores and pharmacies, this is a "must" for mineral health. Most people take tablets daily (about four throughout the day) or make an "iron punch" like this: Mix three heaping tablespoons of desiccated liver in a glass filled with grape juice. Add one tablespoon of buckwheat honey. Stir vigorously or mix in a blender. Drink just one glass daily and you will discover that this "iron punch" can mark the difference between success and failure in your treasure hunt for health and personality rewards!

4. Iodine

Originally, iodine was associated with problems of goiter; that is, the enlargement of the thyroid gland. Today, we know that this mineral has even greater powers in building intelligence and eliminating stupidity! You have about 25 milligrams of iodine in your system. Two thirds (15 milligrams) is in your thyroid gland; the other third is distributed in blood and tissues.

Iodine stimulates the thyroid (a two-part gland that looks like a butterfly, resting against the front of the windpipe) to secrete the thyroxine hormone that regulates metabolism and energy. An iodine deficiency may cause goiter, obesity, sluggish metabolism and lowered mentality.

An iodine shortage (which means a thyroxin shortage) causes impairment of the mind and body, slow mental reaction, dry hair that easily breaks. Other symptoms include rapid pulse, heart palpitation, tremor, nervousness, restlessness, and increased irritability.

Iodine is needed to utilize fat and influence other nutrients. Iodine is found in all sea foods and vegetables grown in iodine-rich soils. Immature salmon has more iodine than the spawning salmon; roe of various ocean fish is another good source of this precious mineral. A wonderful source is found in kelp — dehydrated sea weed. Kelp is available in most health stores, pharmacies and some special food shops. Kelp is sold as a powder so you use it wherever seasoning is required in foods. Another good source is in onions. You should use onions as a garnish with meat and sea foods.

One Spring, I made a trip into Nova Scotia and stopped for a bite to eat in a small town. I noticed that a number of the children who walked along the streets were nibbling on something. They carried small paper bags into which they stuck their hands, removed this item and chewed it. I noticed one little boy coming out of a grocery store with what appeared to be a freshly purchased item in the same paper bag.

Going inside, I asked the grocer about it and he said, "Oh, we all eat dulse. It's a form of seaweed or sea lettuce, made in New Brunswick and the children eat it like candy."

I tried some, found it delicious, and have eaten dulse regularly ever since. It is a wonderful source of iodine; I might also add that the children and adults in this area are remarkably free of skin blemishes, look healthy, are alert and intelligent. It can be used in powdered form for seasoning, in a dried leaf form for nibbling or try chopping it finely and adding it to sauces, salads, soups, and over meat or fish stews. Health stores and pharmacies have dulse, as they do kelp.

5. Sodium

This mineral works with potassium to help maintain the favorable acid-base factor in your system. It also helps maintain a normal water level balance between cells and fluids. Sodium enables your nerves to respond to stimulation and transmit it, and provides strength to your muscles so they can contract. It joins with chlorine to improve blood and lymph health. Its main purpose is to render other blood minerals more soluble and prevent them from becoming clogged or deposited in the blood distribution system.

A sodium deficiency may cause stomach and intestinal gas, weight loss, muscle shrinkage. Carbohydrate foods cannot be changed into fat for digestion. You may have plenty of amino acids, but sodium must process them. Sodium favors the formation and free-flow of saliva, gastric juices and enzymes and other intestinal secretions.

Sodium is found in sea foods, poultry, beets, carrots, chard, and dandelion greens. Since this mineral is needed to build a resistance against heat cramps and heat stroke, it's a good one to have during warm weather. It also helps keep calcium in solution which is necessary for nerve strength. Make a good *natural sodium cocktail* by drinking the freshly squeezed juice of beets combined with carrots and dandelion greens. Munch raw dandelion greens.

6. Potassium

Here is another "balancing" mineral; it works with sodium to help normalize your heart beat and feed your muscular system. It joins with phosphorus to send oxygen to your brain. Sodium and potassium have to have a balance. Sodium is found basically in the fluids circulating *outside* your cells and only a tiny amount is inside. Potassium is found largely *inside* the cells and a tiny supply is outside.

Potassium stimulates the kidney to dispose of body wastes. Your blood needs this mineral, too. A deficiency may cause constipation, nervous disorder, insomnia, slow and irregular heartbeat and muscle damage. Sometimes, the kidneys enlarge and bones become brittle.

Good food sources include all citrus fruits, watercress, mint leaves, green peppers and chicory, as well as blackstrap molasses and figs.

A good health idea is to eat figs regularly. The famed California Black Mission Figs are known for having a powerhouse of potassium. Health stores sell them because they are unsulphured and sun-dried, free of harmful chemicals.

Try California natural white figs (unsulphured and sun-dried) which you may eat, as is, or soak overnight in water and then serve with yogurt. Either way, you'll get a good potassium supply.

7. Magnesium

"I dread warm weather," said the harried housewife, "because the heat is too much for me. I can't stand air conditioning — gives me a chill. Fans? They give me headaches."

This housewife might have endured endless and needless warm weather tensions had she not once attended a country fair in her vicinity. She sipped a special drink and noticed that it made her feel so cool and relaxed. The fair, incidentally, was held on a hot Saturday afternoon; trees offered little cool shade.

"What's in this drink?" She begged the exhibitors to reveal the secret. "Honestly, it's made me feel so relaxed and calm, I don't even know it's summertime."

The exhibitor confided, "I call it my *Nature's cooler.* I take equal portions of freshly squeezed beet greens, cucumbers, cauliflower and mix the juices all together in a blender. Then I add powdered sunflower seeds. That's all. Works wonders, doesn't it?"

The wonders lay in the magnesium content of those foods. Biochemists have labelled magnesium as the "cool, alkaline, refreshing, sleep-promoting mineral." It keeps you calm and cool during hot muggy days. It relaxes your nerves.

Dr. Ruth M. Leverton in *Food,* tells us:

> Magnesium is closely related to both calcium and phosphorus in its location and its functions in the body. About 70 per cent of the magnesium in the body is in the bones. The rest is in the soft tissues and blood. Muscle tissue contains more magnesium than calcium. Magnesium acts as starter for some of the chemical reactions within the body.
>
> It plays an important role as a coenzyme in the building of protein. There is some relation between magnesium and the hormone cortisone as they affect the amount of phosphate in the blood. Animals on a diet deficient in magnesium become extremely nervous and give an exaggerated response to even small noises or disturbances. Such unnatural sensitiveness disappears when they are given enough magnesium.

Dr. Leverton emphasizes, "In extreme deficiencies, the blood vessels expand, the heart beats faster and causes such irritability that the animals die in convulsions."

So you can see that magnesium, by cooling the muscular structure during hot, muggy "dog days" can act as Nature's own cooling system.

Other food sources of magnesium include figs, lemons, grapefruits, yellow corn, almonds, oil-rich nuts and seeds, wild rice, apples, celery. Use vegetable oils for cooking as they have magnesium in fairly good supply.

8. Copper

Although iron is used to make blood, copper must be present to convert iron into hemoglobin. This valuable mineral influences tyrosine, an amino acid and also utilizes vitamin C. In some test animals, it was seen that a deficiency of copper causes lameness, deformities, anemia, easy bone fractures. Skin sores develop and fail to heal. General weakness and impaired respiration are among the early symptoms of a copper deficiency.

This mineral is found in almonds, dried beans, peas, whole wheat, prunes. A top notch source is in calf and beef liver, egg yolks and shrimp. Make it a rule to include liver in your menu at least twice weekly. Or, use desiccated liver powder as a flavoring agent. Mix three tablespoons with a glass of tomato juice for a copper tonic that is sure to make you feel glad all over.

9. Sulphur

This is a mineral the ladies ought to hear about. It's Nature's "beauty" mineral — keeps your hair glossy and smooth, keeps your complexion smooth and youthful. It acts by invigorating your bloodstream, rendering it more powerful to resist bacterial infections.

It works to cause the liver to secrete bile, maintain overall body balance and has an influence on brain power. Sulphur helps maintain hair and fingernail health.

Grandma, back in the good old days, would give a sulphur-and-molasses Spring tonic to her family. She knew her minerals instinctively!

Sulphur works with the B-complex vitamins that are needed for metabolism and strong nerve health. Human hair contains sulphur, too. Sulphur is part of the amino acids that build body tissues and cells and this may explain its power to create beauty, so to speak. A healthy skin is a beautiful skin. You can obtain sulphur in any good vitamin-mineral food supplement sold at most health stores and pharmacies.

Natural food sources include fish, eggs, cabbage, lean beef, dried beans. Include brussels sprouts as a good sulphur source.

10. Silicon

A silicon deficiency may be traced to skin flabbiness, a feeling of chronic fatigue and eyes that are dull and glazed. Silicon is found in hair, muscles, nails, cellular walls, and connective tissues. It joins with other minerals to create tooth enamel and build strong bones. In some cases, it has been seen to build resistance to tuberculosis.

Good food sources are buckwheat products, mushrooms, carrots, tomatoes and liver, as well as whole grains and lentils.

Here are some ways to obtain an adequate silicon supply:

1. Buy some *steel-cut oatmeal* at a health store; prepare as you would ordinary oatmeal and eat for breakfast. This type of oatmeal is not to be confused with ordinary cereal which has been put through a milling process, and thereby robbed of precious nutrients. It is rich in silicon.

2. Place two tablespoons of steel-cut oats into an empty glass. Cover with warm water. Stir a few moments. Let remain standing overnight. The following morning, strain off the water and drink it. Simple, isn't it? Yet, this liquid is a rich source of silicon!

11. Zinc

This mineral is not only a constituent of insulin, but also of the male reproductive fluid which is a slight suggestion of its power. It is made in the pancreas (large gland located behind the lower part of the stomach) where it helps in the storage of glycogen, an energy producing substance. It combines with phosphorus to aid in respiration. It also sparks vitamin action. Zinc helps in tissue respiration — the intake of oxygen and expulsion of carbon dioxide and toxic wastes. Insulin is dependent upon zinc for functioning. Insulin shortage leads to diabetes. Furthermore, zinc helps food become absorbed through the intestinal wall. Zinc is part of a stomach enzyme; it helps manufacture male hormones. Since it is so intimately connected with carbohydrate utilization, a deficiency of this mineral may cause fatigue and "lazy" reaction. Zinc produces energy.

Usually, most of the aforementioned mineral foods contain zinc; you'll find it in liver where it is most abundant.

12. Manganese

Manganese is a mineral that works with the B-complex vitamins to overcome laziness, sterility and marital weakness. It also combines with phosphatase (an enzyme) to build strong bones. Much of manganese is found in the liver. Manganese is needed for good enzymatic function so foods can be digested and vital nutrients extracted for overall body utilization. Manganese helps build resistance to ailments, strong nerve health and in the expectant mother, promotes milk formation.

This mineral is found in green leaves, peas, beets, egg yolks. One of the richest sources is in the unmilled grains. Make it a point to eat cereals made from these grains and chew sunflower seeds.

13. Chlorine

Unofficially, chlorine is called Nature's broomstick. It works by cleaning out toxic waste products from your system. Chlorine acts by stimulating your liver to act as a filter for waste substances. It stimulates production of hydrochloric acid, the enzymatic digestive juice needed for tough, fibrous foods. Chlorine also helps in keeping a youthful joint and tendon condition; it also helps to distribute hormones issued by your endocrine glands.

A chlorine deficiency may cause hair and teeth loss, poor muscular contractibility and improper digestive power. *Good sources of chlorine* include kelp, dulse, sea greens, leafy greens, rye flour, and ripe olives. Remember to use kelp and dulse as flavoring agents in place of harsh table condiments and you'll have a good chlorine nourishment.

14. Fluorine

Natural fluorine is what we talk about. It does help to strengthen teeth enamel, but this is a tricky mineral. Too much may cause abnormal and unsightly teeth mottling. Minute amounts are found evenly distributed throughout the tissues. You can find enough fluorine in ordinary foods such as those listed for the other minerals. It has been noted that when an excess is taken, such as by means of fluoridated water, bones become weak and there is an adverse reaction upon internal organs.

Mineral Balance Must Be Maintained

The chemical elements which make up the body sustenance must be nicely balanced in nutrition or trouble ensues. The efficiency of each mineral element is enhanced by proper amounts of the others.

Yes, in our quest for the secrets of magic minerals, we are discovering the truths of the power of this treasure. We may well agree with famed Dr. Henry C. Sherman who declared: "The importance of minerals in the tissues and fluids of the body is very great. Any considerable departure from normal is incompatible with life!"

MAIN POINTS OF CHAPTER TWO

1. All the minerals work in harmony with the other essential life giving nutrients. A deficiency of one mineral may disrupt the entire chain of life, rendering other nutrients either useless or inefficient.
2. There are close to 30 known minerals, all of which influence your health and personality. Of these, 14 are known as Magic workers because they dominate the health picture.
3. Each of these minerals needs the other minerals, for together, they influence vitamins, proteins, amino acids, enzymes, carbohydrates, fats, sugars, etc.

4. All minerals can either build or destroy an entire person, depending upon their supply or deficiency. This is just one example of their power over health and mental stamina.

5. Some minerals exert a specific action upon a specific body function: magnesium is Nature's own tranquilizer; silicon acts as an overall beauty treatment. Emphasize individual minerals for your specific needs, but remember — *all* minerals are required to build and maintain mental and physical vigor. Try the home tonics and remedies.

A healthy body is the guest chamber of the soul; a sick one, its prison.

Bacon

Minerals
Can Help Fight Arthritis

Arthritis and rheumatism is a disease older than man. Evidence of this crippling disease has been found in the skeletons of prehistoric animals. Arthritis is not a so-called dramatic killer, like heart disease; neither does it have a slow malignancy of cancer. Victims may live to a great old age with this "chronic disease" as it is called. A frequent plea is, "Don't tell me how to live *with* my arthritis. Tell me how to live *without* it."

Precisely, that is the attitude of many tireless nutritionists who attacked the problem of arthritis from all sides and came up with the discovery that minerals play such a decisive role, they cannot be overlooked in the quest for arthritis-prevention and arthritis-cure.

Facts about arthritis

To begin, let's understand the nature of this ailment. Arthritis is the world's leading crippler of humans. It centers its painful and disabling attack on the joints and the vast network of connective tissue that holds the body together. Certain conditions seem to bring on the disease, such as nervous shock, emotional or physical strain, fatigue, exposure to dampness and cold, and chronic infections.

According to the *Arthritis and Rheumatism Foundation:*

More than 12 million Americans are afflicted by some form of arthritis. Nearly half of them are partially or totally disabled. Each year, 250,000 more become victims. There is a sufferer in one out of five families. Although many think of arthritis as an ailment of old age, the disease can strike anyone at any time — from infants to old folks. Rheumatoid arthritis, while it hits all ages, concentrates its crippling in the 20 to 45 "prime of life" years. For some unknown reason it attacks three women for every man.

In terms of human suffering, the cost is incalculable. In time lost from work, arthritis sufferers show a staggering 115,000,000 days a year, a figure equivalent to 470,000 persons out of work for the entire year. It amounts to more than a billion and a half dollars annually in lost wages.

Arthritis also drains away countless millions of dollars from the U.S. economy. An estimated 12 per cent of the welfare dollar goes into bare subsistence allowances to arthritis sufferers unable to support themselves.

Different Types of Arthritis

The name arthritis comes from the Greek, *arthros* and *itis,* meaning simply "joint inflammation." This ailment takes in a lot of different types. According to Public Health Service Publication #29, *Arthritis And Rheumatism,* these are the more prevalent forms:

1. *Rheumatoid Arthritis* About a third of those who visit doctors or clinics for treatment of rheumatic disease have this type. If afflicts twice as many women as men, sometimes runs in family patterns and usually starts between the ages of 25 and 50.

The disease causes inflammation and thickening of the lining of the joints. The lining may grow into the space and fill it. Meanwhile the cartilage covering the ends of the bones may become eroded, and often the bones become brittle and pitted. Finally they may grow together and the joint becomes permanently fused.

Often the first signs of rheumatoid arthritis are fatigue, muscular stiffness, and loss of appetite and weight. Painful swelling then begins at one or more joints; nodules, from the size of a pea to a walnut, may appear under the skin; and muscular wasting and spasm frequently occur. The disease may affect various organs and is sometimes accompanied by fever.

2. *Osteo-arthritis* This is a degenerative joint disease that seems to result from a combination of aging, irritation of the joints, wear and tear. Chronic joint irritation may result from overweight, poor posture, injury or strain. The disease is characterized mainly by degeneration of joint cartilage.

This becomes soft and wears unevenly. In some areas, it may wear away completely, exposing the underlying bone, and thickening of the ends of the bones may occur. Common symptoms are pain, aches, stiffness. Pain is experienced during use of the joints, especially finger joints and those bearing the body's weight. Enlargement of the fingers just below the last joint often occurs.

3. *Rheumatic Fever* This is a treacherous child disease. It is the leading disease killer between the ages of five and 19. Half a million children in the U.S. are handicapped by rheumatic fever and resulting heart disease. Almost all cases start with a streptococcus infection of the tonsils, nose or throat. Danger signs may be fever, pain in the limbs, nosebleeds, jerking movements of arms, legs and face.

Rheumatic fever may cause inflammation of many body tissues including the heart, frequently damaging the heart muscle and scarring the valves.

4. *Gout* This arthritic condition affects the joints of the feet, especially the big toe. Nearly all cases occur in males and it is believed to be caused by a disorder of body metabolism which indicates a possible mineral imbalance. There is an excess amount of uric acid in the blood. Gout usually occurs in attacks lasting days or weeks, during which the victim suffers acute joint inflammation. Between attacks, there is freedom from symptoms. Many years after the onset, chronic arthritis may set in.

Attacks of gout usually follow minor injury, excessive eating or drinking, heavy exercise or surgical operations. Often attacks occur with no apparent provocation.

5. *Fibrositis* This is muscular rheumatism, not affecting the joints directly. It is known by pain, stiffness, or soreness of

fibrous tissue, especially in muscles and around joints. Fibrositis within the muscles is sometimes called *myositis,* and when it attacks the bursae (fluid sacs in the tissues), it is known as *bursitis. Lumbago* is fibrositis in the lumbar region and low back. Attacks may follow an injury, repeated muscular strain, prolonged mental tension or depression.

Tensions Cause Arthritis

"Within recent years the concepts of the causes of arthritis have been broadened to include emotional factors," says Harold Shryock, M.D., in *Happiness And Health.*

It may well be that such factors in and of themselves cannot produce full-blown cases of arthritis. In combination with one or more of other factors, emotional factors do play a definite role in arthritis.

It has been observed that persons afflicted with arthritis fall in approximately the same group in terms of personality type. These are the persons who discipline themselves rigidly. They are conscientious, they have a strong sense of duty, they are tidy and meticulous, and they thrive on accomplishing routine tasks. Going back into the childhood history of such persons, they are usually described as being nervously high-strung. In a person of this personality type with a predisposition to arthritis, almost any emotional shock can bring about an actual symptom of arthritis.

The nervous wife

Dr. Shryock tells the story of a missionary's wife. Her husband was imprisoned during the war. As she waited for his release and return home, she lived in loneliness and anxiety. She was previously in good health. After prolonged anxiety, she noticed pain in the small joints of her hands. These joints became swollen; for a few months, the pain continued. She was examined by a doctor and treated for arthritis. Still, the symptoms continued until her husband returned. Dr. Shryock sums up, "Her symptoms of arthritis disappeared rather promptly after his return."

Stress and arthritis

A group of doctors studied many arthritis patients and found that poor diet may be responsible for weak nerves which, in turn, make the individual incapable of meeting stress situations. Reporting to the *Canadian Medical Association Journal,* (9:15,57), the doctors say that rheumatoid arthritis is a "stress disease and represents a maladaptation of psychobiological stress." Speaking simply, a severe emotional problem can hurl you into a case of swollen joints and arthritic misery.

The doctors point out that some arthritic patients show a definite restriction of emotional expression as well as strong elements of self-sacrifice. Arthritis was seen to follow events which upset the balance between aggressive impulses and their control.

A man who hates his job but must keep it because he has a family to support is forced to swallow his resentment. Repression may lead to arthritis. It was reported, "A fairly severe emotional disturbance of one kind or another had been present before any sign of rheumatoid arthritis" in treated patients.

Some other stress situations which accompanied arthritic symptoms included passing of a beloved person, separation from the family, concealed hostility, inhibited urges. On the other hand, the aggressive persons were free from arthritis!

Effect of Stress On Body Mineral Supply

Stress causes a drain on the body's resources of precious minerals and upsets the entire calcium-phosphorus balance. This has been found to be the key to mineral therapy of arthritis. Osteoporosis, a condition in which bones are porous because of calcium loss, is a forerunner of, not "mate" of arthritis.

Oldsters deficient in calcium

Dr. Henry C. Sherman states in *Nutrition Reviews:*

> It was a surprise to me to see that the majority of X-ray studies of adults past the age of 45 to 50 years showed considerable demineralization of bone and one wondered if low dietary intake

of calcium or of vitamin D might not have been prominent factors in the (cause) of demineralization.

Calcium-phosphorus intake valuable

To build resistance against arthritis and to build reserves of the minerals needed to provide strength against stress, you need to maintain a delicate calcium-phosphorus balance.

A treatment of calcium disorders upon conditions, such as arthritis, is reported by Drs. Martin Frank and Fritz Heppner in the European medical journal, *Langenbecks Archives* (Vol. 274, p. 159). These doctors prepared a bone meal food — made from the long bones of young animals. (In the U.S., calves' bones are used.) The bones are fat-free and hollowed but are not processed before grinding. This calcium rich source was used to build up resistance against arthritic symptoms and conditions. Results were so favorable that we cannot recommend this powerful calcium source too highly.

Just how does bone meal benefit arthritics? It has a treasure of calcium-phosphorus and vitamins A, C and D. Bone meal has carbon, a substance which enables the calcium to be absorbed within your system. This interrelationship aids in the formation of strong bones and strong intercellular substances that are vulnerable to arthritic conditions.

Interesting reports of cures

Drs. Frank and Heppner tell of a 24-year old man who had such an ailing shank, he was put into traction. The entire leg could not endure walking pressure. The bone supplement was given, a daily intake of 20 tablets, for about 2½ months. Then, his cast was removed. The entire limb had become strong and the young man could walk.

Another case was a 47-year old woman who used a cane because of a sick leg. She was given a bone supplement for three weeks — a total of 201 tablets. Afterward, X-rays were taken to show that the symptoms were eased and soon she was reported completely healed.

At the age of 57, a woman fractured her leg. Treatment was partially helpful, but she developed a form of arthritis. She could not walk without a cast. Bone meal therapy was begun — one tablet three times a day for two months. At the end of that time, her leg was completely healed and she could walk with no problems.

Here is an unusual situation. The woman was 26 and pregnant. During the last few months, she had pains in her left wrist. Splints and medication were useless. She had the same arthritic pains during lactation — they ended with the lactation. When she was again pregnant in a year, the same trouble began. She had recurrent dental caries that refused to respond to treatment.

This time, the doctors gave her the bone supplement — for three months, she took one tablet three times daily. After 12 days of this calcium-phosphorus therapy, X-rays showed her wrist returning to normal. Pain vanished. Complete use of the hand was restored. The dental problem was solved.

The doctors recommend the use of bone meal for all forms of bone problems either at the onset or when the condition has already taken hold. The sooner bone meal is introduced to the body, the speedier the balance is maintained and the quicker the possibility of relief.

A country doctor speaks

William N. McCartney, M.D., in *50 Years A Country Doctor* says of bone meal:

> It is a natural food, physiological, harmless, can be given safely in any dose. In certain conditions it is as near a specific cure as anything we are likely to meet within this vale of tears
>
> I have treated many cases of delayed union in fractured cases. In no case where the bones were in reasonable apposition have I failed to get sufficient callus (mineralization) formation and an eventual good union.
>
> It is inexpensive. It is safe to use in almost any conceivable condition where such treatment is indicated.

This makes good sense from an old-fashioned country doctor, a breed that unhappily will soon vanish as did the horse and buggy.

Considering that tensions lead to arthritis, we can see how valuable calcium may be to the nervous system. It helps build nerve health and make you resistant to constant pressures. Bone meal is the answer!

You can obtain bone meal at most health food stores in tablet form or in powder to be used as a sprinkling agent on foods. Bone meal flour should be used for baking or any recipe calling for flour.

Cherry Juice for Arthritis Relief

Minerals, together with vitamins in cherries appear to exert a truly magical influence on arthritis. Ludwig W. Blau, M.D., in an article entitled "Cherry Diet Control for Gout and Arthritis" in the *Texas Reports on Biology and Medicine* (Vol. 8) tells of an astounding cure among arthritic patients who were given cherry juice!

Dr. Blau adds that "apologies are offered for unsatisfactory clinical and laboratory data and control," yet he feels that this discovery merits the "property of publishing the information available."

Twelve gout patients were remarkably relieved by taking cherry juice. The blood uric acid level dropped and "no attacks of gouty arthritis have occurred on a non-restricted diet in all 12 cases, *as a result of eating about one-half pound of fresh or canned cherries per day.*"

Dr. Blau tells of astonishing cures by the eating of either canned cherries, sour, black, Royal Anne, or fresh Black Bing varieties. One arthritic patient just drank the juice and the curative powers were equally effective.

Other researchers reported possible cures by the drinking of cherry juice. One tells of an experiment among residents of Sturgeon Bay, Wisconsin. They cooperated and drank cherry juice daily. "Outstanding results were reported." It is reported that a few local dentists suggested cherry juice to their patients; one dentist said that it was a useful treatment for pyorrhea.

"To date," this research report states "there is no definite scientific data on just how the juice aids in relieving pain caused by diseases where improper balance of calcium is evident. However, it is believed that it may be the pigment in the cherries that brings relief."

According to Dr. Morris B. Jacobs in *Food and Food Products,* cherries contain malic acid and a surprising supply of pectin — this is the substance in fruits used to make jelly harden and "jell."

Arthritic patients should avail themselves of cherries and juices. Daily, eat up to one-half pound of cherries. Daily, drink one glass of the juice. Most stores sell bottled cherry juice; you should seek out cherries and juices that are free from insecticides and harsh artificial sprays. The labels should tell you about this; or, be on the safe side and buy raw cherries and bottled juices in a health food store.

New Diet for Arthritics

Since minerals function best in a comprehensive health plan, your entire body should be nourished with all valuable nutrients. A hopeful new diet plan for arthritics appeared in the *Journal of the National Medical Association* (7:59) with regards to 98 arthritics who appeared for treatment. The blood sedimentation rate dropped. This is possible with adequate mineralization. Cholesterol levels either controlled or dropped. One diabetic patient gave up insulin. Blood pressure levels were normalized. How was this possible?

Drs. Charles A. Brusch and Edward T. Johnson, M.D., who conducted this plan, start out by saying that "there was complete curtailment of soft drinks, candy, cake, ice cream or any food made up of white sugar. Those who felt that the sacrifice of coffee was too great were allowed black coffee — 15 minutes before breakfast."

If there is a magical secret here it is evident — white sugar and starch upset the calcium-phosphorus ratio and this opens the way to arthritis. Here are the general diet rules which the arthritic patients observed:

1. All daily water intake was restricted to morning awakening, especially at warm temperatures and about one hour before breakfast.
2. Room temperature milk or warm soup (not creamed) were the *only* liquids allowed with meals; these were allowed any time, too.

3. Cod liver oil, mixed either with two tablespoonfuls of fresh, strained orange juice or two tablespoonfuls of cool milk, was taken on a fasting stomach at least four, but preferably five or more, hours after the evening meal and before retiring, or one or more hours before breakfast upon arising and at least 30 minutes after water intake. Diabetics and heart patients took the oil only twice weekly. The cod liver oil mixtures were shaken well in a sealed glass before taking.

4. Tablets, pills or supplements of any kinds were permitted either with water upon arising, with milk or soup at mealtime, or with milk or soup at any time.

5. No sugar allowed. No sugar-containing foods allowed.

6. No coffee, except before breakfast.

The success rate for this plan is high. The doctors reported that there was noticeable skin, hair and scalp improvement, cerumen (ear wax) correction, diminishing of inflammatory ear conditions. Of course, arthritic symptoms were also eased. Here again we can see that health is a *complete* picture of all types of treatment and care. Sugar, a highly concentrated carbohydrate, is destructive to minerals and according to this particular diet, when prohibited, allows the body to build up a store of precious minerals. These magic minerals help to build resistance to arthritis and also help overcome the ravaging effects of the disease. So remember: in any diet plan to combat arthritis — NO SUGAR. NO FOODS CONTAINING SUGAR. To substitute, use natural sweetening agents such as pure honey.

Sleep and Arthritis

The housewife awoke shortly after midnight and discovered that her entire arm was numb from shoulder to wrist. She spent a troubled night. "I said nothing to my husband the next morning," she relates, "because I didn't want to worry him." The numb pain went away the following day.

Three nights later, the housewife again awoke and felt the stinging, almost frightening pain. Now it seemed to cover her entire shoulder span and back. She feared arthritis and this time decided to confide in her husband.

He suggested she obtain an X-ray to see if such a condition did exist. Then he added, "If you feel the pain when you awaken, it's possible that sleeping on the arm is causing a painful pressure. Maybe you ought to try and sleep on your back." .

It was known that the wife slept on her side, usually with her arm bent, her head resting in its crook at the elbow. The wife had a complete examination and it was reported that she had *no* symptoms of arthritis.

She decided to alter her sleeping patterns; it was quite an effort but she managed to overcome habit. "No more shoulder pain," she declared happily after she had avoided sleeping on her arm for more than a week.

Sleep-caused arthritis

Patients come to doctors telling of waking up in sleep with so-called paralyzed arms. Symptoms are said to resemble arthritis. The patients are so afraid of getting this ailment, they suffer from insomnia and the body becomes further weakened. This condition is called *Brackialgia Statica Paresthetica* — numbness in the arm during sleep. Also called "sleep arthritis," it is caused from pressure on the nerves and blood congestions caused by this same pressure on veins of your limbs.

Dr. Emanuel Josephson once stated that if the arm and shoulder are subjected to pressure during sleep, it can lead to bursitis, a form of arthritis. Why? This pressure causes an injury to the shoulder's lubricating system. A delicate sac in your shoulder joint is moistened by an oily fluid. Pressure on the shoulder muscle during sleep may cause a breakdown of its lubricating system, causing a situation of subdeltoid bursitis. Many such victims have to submit to surgery.

You may have heard of "Drunkard's Neuritis" or "Saturday Night Neuritis." This is a condition in which a drunkard or alcoholic falls asleep in a hallway; naturally, no cushions are available so he uses his arm. The body circulation is at a very low ebb during sleep (much lower in alcoholic sleep) so if the man is suddenly awakened, his arm is so paralyzed, he can hardly move. Many such people have to go to hospitals for treatment. Not only alcoholics suffer this way, but ordinary working men, too.

To help prevent *idiopathic nocturnal paresthesia* (a form of numbness that comes on during the night for no apparent reason) sleep on your back, or on one side, but do *not* use your arms for cushions. Do *not* sleep in any curled up position since this, too, causes stagnation in the circulation and creates a peculiar form of sleep-caused arthritis. You have to tell yourself, one hour before you go into bed, that you will not sleep on your arms and use a back position. Self-hypnosis takes time but you must persist in drumming it into your subconscious.

Mineral Baths for Arthritics

Mineral baths have always been used for ailments, especially arthritis. (See Chapter Sixteen for complete story of healing power of spa baths.) Minerals in the waters are valuable for arthritics. Heated baths are even more effective.

Walter S. McClellan, M.D., in *Cyclopedia of Medicine, Surgery, Specialties,* says, "The treatment of a patient with rheumatoid arthritis with physical medicine including heat, massage and exercise stands out as one of the most universally valuable forms of therapy. Hydrotherapy (baths) offers a valuable adjunct both for the provision of heat and a medium of exercise."

We know that hot mineral baths relieve pain, loosen tight muscles, ease aching joints. Moist heat seems to be more effective for arthritis than dry heat. Here are three reasons why:

1. Increased elimination of waste products through the skin and kidneys.
2. Improved circulation of the blood and other body fluids, because the heat expands the blood vessels.
3. Mechanical breaking down of adhesions and softening of any thickening in muscles and tissues.

Moist heat loosens the joints, permits body minerals to flow freely and do their work in preventing, easing, and overcoming arthritis.

The mineral sulphur is most valuable. This was demonstrated in a treatment used under the guidance of three researchers at the Mayo Clinic. Reporting to the *Archives of Dermatology* (Vol. 20, p. 158), the doctors stated that after the patients had a hot sulphur bath, the mineral content was increased in their bloodstream.

Sulphur is important in overcoming arthritis. According to tests conducted by two researchers, the cystine supply of arthritic patients is far lower than healthy ones. Cystine is a form of protein which has a lot of sulphur. So, the mineral, sulphur, is valuable in your anti-arthritis program.

In a reported test, 60 arthritic patients were given a bath ingredient containing sulphur as the chief mineral. They were told to use it nightly, for 20 minutes in a hot bath, before retiring.

A second set of 60 arthritic patients were told to take ordinary hot baths with no dissolved mineral ingredients. Results? The 60 patients who used the mineral baths reported various degrees of relief. That is, 51 reported relief, the others were slightly benefitted. As for those who took ordinary hot baths, only 42 reported *some* relief; the rest were still suffering from arthritis.

Incidentally, those who used sulphur said they could sleep better at night!

Says Dr. McClellan in *Rheumatic Diseases,* "The program built around mineral waters and associated treatments, particularly when occupational therapy and corrective exercise are included can be of real benefit in the rehabilitation of many patients with arthritis."

You can obtain mineral bath salts at just about any pharmacy; try hot mineral baths in your own home, nightly, for 20 minutes, before going to sleep. It worked for others. It may work for you.

SUMMARY OF CHAPTER THREE

1. Arthritis does not respect age or sex. It can strike young and old; it can cripple and disable.
2. Tension frequently is the forerunner of arthritis. Avoid noisy environments. To work off bottled up tensions, try vigorous sports, athletics, outdoor endeavors.
3. Bone meal helps normalize the delicate calcium-phosphorus balance that is needed to resist arthritis.
4. Fresh, raw, unsprayed cherries and juices are valuable to your mineral buildup. Daily, eat up to one-half pound of fresh cherries, drink several glasses of cherry juice daily.

5. Eliminate white sugar and foods containing white sugar from your diet. The same goes for white flour products. Try the special diet plan outlined in six easy-to-follow steps.

6. Never use your arm for a cushion. Pressure may choke off circulation and lead to arthritic conditions. Sleep on your back or any other comfy position which does not hinder the free circulation of guardian minerals in the blood.

7. Sulphur hot baths are important. Heat will open your body pores to allow some sulphur absorption, replacing a possible deficiency.

FOUR

How Minerals Help Release from High Blood Pressure

"Watch your blood pressure!" Usually, this is a warning passed off as a joke if the other person is about to face or is in the midst of an irritating or exciting situation. It's no joke to have high blood pressure. In fact, it's dangerous! In particular, high blood pressure is serious after the middle years when hardening arteries, pushed by abnormal blood pressures beyond their expansion capacity, prepare the victim for long years of confinement as an invalid — or sudden death.

What is High Blood Pressure?

High blood pressure is also known as hypertension. *Hyper* means high; pressure is a kind of tension, so hypertension means high blood tension or pressure. Your heart beats about 104,000 times in every 24 hours. In one day it pumps about 60 barrels of blood through the blood vessels.

The American Heart Association in a release, *Questions And Answers About Heart and Blood Vessel Diseases,* explains it thusly:

1. *What is meant by blood pressure?* Blood pressure is the force which keeps blood flowing through the arteries. It is

generated by the heart as it pumps, or beats, and is maintained by the elasticity of the artery walls. Each time the heart contracts, blood pressure goes up; each time the heart relaxes, the pressure decreases. Everyone has blood pressure. Without it, the blood couldn't circulate.

2. *What is normal blood pressure?* Normally, the pressure in the arteries ranges between 100 and 140 systolic (contraction pressure) and between 70 and 90 diastolic (relaxation pressure), although these limits vary at different times and in different people. When a doctor takes blood pressure, the systolic pressure is written first, and then the diastolic — for example, 130/90 (130 over 90). Blood pressures up to 140/90 or 159/90 are usually considered normal. However, blood pressure in all human beings varies from day to day, and even from hour to hour.

3. *What is hypertension?* Hypertension, or high blood pressure, means that pressure is too high in blood vessels and is persistently high. One or two high blood pressure readings do not necessarily indicate hypertension. A doctor must take periodic readings to find out if hypertension really is present and what kind of treatment, if any, is necessary.

Furthermore, we learn that during the period of years, the heart suffers an added strain that may lead to enlargement. If enlargement progresses, the heart loses its efficiency powers and may fail. In some people, high blood pressure may cause a stroke, in others, a heart attack. It is estimated that after the age of 45, about one out of every four persons in the U.S. has high blood pressure. High blood pressure places an increased strain on the heart and blood vessels. Close to seven out of ten people with high blood pressure die of heart attacks.

Early Symptoms

Headaches are the first symptoms; the typical hypertension headache occurs in the back of the head and the upper part of the neck; it is most severe in the early morning. Dizziness is another symptom; shortness of breath is a symptom that is caused by the additional work imposed upon the heart. Some hypertension victims show no symptoms which reveals how "sneaky" this ailment can be.

Typical Hypertension Personality

Emotions are frequently to blame. Some persons react more strongly to the stresses and strains of life and are wide open to getting high blood pressure. The individual who works continuously and consistently toward his strict ideal of success is in danger of becoming intolerant of individuals or circumstances that tend to interfere with his progress to success. He tends to be aggressive in his struggle for accomplishment, but back of the aggression there develops an anxiety which, because of its emotional counterpart, tends to upset the physiologic balance within the blood vessels of his body until he becomes not only a candidate for, but a victim of, high blood pressure.

Kidney Health *vs.* Blood Pressure

In hypertension, the kidneys, for some reason, send into the bloodstream, substances which start a chain of chemical events that ends in raised blood pressure. Normal kidneys need minerals for function to secrete such substances as *renin* and *anti-renin* in balanced amounts. Malfunctioning or mineral-starved kidneys secrete more renin. This excess often causes high blood pressure.

The kidney (actually, two large glands in the small of the back, serving the purpose of filtering the bloodstream and removing waste products in the manner of a sieve) may be the key to reducing blood pressure.

Dr. Edwin L. Prien stated in a news article that people of the southern states suffer more from ailing kidneys than the north. Why? Southern soil, especially along the Gulf Coast (except Florida) is usually deficient in magnesium. It is thought the absence of this mineral is responsible for weak or ailing kidneys.

Magnesium is found in figs, lemons, cold-pressed vegetable oils, and green vegetables. Cucumbers are a good source. Here's a good tip — drink a small glass of freshly squeezed cucumber juice every single noon time. This helps calm your entire nervous outlook and helps your kidneys work as they should.

The Case of the Professor Who "Munched"

One professor in a large Eastern university was becoming erratic. He had throbbing headaches, extreme fatigue, suffered from dizziness. He not only taught classes but delivered lectures on weekends. He was in the midst of writing a serious book.

His wife was worried. "He's nervous, irritable, tosses and turns all night. I know he's taken on too many responsibilities and he wants to ease up. But it'll be at least five more months until he finishes up his backlog. He's in too deep to try and get out now."

The librarian's wife who heard this complaint begged to intrude. "You know, I spoke to someone else who had high blood pressure. Don't look so stunned. From what you've said, it appears your husband is suffering from hypertension or high blood pressure. I know you'll have it difficult in getting him to a doctor. He's so nervous and wrought up, you can't tell him anything."

The professor's wife asked what could be done. "In five more months," she stifled a sob, "it may be too late to help him."

The librarian's wife suggested, "This friend told me he took garlic. Yes, that's right — garlic. He would chop up garlic very fine, mix it with diced or finely chopped parsley to neutralize the odor, and he'd eat this all day long, just as some people nibble on candy."

"Did it help?"

The woman nodded. "He became so relaxed that he was a better person to live with. He was more receptive to a doctor's help, afterwards."

What about the Minerals in Garlic?

Actually, garlic is a hardy bulbous perennial belonging to the onion family. Some refer to garlic as a herb. Its chemical makeup includes nearly all valuable minerals, especially iron, copper and other blood-building essentials. It is an ancient folk remedy. Research shows that the Babylonians in 3000 B.C. recognized the curative powers of garlic. King Herod, during the days of the Egyptian empire, is reported to have spend a young fortune for garlic to feed his hard-working pyramid-building workers. The Vikings and the Phoenicians put garlic in their sea chests at the start of their lengthy sea voyages. Throughout the years, the mineral properties in garlic have been recognized as effective in reducing hypertension.

G. Piotrowski, M.D., a member of the University of Geneva medical faculty, writing in *Praxis*, a European health periodical (1:1,48) tells how he used garlic on "about a hundred patients" who had high blood pressure. He found that it was very successful. The minerals in garlic, it appears, dilate the blood vessels so that the flow is not so forceful.

Dr. Piotrowski refers to the work of a colleague, Dr. Schlesinger who secured a blood pressure drop in a patient within 15 days of garlic treatment. He, Dr. Piotrowski, starts treatment with large amounts of garlic at the beginning, and gradually decreases over a period of three weeks. He then continues smaller doses until all hypertension symptoms are gone.

The doctor concludes that useful properties (minerals) in garlic are beneficial for reducing high blood pressure.

Drs. David Stein and Edward H. Kotin reported to the *New York Physician* (9:37) that they regard garlic as having therapeutic properties; not only does garlic have valuable vitamins but such essential minerals as copper, zinc, sulphur, iron, calcium and chlorine. The two doctors tell of using garlic on 12 patients who suffered from all sorts of ailments including hypertension, short breath, asthma, constipation, nervousness, etc. In every treated case, there was relief. Sometimes it was within a week and almost always, within a month. The two doctors conclude that garlic is an excellent medicament for employment in a diversity of conditions. "We believe that the vitamin and mineral factors do much to cause this to be a drug of noteworthy usage."

The Healthy Professor

The professor in our case history was prevailed upon to try chopped garlic, and use it with parsley and watercress which not only neutralized the strong garlic scent, but provided even more precious magnesium, phosphorus, potassium.

Results? The happy wife told her friend, "Now he's just wonderful to live with. It's remarkable how a simple thing like garlic can help."

How best to take garlic

This is a food and you may eat it daily. Use diced garlic as flavoring agents for meats, fish, cheeses, and vegetable salads. Garlic perles are best. Swallow one as you would a peanut or seed. Health stores sell garlic perles, capsules, powders. Added to your daily food intake, you have taken a constructive step for health.

Garlic for high blood pressure works much more effectively when combined with watercress or parsley. One herb seems to complement the other, whether taken in tablet form or used as salad ingredients.

Garlic helps slow the pulse and helps tune the heart beat rhythm, relieving annoying symptoms, such as dizziness, numbness, breathlessness and insomnia.

In addition, remember the values of getting a good eight hours of healthful sleep nightly; drink lots of water to keep your kidneys well flushed and control your emotions.

Food Allergies

Arthur F. Coca, M.D., author of *The Pulse Test,* maintains that food allergies tend to raise blood pressure. He suggests you test yourself in this way:

Select a time about 90 minutes after you have eaten. Now, eat a little bit of a food you think you may be allergic to. Take your pulse rate as soon as you swallow this food. Then, 30 minutes later, again take your pulse. Wait for 30 more minutes and take your pulse once more. You do this by finding the pulse on the underside of one wrist. If you note your pulse had increased appreciably, then it is possible that this particular food is responsible. Eliminate it from your diet. Numerous people have tried this test and found that it worked.

Raw Fruit Minerals

The Magic 14 minerals are abundant in most fresh raw fruits as well as many vegetables. A special diet of these mineral-rich edibles of Nature was used on patients by Dr. Alice Chase. In her book, *Nutrition For Health,* she relates:

The sufferer from high blood pressure must be put on the kind of food that will bring about intensive elimination from the cells and the fluids of accumulated metabolic wastes. I have used a raw food dietary which is the only type of dietary that can bring about remarkable changes from disease symptoms to normal health.

This can happen only when the hypertense person is kept for a long time on a fruit diet and very little else. *The fruits must be raw and fresh.* The subacid fresh fruits should be the main staples when they can be obtained — apricots, peaches, cherries and the citrus fruits, such as pineapples, oranges and grapefruits. Perseverance with a fruit diet for several weeks works wonders. Not only does blood pressure come down, it stays down.

Dr. Chase says that one must cultivate daily eating and living as a fine art. "While fruits can help the body *to burn up* wastes that cause arteriosclerotic hypertension, or hypertension of nervous origin, it can do so only if the correct relationship is worked out between the body and food intake."

How to do this? You must be comfortable before you eat. You need a good appetite for the fruit. You must eat the fruit with relish. Do not eat when tired or in pain. Minerals in the fruit work in the presence of a happy mind.

Dr. Chase tells of a young man who came to her clinic. He was fatigued, sleepy, pale. He had high blood pressure and an enlarged heart that extended over an area of about two inches downward and to the side.

She put him in a well-ventilated sunny room with an open balcony. Immediately, she started him on a mineral-rich diet of fresh raw fruit juices and raw vegetable juices. No other foods were allowed, and he could sleep as late as he wanted to.

During the first two weeks of this mineral diet, his blood pressure dropped to about 175. He became energetic. His skin color changed from white to pink. He had developed some ambition. After two weeks, he was given a raw vegetable salad in his diet, a pint of milk a day and (once a day) steamed vegetables with baked potato or steamed brown rice. His condition improved remarkably. He was on the road to full recovery, but the family decided to take him out of the clinic.

In this case, Dr. Chase unhappily reports that the decision was fatal. If the young man had stayed and remained on the mineral-rich diet, he would have been cured and survived.

Mineral Diet

In another case, Dr. Chase tells of a woman who had high blood pressure and was treated with a maintenance diet — rich in all healthful minerals and other nutrients needed by the body. Here is the diet prescribed:

> *BREAKFAST:* One glass of pure fruit juice. One glass of hot water with juice of half a lemon. Honey for sweetening lemonade. No cereal. No eggs. No milk in the morning. Fresh raw fruit was allowed anytime from breakfast to lunch.
>
> *LUNCH:* A small raw vegetable salad; a glass of freshly squeezed raw vegetable juice made from a combination of carrots, celery, lettuce and pineapple. A baked potato or slice of vegetable nut meat. Two steamed green vegetables. Raw fruit for dessert and an occasional piece of home-made pie.
>
> *DINNER:* One egg. A glass of milk or buttermilk. A small green raw salad. A cup of hot vegetable soup without salt or a cup of Postum.

This diet reduced Mrs. D.'s blood pressure, relieved her constipation, eased her hemorrhoids.

The mineral-rich diet appeared to have created a magic transformation. Yes, we can readily appreciate the values of these mineral when used in the body to combat ailments.

How To Handle Tensions

It is true that nervous situations will raise blood pressure. Proper mineral-rich dietary plans will strengthen your entire nervous system so you can better meet tension-causing problems. You must also self-discipline yourself in learning an old rule — the strongest tree in a forest is the one that bends in both directions to a windstorm. Be that type of tree. Don't remain rigid and firm and stubborn. The greater your resistance, the greater the pressure. Roll *with* the tide, not *against* it.

Here are some tips on meeting tensions:

1. *Try not to worry.* Nervous tension, fears, anxieties, all tend to push up your blood pressure. Keep away from people who make you nervous or upset you.
2. *Keep a normal weight.* Obesity and overweight tend to strain the heart, force it to pump more blood and raise pressure.
3. *Keep away from smoking and alcohol.* Both nicotine and alcohol can raise blood pressure.
4. *Get needed sleep.* If you can arrange it, nap during the day. Nightly, sleep a full eight or ten hours. Blood pressure goes down during sleep. The longer you stay awake, the higher it may go.
5. *Rest before you are tired.* Don't wait until fatigue or exhaustion forces you to collapse. Avoid tenseness and irritability of fatigue. Rest at intervals.
6. *Moderation.* Just one word — MODERATION — in everything you do! This is a wonderful way to lessen nervous tension.

REVIEWING MAIN POINTS OF CHAPTER FOUR

1. A nervous personality is a sure victim for hypertension. Recognize the symptoms and correct your situation.
2. Use garlic for its mineral rich properties in normalizing blood pressure. Munch it frequently; take tablets daily, use it as a flavoring agent in foods.
3. Some food allergies cause a pulse increase and pressure rise. Take your own pulse and test which foods cause such a reaction. You may be allergic to them.
4. Fresh raw fruits, fresh raw vegetables and freshly squeezed juices from these foods are Nature's treasure store of the minerals you need to reduce hypertension. Daily, drink as many glasses as possible; include a raw fruit salad with every single breakfast. A raw vegetable salad for each dinner meal. For lunch, eat either raw fruits or vegetables; alternate for variety.

5. External influences and outside surroundings raise pressure. Fight when you have to, but be gentle about it. Accept the inevitability of circumstances that are beyond your control. You'll be doing your blood pressure, and yourself, a favor.

Happiness lies, first of all, in health.

G. W. Curtis

FIVE

How To Mineralize Your Glands
for Happy Health
and Personality

The precious minerals including calcium, phosphorus, magnesium all aid in the vital function of digestion. So essential to health and happiness is this process that our forefathers were fond of the dinner table prayer, "Lord, give me a good digestion...then give me something good to digest!"

What you put into life and get out of it is in a large measure determined by the efficient dynamics of your digestive processes. From birth on, a large portion of human energy is devoted to getting nourishing food and making the best use of it.

Good digestion depends upon the magic power of minerals. You may eat the best quality food, prepared under the most natural of methods, but if this food is mineral-deficient then your digestive process cannot extract those vital substances needed to give you youthful mental and physical energy.

The main character in this drama is the hormone system — those mysterious, yet powerful, substances secreted by your glands. Hormones and glands, when properly mineralized by foods, have the power to turn gloom into cheer, fatigue into energy, idiocy into intelligence. Lives have been snatched from the Grim Reaper when treatment was directed at feeding the right minerals to the glandular network in the body.

If more folks asked, "How are your glands today?" then more of us would be more joyful and healthy. Glands *do* rule your mind and your body.

Glands and Your Personality

The famed gland specialist, Herman P. Rubin, M.D., *in Glands, Sex and Personality,* declares,

> It is a fact that the selection of a diet has infinitely more to do with the physical and psychical make-up of an individual than has ever before been recognized. And, one of the principal reasons for this is the influence on the glands, controlling growth, stamina, energy, expression, virility and longevity.

The components of your character are determined by glands, Dr Rubin adds,

> You can take it for granted that your thyroid, pituitary and sex glands have exerted potent influences in shaping your personality. They are closely involved with growth and nutrition; our personalities grow, too, and need good nourishment.
>
> Personality defects are quite conspicuous in marked cases of thyroid and pituitary deficiency, leading to mental sluggishness, lack of spark and animation. Coupled with sex-gland deficiency, the consequence is a personality — or, if you wish, a biochemical oddity — that is difficult indeed to love.

Today, modern nutritionists and medical experts have discovered that your glands need minerals as well as certain food substances in order to properly function and help create a healthy and happy personality.

Test Your Personality Power

To determine whether your personality power is being weakened by a deficiency of minerals, here is a little quiz for self-analysis. Answer honestly or your efforts will be to no avail. Just answer "yes" or "no."

1. Do you forget names and places?
2. Do you feel tired after just a few hours of ordinary mental and/or physical work?

3. When you awaken in the morning, do you feel a dull thud in your head and a lack of incentive to face the tasks ahead?
4. Is your skin and hair health of poor condition with loss of lustre, gleam and sparkle?
5. Are you always losing your temper, snapping back at others, being grouchy and nasty?
6. Do times occur when your nerves are screaming and you just cannot relax yourself?
7. Is your attitude negative, defeatist, fatalistic? That is, have you decided that life is at its worst and you were given a raw deal, so why fight against it all?
8. When faced with disappointment and rejection, do you fall into a fit of despondency and feel so depressed, you cannot come out of your shell?
9. Do you get angry if the joke is on you and do you have a strange urge to hurt the feelings of others?
10. Are you a victim of an inferiority complex in which you maintain you are not as good as others and resign yourself to your failure in life and/or family life?

How to Analyze Your Personality Answers

In self-analyzing your personality powers, write down the numbers one through 10 on a sheet of paper. Answer each of the aforesaid questions with an *honest* and *truthful* "yes" or "no" beside each number. Now, if you have fewer than two "yes" answers, it means you have a slight personality defect which may increase. If you have between two and five "yes" answers, it means that your personality is split in half and may become worse if uncorrected. If you have more than five "yes" answers, then it indicates that your personality is ailing and you would be wise to look to your glands for possible mineral deficiency.

How Do Glands and Hormones Determine Personality?

Exactly what are these glands and how do they determine your personality to the extent that financial, marital and social success are so influenced? To begin, a *gland* is any body organ that manufactures a liquid substance that it secretes from its cells. Some glands, such as the endocrine or ductless glands, do not issue any liquids but leave them to be picked up and transported via your bloodstream to other body parts.

A *hormone* is the name of the liquid substance issued by the glands. These hormones influence just about all of your mental and physical activities. The word "hormone" is taken from the Greek *hormaein* which means "to excite." Just a tiny few drops of any secreted hormone has the magical power to stimulate body growth, activity, development, tissue nutrition, sexual vigor, muscular tone, resistance to fatigue as well as numerous mental activities. Hormonal production in your body is influenced by an adequate mineralization.

How Eight Major Glands Control You

You have eight major glands which create the "interlocking directorate" of your body. These are called the ductless glands because they send their dynamic hormones (chemical messengers) pouring directly into your bloodstream. These dynamic eight glands *must have minerals*. A deficiency of these can wreck your health and personality. Each of these glands has its specific function, but all eight are ruled by the master gland or the pituitary. Let's see how they work to build mental and physical health and give you the personality power that will make you stand out in competition with other people. Each gland will be discussed in the following pages.

1. Pituitary Gland

At the base of your brain, directly behind your nose is a tiny "pea" which serves as your pituitary gland. This is known as the master of your entire personality because it issues 12 different hormones. These hormones normalize your blood pressure, improve your muscle tone, build a strong bone structure, and give power and strength to your nerves. You can enjoy an improved sense of smell, better vision, better hearing with a healthier pituitary gland. Also, this gland normalizes passage of urine and waste substances and gives you a mental desire to do work and have recreation.

Gland specialist, Dr. Herman H. Rubin states, "While the thyroid makes available the supply of crude energy by speeding up cellular processes, the pituitary is responsible for the transformation, expenditure and conversion of that energy into a healthful, youthful vitality."

A malnourished pituitary may cause premature aging, loss of enthusiasm. Abnormal malfunctioning may create either a midget or a giant. The front (anterior) portion of the pituitary controls the sex-regulating hormone.

In pubertal boys (around 13 or 14), this gland issues hormones that will develop the sex organs, change the voice, grow body hair and promote other signs of healthy young manhood. In the pubertal girls, the pituitary hormone is responsible for the secretion of the lactogenic hormone in her mammary glands to prepare her for eventual motherhood, in addition to other signs of maturity.

Other pituitary hormones regulate the storage and distribution of fat; an internal imbalance may lead to overweight. Remember the old-fashioned carnival side show which featured the dwarf, giant, and fat lady? Hucksters reaped profits from a malfunctioning pituitary gland.

If your pituitary is "starved," it means your brain is being under-active. You feel sluggish. You have nervous disorders and also display an abnormal desire for sweets. Directly above this gland is the *hypothalamus* — the appetite and sleep control center of the body. The hypothalamus is a substance of the brain that depends upon the pituitary for nourishment. If there is a mineral deficiency, it means you may suffer from poor appetite and insomnia, among other things.

Your pituitary requires a calcium-phosphorus balance, together with the valuable Vitamins A and C. This gland also must have potassium, the mineral that joins with phosphorus to send precious oxygen to your brain. Your pituitary will do all this if it has sufficient minerals to work with.

A powerhouse supply will be found in a powerful mineral supplement known as "dolomite." Sold in most health food stores, dolomite tablets are rich sources of organic minerals needed by your pituitary. If you take just three tablets daily, or as directed on the container, together with a glass of freshly squeezed cucumber-lettuce juice, you will be doing a wonderful favor for your pituitary and your personality!

2. Thyroid Gland

Directly before your windpipe and located in your throat is your thyroid gland. It issues the hormone, thyroxine which is formed by iodine, the precious mineral that combines with an amino acid (digested protein) and then still another valuable protein byproduct. Do you see how *all* nutrients must be present to function? When these amino acids join with iodine, then the hormone is sent to all body parts via your bloodstream.

Thyroxine determines growth, regulated metabolization (burning) of foods, influences your emotions and personality, and has been seen to regulate the reproductive or sexual functions. If you are mineral-deficient, then a malfunctioning thyroid means you gain unnecessary weight, risk a slow heart beat which, in turn, causes poor circulation. This spoils skin and hair health. If you complain that your hair is dry, cracks easily, falls out abnormally and looks generally lifeless, then look to a possible thyroxine deficiency. Coarse or chapped skin is also traced to a thyroxine shortage.

Thyroid malfunctioning may lead to constipation, senility, or lowered body metabolism. Hypothyroid (low activity) may cause the ailment known as myxedema. It leads to "cretinism." These victims are mentally and physically slow, have low blood pressure, and look prematurely aged.

There are about 25 milligrams of iodine in your body which are needed by your thyroid. If you are tense or subjected to excitement (even ordinary daily endeavors can be tenseful), your thyroid secretes more of this hormone. Thus, more iodine is needed to meet the challenge. You also need more iodine-produced thyroxin during situations of growth, ailment, infection, adolescence, menstruation, pregnancy, increased activity.

The case of the "slow to learn" school girl

Her name is Nancy. She was a bundle of joy at her birth; her parents delighted in her, hoped for the best. In an effort to become good parents, they joined all sorts of PTA clubs, civic groups and organizations. Nancy was a bright child when she started in school. Everything appeared to run smoothly.

One morning, Nancy was late for class. She had gone to the wrong room and a teacher found her wandering in the hallways, confused. Several weeks later, she became aggressive and hit a few playmates in the schoolyard. Her attitudes and personality wavered from one extreme to the other. She was irritable.

The school nurse examined her briefly and asked her parents to stop in. Consulting her chart, the nurse said, "Nancy's coloring is poor. She has a dull gleam in her eyes. She hasn't gained much weight."

The anxious father asked, "What of her school work? The principal said she might have to be placed in a delayed class. Our girl isn't 'slow,' but needs a little time to catch up."

The mother could not understand it. "We do so much for her; it's true she's looking pale but we thought it could be the long winter months of being indoors."

The nurse asked that Nancy be examined by the school physician. Meanwhile, it was suggested gently that she be considered a "slow" child and taken out of regular classes. Needless to say, her parents were beset with grief. They had put their hopes into Nancy and this was a bitter disappointment.

A battery of tests were made and still no clue was found. Fortunately, an astute laboratory technician recalled that his little sister once was diagnosed as having a thyroid deficiency. "Not until they sent her to a special school did they find out she wasn't even retarded — just her glands."

This little hint saved Nancy. Hormone specialists made tests and found that she had an abnormally low thyroxine count; *she showed a severe iodine deficiency.*

Nancy's mother admitted. "Well, I'm always so busy with school clubs and all, I guess I didn't give her enough fish. You have to be careful with cooking fish and I just didn't have time for precision cooking."

The school doctor and nurse prescribed special iodine capsules to be taken by Nancy. Within two weeks, she emerged from the shell, so to speak, and resumed life with energy and vigor. In fact, she spurted ahead so rapidly, she skipped a class and was promoted ahead of time.

Iodine sources are sea foods as well as a mineral capsule. One powerful organic source is in *kelp*. A form of dehydrated sea weed, it is harvested from the depths of the ocean where minerals flourish like buried treasures! Kelp is sold at most special food stores or health stores. It is available in a capsule form or in a convenient powder. Use kelp in place of *all* sharp seasonings and wherever a recipe calls for salt. Kelp is Nature's wonderful tonic to feed iodine to your thyroid gland.

3. Adrenal Glands

You have two adrenal glands: shaped like Brazil nuts, they sit astride each kidney. The adrenals issue adrenalin, known as the "emergency hormone" and related closely with a healthy automatic nervous system.

A famous doctor, Justus J. Schifferes, explains, that in times of personal danger or emotional stress, extra adrenalin is released into the bloodstream, where it quickens the heart beat, increases the energy-yielding sugar in the blood, slows up or stops digestion, pours blood into the massine muscles, dilates the pupils of the eye for greater perception, and may even cause the hair to stand on end. All of this prepares the body to meet an emergency — by fight or flight!

Want to *see* adrenalin in real action? Watch the hair on the back of a dog stand up when a stranger (or cat) arrives at the door. Want to *feel* the power of adrenalin? In a moment of terror, don't you feel goose pimples up and down your body? And, when you eat during a time of anger or upset, don't you feel the heavy lump in your stomach? Your food cannot digest. Adrenalin has been diverted to meet the stress situation and cannot aid in digestive processing powers.

The adrenals also influence a normal mineral balance between blood and body tissues. It was found that two out of ten allergic patients have an endocrine imbalance. Modern nutritionists maintain that a disturbed or upset glandular system may be responsible for allergies. It has been found that adrenalin has the power to open up the air passages in the lungs to relieve asthmatic convulsions.

Healthy adrenals will give you a healthy complexion. A deficiency of adrenalin may cause the skin to develop deep lines, grow sallow and dark (sometimes causing Addison's disease which darkens skin pigment), and cause congestion and swelling of the nasal passages. A deficiency of adrenalin (called hypoadrenia) leads to chronic tiredness, poor appetite, weak pulse, and low blood pressure.

There are hundreds of toxic substances that wait to invade the bloodstream. It was found that adrenalin will neutralize these poisonous substances and build resistance to infection.

A severe deficiency may be responsible for a complete mental and physical breakdown because the precious minerals are out of balance between body tissues and the bloodstream.

Experiments were conducted by the Worcester Foundation for Experimental Biology. Patients were schizophrenics — a split personality with peculiar behavior symptoms, also known as dementia praecox. These patients showed symptoms of a malfunctioning adrenal gland. A mineral deficiency was responsible for stress-tension which caused the adrenal glands to secrete more adrenalin to meet the challenge. This caused an exhaustion of the hormone and led to mental disorders. When adequate vitamin-mineralization was provided, schizophrenia was relieved by means of normalizing the adrenal glands.

Do you see how the entire personality can be wrecked by mineral starvation? You need potassium and magnesium, among the major minerals, as well as the calcium-phosphorus balance. While a good mineral supplement is the best way to maintain glandular health (all pharmacies and health stores have mineral supplements), you might avail yourself of still another powerhouse. It is little known here in the United States, but quite popular in such parts of Europe as Greece, Albania, Yugoslavia, countries where mental illness is virtually nil.

The mineral magic of goat's milk

Goat's milk, with its unusual characteristics in the mineral globules, acts as a super-charger in the glandular system. This may account for the robust, healthy and youthful appearance of many Europeans who drink goat's milk from childhood. Nature has provided a *wonderful balance* of precious minerals in goat's milk. These work together with pantothenic acid (one of the B-complex vitamins) to feed the adrenal glands and enable them to issue more adrenalin during stress situations.

Daily, drink one or two glasses of goat's milk. To find a local supplier, ask at any health food store, or write to your State Department of Agriculture and ask for sources of supply.

4. Pancreas

Here is a narrow gland that lies across the back of your upper abdomen. The major part of the pancreas consists of glandular tissue that issues enzymatic juices by way of a duct into the upper intestine. The pancreas secretes *insulin* — the substance that aids in sugar storage in the liver for use in energy requirements.

A malfunctioning, mineral-starved pancreas secretes little or no insulin. This means that sugar, the sole source of brain and nerve power, can neither be stored or burned. It is passed off through organs of elimination. An insulin deficiency leads to extreme tiredness, weakness, dizziness and excess weight since sugar is not burned, and some is converted into fat before being passed off from the body as waste material.

Diabetes is traced to an insulin-weak pancreas gland. In due time, the cells that make insulin will wear out because they have the heavy job of digesting more quantities of sugars than that for which they were originally created.

An unusual mineral tonic for those insulin-poor

In a few test conditions, insulin-poor patients were given a combination of tea made from blueberry leaves and powdered dehydrated cactus juice. Improvements were remarkable. Such medication is under strict medical supervision, however. Yet, it is believed that numerous minerals in blueberries and cactus worked a wonder cure.

Insulin, so we see, is the "spark" that lights the flame to burn sugars and starches to convert them into heat and energy.

A possible pancreas malfunction may be seen in various conditions, such as brittle nails, poor teeth, sore and bleeding gums, lip and tongue fissures, skin ailments, excess mouth dryness, craving sweets, weight loss, headaches, giddiness, nervous irritability and a feeling of numbness or tingling in the extremities.

The pancreas must have the minerals found in blackstrap molasses as well as in peanuts, pumpkin seeds, and nut butters. Ordinarily, for a nut butter, you would first think of peanut butter, but for a powerhouse of minerals, try cashew nut butter found in most special or health food shops. The minerals in sunflower seeds, as well as those in oils derived from seeds (corn, peanut, safflower, wheat germ), combine with vitamins B1, B2, niacin, pantothenic acid, and B-6 to spark the function of the pancreas. Do your cooking with vegetable and seed oils for a solid mineral intake. Avoid white flour, white sugar, candy, cake, chewing gum, pastries, soft drinks, noodles, spaghetti and macaroni. Starchy and sugar foods cause destruction of precious vitamins and minerals.

5. Parathyroids

These are four glands that are so very tiny they can hardly be seen. The parathyroids are found behind the thyroid gland, in the upper chest, between the tonsils and thymus. If removed or damaged, they cause bone malformation, tetany (cramps and convulsions), and severe calcium deficiency. This means that the victim is nervous, easily irritated, has a poor heart beat, poor appetite, and abnormal hair loss. Visual disorders may include cataracts. Hearing fades.

The parathyroids measure about the size of a small pea. These glands work closely with the use of calcium and phosphorus and their hormone arranges to store calcium in your long bones. If you face an important mental or physical task, calcium is sent out of the bones by means of parathyroid action.

Your kidneys may suffer if your calcium metabolism is awry because of unhealthy parathyroids. Conversely, if the quantity of calcium-phosphorus is improper, the entire hormonal system is also upset.

If you seek a wonderful treasure of calcium and phosphorus to "feed" your parathyroids, look to bone meal. Made from dehydrated cattle bones, this food is rich in the aforementioned minerals as well as Vitamins A and D, all of which combine to normalize hormonal powers. Most health stores have bone meal. Take capsules daily with your three meals and use the flour for cooking many delicious foods.

6. Female Ovaries

The ovaries are olive-sized; one is situated on each side of the female womb. These glands secrete the estrogen and progesterone hormones. Harold J. Hoxie, M.D., in *Life And Health* (Vol. 71, No. 1), explains:

> Estrogen stimulates the growth of the female genital organs, the breasts and the pubic and axillary hair. It stops the growth of the long bones at puberty, sensitizes the muscles of the uterus (womb) to pitocin (hormone) from the posterior pituitary, and is a primer for the action of progesterone.
>
> Progesterone is secreted by the corpus luteum that forms after an egg cell leaves an ovary. It is essential to pregnancy, preparing the lining of the uterus for implantation of the fertilized egg cell. It stops menstruation and causes the breasts to grow. If fertilization does not occur, the corpus luteum dies and the fall in progesterone secretion brings on the menstrual flow.

You can see how female fertility and monthly regularity is interwoven with this gland. An estrogen deficiency may cause a flat-chested condition. A progesterone shortage may cause female sterility.

These hormones create a soothing, tranquil influence on the female organs. It was also found that numerous miscarriages were responsible because of a hormonal deficiency.

One young woman found she could not bear children, although her four older sisters had healthy broods. "I felt so useless, I would have divorced my husband if he consented. But he said that there must be a solution to the problem." Several doctors pronounced her healthy.

It was by chance that she happened to attend a lecture series for public health nurses who were preparing to go abroad. The lecturer pointed out that diet influenced health, personality and even fertility. He found that the rate of sterility was very low in countries where food supplies were meager. "Agriculturists noted the people ate all parts of the vegetables including beet greens and roots. Tests proved that the roots were rich in manganese and zinc."

The childless wife, becoming interested, inquired further. She was told that they unite with vitamins and normalize tissue respiration and also help in manufacturing hormones. These minerals are found in green leaves as well as in roots and parts of the vegetable generally discarded. A good source was in unmilled grains, especially *millet*.

The childless wife conceived after taking special mineral supplements. She then said, "I ate a bowl of millet cereal every morning. Then I ran beets, celery, and cabbage through an electric juice extracter and drank the fresh juice throughout the day."

It is possible that the minerals in the fresh vegetables combined with Vitamin E in millet to stimulate the function of the ovaries. At any rate, make fresh vegetables and their roots and greens into a juice and drink daily. Also, unmilled millet grains are sold at most large food markets or write to your State Department of Agriculture for a source. Millet is a delicious cereal similar to oatmeal. It is a good supply of Vitamin E which is needed by your glands for reproductive power and fertility.

7. Male Sex Glands

In addition to the reproductive organs, these consist of the testes (gonads) which issue hormones to produce fertility. The male hormone is called *testosterone*. This hormone makes him virile and fertile, and creates body shape. The main substance of the testes is a mass of tiny coiled tubes. If placed end to end, they'd extend for more than 300 yards. These tubules are lined with cells that produce spermatozoa. Between these coiled tubes are tiny isolated cellular groups which pour forth the male hormone (testosterone).

A deficiency may cause prostate gland disorders, a flabby muscular condition, premature aging, and poor mind power. The hormone has the power to give vigorous tone to all body muscles, provide strength to bladder and stomach.

A testosterone extract has been made from the sarsaparilla root. This is a tropical American climbing plant with roots so deep that they extract the precious minerals from the soil that are imparted to its seeds. It has been found that some of the minerals in foods prepared from sarsaparilla helped stimulate a healthy male hormonal system. Zinc, the mineral found in male reproductive fluid, is abundant in sarsaparilla; also, this plant has B-complex and C vitamins which unite with minerals to create a strong hormonal power.

Try sarsaparilla tea which health stores sell in handy tea bag form or in loose granules and seeds. It may be just what the male sex glands need for mineral toning.

8. Thymus

This gland is found on the upper part of your chest. Actually, it is on the windpipe beneath the thyroids. The purpose of the thymus is to metabolize the minerals in your body, particularly calcium and phosphorus. When your thymus has enough minerals, it produces white blood cells which then build your resistance against disease. Minerals unite with the B-complex and Vitamin C nutrients and protein to function adequately.

A deficiency of minerals may react upon the thymus and cause frequent nosebleeds, excess bleeding from small scratches and bruises. Remember dairy foods for good mineral intake. Cheese sandwiches are a must. Also, include sunflower seeds because they have many minerals in Nature's balance with vitamins.

Louis Berman, M.D., describes the thymus gland as being a storage organ "affording a certain amount of protection against the deleterious effects of a lack of food."

Diet Can Help Make You a Popular Leader

Diet has a big part in your success or failure. Dr. Berman reflects that Julius Caesar was a careful eater. He spurned wine and preferred barley water. On the other hand, an improper diet and a poor mineral-glandular system can make one a *ruthless* and cruel leader.

As an example, we have the iron-fisted militarism of Prince Otto von Bismarck (1815-1898) who founded the German empire. He always indulged in enormous meals and when he was 68 years old, the Iron Chancellor tipped the scales at 247 pounds!

"There are those," says Dr. Berman, "who would correlate these prodigious indulgences in food with the coarse brutality and the 'blood and iron' policy of the Chancellor." Of course, we know that Bismarck lacked humanity and compassion.

A contemporary of Bismarck was the British leader, Prime Minister William Gladstone (1809-1898) in Queen Victoria's court. Gladstone had no warlike tendencies, was beloved by his people. He had simple eating habits and would chew each item very carefully. "How much," asks Dr. Berman, "were Gladstone's liberalism and abstemiousness connected?"

Mahatma Gandhi was a great man who said that he had to regulate what went into his stomach in order to control what entered his brain. He ate only goat's milk and dried fruit, such as dates. Considering Gandhi's type of life, Dr. Berman thinks this to be the ideal diet which creates restfulness, not restlessness. "For one who seeks a life of meditation rather than of energy and action, such a diet is ideal."

Diets and glands

Dr. Berman explains the diets eaten by these leaders in this way:

> There are as many types of leaders as there are kinds of causes which they lead. But the kind of cause they lead is correlated with the constitution of their ductless glands, and so, with what they feed themselves. To this must be added the consideration of the climate of the times in which they live. Could any great man have been great if he had lived out of his time? Would Napoleon, in 1960, have been a great general, would Lincoln have been a great president or would Washington have been "first in the hearts of his countrymen"?

So we see that hormones act as catalysts by promoting internal reactions and speeding up or slowing down body processes. Many corporation executives may owe their success to a healthy hormonal system that was fed minerals.

Personality and glands

The nature of the food supply may be a possible factor in the production of the disturbance of the glands of internal secretion. In handling such a condition, a diet calculated to affect the endocrine gland in question becomes a necessity.

The correction of dietary defects, especially in the vitamin-mineral content, is essential. Whatever affects the endocrine glands, harmfully or favorably, affects the character and personality of a person in a similar manner.

Simple Diet Plan

J. D. Walters, M.D., a tireless worker in the field of minerals and glandular balance, presents a simple diet plan.

He was able to relieve, and sometimes cure, his patients by means of restoring a mineral-balance. His patients were told to reduce the intake of cooked cereals and cooked vegetables. They were to step up use of cold-pressed vegetable oils, raw nuts, and sunflower seeds. Also, they would use cod liver oil, unheated salad oils — *no* cooked fats. They reduced starch foods. Daily, they took about three teaspoonfuls of mineral-rich wheat germ oil, together with nutrients derived from yeast, rice bran, wheat germ extract, and liver. *No* smoking was allowed.

It was found that when this special mineral-balance plan was followed, all complaints vanished. But, when this was stopped, the illnesses recurred. In brief, here are seven recommendations according to Dr. Walters as a means of restoring hormone balance:

1. Serve foods in their original state when possible.
2. Cook meals at low heat when possible, because high heat destroys nutrients and some precious minerals.
3. Cook vegetables with a minimum amount of water, at a low heat, for as short time as possible and save the water for other cooking uses. It is rich in minerals.
4. Eat protein foods to build tissues.
5. Avoid the use of carbohydrates. Use 100 per cent whole grain products.
6. Avoid the use of sugar and *all* sweetened foods.
7. Consider nutrients, such as minerals, not calories, when you plan the foods you eat.

ESSENTIAL POINTS OF CHAPTER FIVE

1. Minerals in gland and hormone activity can make or break your personality.
2. A mineral-starved personality means you are grouchy, sleepy, prematurely aged, mentally sluggish. An executive can topple from his high post if he is mineral deficient. A housewife can become a family terror without minerals. Mind and body are influenced by the absence or presence of minerals in diet.
3. There are eight basic minerals, each of which serve a vital purpose in keeping you alive and functioning both in body and mind.
4. Whole empires have been shaped and destroyed because of the dietary influence on the glandular system of its leaders.
5. Eat wholesome natural foods as described in Chapter Five for specific gland power.

Life is not merely to be alive, but to be well.

Martial

SIX

How Minerals Add Life to Your Years

How would you like to live forever? This sounds like a great idea. Is there a catch to this promise? In a way, yes. Actually, we would *all* like to live forever in a healthy, disease-free state of mind and body. It is one thing to grow old; it is another to grow senile or become an invalid, bedridden and dependent upon others for our needs. Surely, this is not a hopeful way to live forever.

The point is that you want to add life to your years as well as years to your life. You want to feel young as you enter your senior years. Life should be prolonged, but it must be free from the threat of arthritis, heart disease and numerous degenerative ailments.

Dr. Henry C. Sherman maintained that "old age can be deferred and man's life span lengthened. The indicated improvement of the adult life expectation from 70 to 77 is apparently well within the scientific probabilities for those who use the newer knowledge of nutrition in their daily food habits, beginning early enough in life. It is not merely a longer lease on life that is offered, but a life cycle both longer and lived on a higher plane of positive health, efficiency and happiness throughout."

Diet and Longevity

W. Coda Martin, M.D., declares:

It is then apparent that when we learn to eat day after day, month after month, year after year, all the essential nutrients, a higher degree of health will result and there will be a marked decrease in the degenerative diseases, and a prolonged, healthy life span will follow.

Food intake should be based on what materials the body needs for its health and efficient function rather than on present-day perverted taste habits. The diet should be low in carbohydrate, low in fat, high in proteins, and high in foods that contain natural vitamins and *minerals,* such as whole grain products in the form of bread and cereal, fruit and fresh vegetables, and the intake of refined foods and sugars must be restricted or eliminated entirely.

Arteries and Age

You have heard it said that man is as old as his arteries. This refers to the quality of the tissues of which these blood vessels are composed. Hardening of the arteries, also known as arteriosclerosis or atherosclerosis is a disorder accompanied with increasing age. So we can see how young arteries can keep you feeling and looking young.

Arteries are the elastic tubes through which fresh blood, reinforced with oxygen, is carried from the heart to various body parts. The elastic arteries can contract or expand as the heartbeat pushes more or less blood into them. Blood-filled arteries are essential to life. The major heart artery is the aorta, which is about one-half inch to one inch wide at the place where it leaves the heart's left sector, then starts branching out into smaller arteries which carry blood to the head, stomach, limbs, etc. It is said that women's arteries are wider than men's; perhaps Nature did this to accommodate the greater strains of childbirth.

But note this — wide arteries can also keep you younger and freer from premature aging and senility.

What happens to arteries that predisposes to premature aging? According to the American Heart Association in *Questions And Answers:*

Atherosclerosis is a form of arteriosclerosis, or hardening of the arteries. In atherosclerosis, the canal, or passageway, in the arteries becomes narrowed and roughened by fatty deposits in the artery lining, impeding the free flow of blood. Atherosclerosis of arteries that supply the heart muscle with blood is called coronary atherosclerosis, and it underlies most heart attacks.

Atherosclerosis develops over a long period of time; it may be present in a young person but not become apparent until middle age or later, when a complication, such as a heart attack, occurs.

How Cholesterol Can Affect Your Health

Cholesterol is a substance that is like a fatty deposit. It accumulates in the artery walls, reducing the amount of space in the arteries and veins for the blood to circulate. Cholesterol is nothing new. It is found only in animal fat, but your body can make it from sources other than fat. Cholesterol is a compound which is also a factor in gall stone trouble.

If too much cholesterol is deposited in the big arteries that feed blood to the heart, it causes a flow impediment or blockage. It may lead to such symptoms as chest pressure and constriction in the heart region.

If too much cholesterol is deposited in the arteries and veins leading to the brain, blood and oxygen flows are reduced, and this creates senility and premature aging.

The same senile condition is found in limbs that are no longer agile, a mind that does not work, ears that cannot hear and eyes that grow weak. Thousands of arterial miles are spread throughout your body in a giant network. Choke one road, and the section of your body that needs that road for life will become affected.

Medical authority states that you do need cholesterol; it is a valuable part of nerve tissue. It also fights elements that destroy red blood corpuscles. Cholesterol is needed to reduce excessive cellular wateriness. But if your arteries become too clogged with cholesterol, then circulation is hindered, literally choked.

An important fact to remember is this: *heavy starches and animal fats cause cholesterol deposits to form in the body, especially in the arteries, but an abundant supply of the right minerals will help to liquefy excess cholesterol to be excreted and keep your arteries elastic and youthful.*

What minerals reduce cholesterol

A thyroid preparation as well as a mineral supplement, together with vitamins, helped reduce cholesterol deposits in a report made by Murray Israel, M.D., in the *American Journal of Digestive Diseases.* The minerals in the supplement lowered the cholesterol and also eliminated these aging symptoms: fatigue, nervousness, depression, irritability, weakness, forgetfulness, poor concentration ability, drowsiness, insomnia, headache, dizziness, short breath, heart palpitation, leg pains, numbness, backache.

Dr. Israel seemed to feel that production of the thyroid gland hormone decreases with advancing age. Therefore, he gave his patients a thyroid supplement which actually did the trick and added life and years to these oldsters.

Furthermore, according to *Lancet* the *British Medical Magazine* of July 1959, examination of patients who died of arteriosclerosis also had goiter — another clue that certain minerals could have snatched these folks from the Grim Reaper.

Since the thyroid gland regulates metabolism — the body process that metabolises cholesterol — we can see how minerals are valuable. Remember to keep kelp and iodine-rich sea foods in your diet.

Avocado — The Miracle "Youth" Food

While doctors and dietitians have been searching for an adequate substitute to replace cholesterol-rich animal fat, there has been silently growing on large leafy green trees in California and Florida, a humble green fruit called avocado that fills the bill for this need.

"Called avocado pear or alligator pear, it is composed primarily of water and *unsaturated fat, or oily substance,* which makes it smooth as butter, delicate in texture and flavor — a prize for anyone looking for a low-cholesterol-producing fat," reveals J. DeWitt Fox, M.D., in *Life And Health* (Vol. LXXX, No. 4).

The avocado is considered to be superior over other vegetable oils in helping liquefy cholesterol in the human system. Although other oily fats are good for the health, they have the disadvantage that they cannot be spread on bread. Among these is the popular safflower oil, a light oil highly recommended for cooking and salad dressings, but so thin it will run all over bread. Into the same category fall other oils, such as peanut, soy, corn, and olive. These oils are relatively unsaturated, but they cannot be used as a spread for bread.

Mexicans have long enjoyed the avocado which they call *aguacate*. It is said that Fernando Cortex (1485-1547), the Spanish conqueror of Mexico and Lower California, knew of the avocado and attributed the strength of his army to its nutritional powers. The personal historian of Charles V of Spain said of avocados, "They are pears which are unlike pears, similar to butter, and very good eating and of good taste."

How Avocados Work With Minerals

Just how can avocados work to help keep you young? Its rich mineral and vitamin content make this possible. Here are some miracle powers of this mineral-rich fruit:

1. *Vascular-disease prevention*. Just what the doctor ordered to lower the fat content of the blood and avoid cholesterol. It can stem the tide of blood vessel disease.

2. *Overweight control*. The avocado has only 165 calories per 100 grams while butter has 733. It has a way of *reducing your appetite,* helping to normalize digestion and giving you a feeling of satisfaction after eating. The minerals make you feel contented and less prone to overeating and gorging of food.

3. *Benefits for heart patients*. The avocado has little or no sodium, contains fewer calories than most solid fats and is generally considered ideal to help reduce weight and strain on the heart resulting from overweight, high blood pressure and erratic heart action.

4. *Benefits for diabetic patients*. As a fruit, the avocado is low in carbohydrates — only 5 per cent as compared with other fruits that have up to 20 per cent as carbohydrate. Since diabetics may experience high-cholesterol levels, many doctors say they will benefit from the avocado's anti-cholesterol combative powers. Also, the avocado contains a weight-reducing factor that many diabetics may require.

5. *Skin health benefits*. Avocado oil is most beneficial for face, hand and skin creams because it has a light texture which prevents

dry skin; oil of avocado also helps control skin blemishes. Cosmetic creams sold in some pharmacies contain avocado oils which help keep skins smooth and retain youth.

6. *Ulcer diet.* The avocado is a perfect food for an angry stomach and a duodenal ulcer. It has been recommended in the diet as a *preventative* measure against ulcers. This is a health tip very well worth remembering.

7. *Convalescent patients.* Minerals in the avocado make its fruit fat bland and easily digested. This means that even surgical patients tolerate it without digestive upset or gas. After the convalescent period of a patient who has had his gall bladder removed, it is an ideal food. He is able to eat it in place of other fatty foods.

8. *For oldsters in general.* If a senior citizen has a dental problem and cannot chew hard foods, avocados are great. They just about melt in the mouth.

9. *Baby food.* Yes, infants need mineral-rich avocados, too. This fruit has a flavor and texture that they will like because it appeals to their fickle taste buds.

10. *Acne problems.* If you or your teenager have pimple problems, switch from hamburgers and french fries, candies, and chocolate malts to avocado. Spread it on brown bread, use it in salads with fruit or as a dip for corn chips and watch those pimples disappear. Recent research shows that when saturated animal fats are withheld from the diet and unsaturated oily fats are used, there is no more acne. Avocados are just such an unsaturated fat. The avocado's easily digested fat does not clog tiny oil ducts in the body as animal fats do.

How to use avocados

Toast slices of pumpernickel or other breads and smear with avocado. Sprinkle with lemon, garnish with a tomato slice, some chopped onions and you've got a delicious mineral-rich treat. Or, try avocado on the half-shell with pineapple and other fruits. Combine it with orange, grapefruit and cherries for a fruit salad. Or, add slivered or cubed to green tossed salads.

If your family can't get used to new things, then introduce the fruit in the form of avocado mayonnaise. You whip avocado together with lemon juice and honey. Add vegetized salt or kelp, and serve with a fresh sliced tomato."

How to buy avocados

If the fruit is soft, it has its greatest mineral supply. Buy firm fruit if it is not to be used at once. Let go soft at room temperatures. Store avocados in the refrigerator, but never freeze them. Always prepare avocados just before serving. To prevent darkening on cut surfaces, sprinkle fresh lemon or lime juice. Unusued portions may be wrapped and kept in the refrigerator for a short while. Just about any fresh fruit and vegetable outlet will sell avocados.

Sauna Bath Magic

A doctor in a recent publication tells us that a means of dilating the blood vessels to keep them young and elastic is available. The Sauna bath has been used for years in Finland and now in the United States it is becoming ever more popular.

A Sauna is a unique heat room made of redwood or cedar, which has a heater and a dehumidifier capable of running the room temperature up to 190° F. with only 3 per cent humidity. The procedure is to sit in the room for ten minutes, run out into the snow (and they do this in Finland) or take a brisk cold shower. Then, back into the Sauna for ten more minutes, follow with another shower, and then stretch out in a cool room for a fifteen minute snooze or rest.

The effect of such a hot-and-cold procedure is to open and dilate skin blood vessels as blood is rushed to the surface, then whisked through the body in an effort to cool the body. Body temperature rises to 103° F., and may remain for an hour or so somewhat above normal.

The sudden cold causes constriction of the blood vessels and quick flushing of fat, cholesterol, and waste through liver and kidneys for rapid elimination.

The Sauna bath is good for its relaxing and refreshing powers, and it dilates the blood vessels. This is the ticket to youth!

If you can afford it and have the facilities, you can have a Sauna bath built on your premises. Inquire at any major housewares department store. You may care to go away for a vacation at a resort featuring the Sauna bath. Ask your local travel agent for names of such resorts. Some accommodate guests for a weekend, a week, a month or longer. Look in the classified pages of your telephone directory under "Steam Baths." Ask some of these establishments if they have Sauna baths. You may find one in your own area.

Since hardening of the arteries is responsible for aging and senility, you should put forth every effort to prevent this debilitating degenerative disease. Aging is not an overnight blight. It starts early and progresses, unless you do something to help halt the ravages. A Boston specialist has stated that most people expect their bodies to degenerate automatically with age and develop such frightening diseases as arthritis, eye cataracts and heart attacks. Disease is not caused by aging. The damage is caused by strain to an organ or bad nutrition.

Think yourself young

It is a sad truism that most people think themselves old! They fear advancing years and automatically deplore ailments and sicknesses. This is negative thinking. A research report on aging, according to the Royal Bank of Canada *Newsletter* put it this way:

> So far as health goes, the remedy is simple: stop thinking of ills as merely applying a temporary patch to a worn fabric, and think positively of how to keep that fabric in shape for a long and comfortable use. A man of 65 may be as vital as the average man of 40 and may show no sign of old age except the accumulation of wisdom.

It is well known, too, that worry is a greater killer than work. No one dies of work he enjoys! Use a young attitude! Begin early *and improve mineralization of your diet.* It is never too late!

"Security Killed" Executives

One of the nation's largest engineering concerns decided to do something for its executives by setting up a security plan. It not only consisted of a pension, but also provided for medical care (hospital and doctor bills included), as well as burial expenses. The plan went so far as to invite its participants to select funeral arrangements and burial sites in advance.

The company's president was pleased...for a while. Then someting peculiar happened. An important vice-president died in his sleep. A treasurer suffered a fatal stroke. Two young executives fell ill and were hospitalized for four months apiece. Within one year, eight members of the Board of Directors succumbed to illnesses.

The president, himself, complained about a feeling of weakness. He visited a fraternity friend of his; several decades ago, the friend had been a medical student and now was currently a leading Chicago specialist.

"I don't understand it," complained the president. "They're all dying and I thought the security plan would help ease their tensions."

The doctor smiled. "You know, man is the only animal who plans to die! That's right. Man buys insurance, annuities, hospitalization, even burial plots. He gets ready to die — and he does. Animals are smarter. Animals prepare to live and maybe that's why so many of them reach ripe old ages."

"Who told my colleagues to die?" protested the president. "They all approved of the plan."

The doctor nodded and then went on, "Of course. I've had many patients who told me that their parents lived until 64 and their grandparents died at that same age. I know very well my patients will never go beyond 64. It's an unhealthy dying pattern. I know other people who tell me of a family pattern of heart attacks, strokes, even accidents. They, themselves, reach the end in the same manner. Know why? Their minds are telling their bodies how long to live!"

"What can I do?" The president feared he, too, might exit this way.

"Change the whole security plan. Don't mention a word about burials or funerals. Make it a comprehensive financial plan that includes health benefits. But be clear to say that extensive illness will deplete this reserve sum. Death will give the survivors even less!"

The company president followed this advice. In the next three months, *no* illnesses and *no* deaths were reported.

This is the power of the mind — it can be constructive or destructive. The body is merely a vehicle which houses a spirit that moves it from place to place. The spirit rules the body. The body will survive hardship, banish obstacles or destroy itself, if the spirit so wills! Build a renewed desire to live and enjoy renewed vigor. Banish all thoughts of the "ease of dying" and you can enjoy a healthy lifespan.

Statistics show that most folks die after retirement. Why? Because they've nothing to live for. They just sit on a porch and wait for the end. This is an unhappy personality defect that attitude can correct.

Nine-Step Anti-Senility Plan

You can add life to your years with a sound mineral diet. Minerals need other nutrients as sparkplugs to release their power, so you need a balanced mineral diet. Here are nine steps suggested by a famous physician. Note carefully the plan for certain vitamins which work with minerals in helping to add dynamic life to your present age span.

1. Delete from the diet any food which has the basic chemistry altered by the removal in its preparation of those elements (usually minerals) essential to human nutrition.

2. Do not depend on "enriched" or fortified foods. (Read the labels on your present food packages.) These food replace only a small fraction of the vitamins and minerals removed in the process of its refining or manufacturing.

3. The diet should be high in "protecting" foods. These foods include fresh fruits, vegetables and dairy products, whole grain bread and cereals. A large portion of the fruits and vegetables should be eaten in the fresh raw state to assure an adequate intake of the important enzymes and minerals.

4. The daily diet intake of lean meat, fish, fowl and eggs should be sufficient.

5. Milk and dairy products are necessary in the daily diet. Whole *unpasteurized* milk is preferable. (Ask your State Department of Agriculture for certified producers of unpasteurized milk products.)

6. The intake of fresh fruits should be adequate.

7. For adequate intake of important B-complex factors, the diets of older people should be supplemented with a good natural source

of these elements, such as (1) *desiccated whole liver*. This substance contains not only all the known and identified fractions of the B-complex but also a number of unidentified substances that are at least as important to nutrition as those already known. It also contains the anti-fatigue factor (minerals) which is so important in elderly people. (2) *Brewer's yeast,* which is probably the cheapest source of the natural B-complex and is also high in complete proteins. (3) *Wheat germ* is another excellent source of the natural B-complex and also rich in vitamin E.

8. This recommended diet should supply sufficient vitamin A and D, but if there is a doubt, supplement it with a preparation of liquid natural A and D vitamins for better absorption, such as cod liver oil.

9. Organically-grown foods are advisable when available for consumption. Organically raised foods have 20 to 40 per cent greater vitamin and mineral content than those grown in depleted commercial soils. They are also free from chemical insecticides and pesticides which accumulate in human fat and produce liver damage. For optimum health this type of food is essential. Organically-grown foods contain many unknown protective elements that have not yet been identified. Many feeding tests in humans and animals have proved this fact. If this type of food is not available, a vitamin and mineral supplement is recommended.

It is important that the diet have optimum mineral content to protect against degenerative diseases and prolong the life span.

For mineral-rich desiccated liver and for nutrient-rich Brewer's yeast and wheat germ, visit any health store. Ask your State Agricultural Department for outlets of organically grown fruits and vegetables.

It's wonderful to reach the sunset years of life — and keep on enjoying that perpetual sunset. Minerals will help you keep that sun from going down too soon!

IMPORTANT TOPICS OF CHAPTER SIX

1.   You can enjoy prolonged, healthful years of life with a low-starch, low-fat, high-mineral, high-protein diet plan.

2. Your arteries need to be elastic and young, if you want to feel the same.

3. A thyroid gland extract containing minerals helped reduce cholesterol in test cases and generally improved health.

4. The avocado, a simple fruit known for almost seven centuries, is a mineral-rich powerhouse of youth building factors. Include avocado in your daily meals.

5. Take a tip from our friends in Finland — the Sauna bath can keep your blood vessels young and elastic along with your mineral diet.

6. Think yourself young. Prepare for life, not death.

7. Minerals should "star" in your eating plan as set out in the nine-step plan.

SEVEN

How Mineral Dynamic Action (MDA) Fires Up Your Energy

When you discover the "buried treasure" what should be first on your list of purchases of what you always wanted? No doubt, it is *energy!* Ask yourself these questions: Do you go through your tasks with limitless energy? Are you always alert, abundant with good health, a picture of incentive? Are you the life of the party, an ever-welcome member of the household?

Or, are you one of those who feel tired all the time? Is each step a mile? Do you complain of extra work on your job, in your home? At night, do you collapse in bed, feeling all worn out? And, when you awaken, are you just as tired as the night before? If you answer "yes" to any of these questions, it means that you lack energy. This is not the type of fatigue that comes from ordinary mental and physical work. No, indeed not. This is a form of chronic fatigue *traced to a mineral deficiency.* It is an insidious and sneaky fatigue that robs you of personality, health and well-being. Small wonder that you will want to use your discovered treasure to acquire energy.

Low Blood Sugar

As the name implies, low blood sugar is a condition in which you have a subnormal amount of sugar in your bloodstream. This is known as *hypoglycemia.* The mineral zinc as well as magnesium and manganese work together in the metabolization of sugar in your system to give you energy. Here's how it works. As soon as sugar-containing foods are swallowed, enzymes are sparked by the minerals to start the process of digestion. Minerals work with calcium and phosphorus as well as with zinc in order to break down the sugar in your intestine. This sugar seeps through the tiny capillaries along the intestinal walls. Here, minerals transform the sugar into *glucose*.

Now iron and copper work together to send glucose, via your bloodstream, to all parts of your body — brain, heart, hormonal system, etc. Minerals are constantly at work in transporting this steady glucose supply. Without it, your brain and nerve cells could starve!

Phosphorus also helps send glucose to your central nervous system which can absorb oxygen only with this substance. Iron helps send glucose in the bloodstream to the region of your heart so the beat can be regulated. Even the subconscious mind is influenced by a normal blood sugar level.

After the minerals have sent an ample supply of glucose into your bloodstream to give you mental and physical energy, there is some left over. Minerals help send this excess to your liver; the stored glucose is called *glycogen,* formed by hooked-up molecules of glucose. To do this, iron, copper, phosphorus, zinc as well as potassium all join hands to form and store glycogen in your liver.

Suppose your bloodstream needs some stored glucose. Minerals join together to alert three glands — the pancreas, adrenals and pituitary. Minerals influence the pancreas to issue insulin which enables body cells to absorb and utilize the sugar. (Minerals also act to cause insulin to remove unwanted sugar from the blood and store it.) Minerals now signal the adrenal and pituitary glands to issue hormones to split the liver glycogen into usable glucose. These minerals-inspired hormones trigger your liver into manufacturing blood sugar from fat and protein food elements. You can see how minerals play a star role in this energy producing drama. Hormones, activated by minerals, assure a steady glucose supply.

Muscles Need "MDA" Action

Your overall muscular structure requires glucose. Suppose you sit quietly at your desk for several hours. Now you have to get up to open file cabinets, drawers, do typing, work on a machine. This demand for physical work requires a sudden burst of glucose into certain muscles.

Minerals will store some glucose in your heart, but when this energy-producing substance is needed, your heart is activated by iron and copper to take glucose from your bloodstream. If you have a low blood sugar level, the heart is forced to draw upon its own storage. This shows a reaction. It may not be serious but if your heart is "starved" by serious blood sugar deficiency, it may be injured.

A diabetes specialist, stated that prolonged hypoglycemia is more frequent than we suspect. He named, among symptoms, weakness and a disordered heart action. These compound the effects of heart disease and the victim becomes susceptible to a heart attack.

MINERAL DYNAMIC ACTION, or "MDA," is the force that energizes the entire manufacture of vital blood sugar to give you mental and physical action. Without minerals, or with a deficiency of just potassium or iron, sugar cannot be properly metabolized and the entire energy system of the body begins to suffer. MDA is your golden coin of youthful energy in the sought for treasure of health!

Minerals, by means of MDA action-producing energy, combine with essential proteins to give you pep and vigor. Again we can see how minerals become the vital link in the chain of health. Minerals aid in breaking proteins down into usable amino acids that then create sugar metabolization.

An eminent medical authority explains that it has been found that a meal consisting of protein and fat but with *no sugar and starch* never caused low blood sugar. The addition of sugar and starch to such a meal could readily produce low blood sugar.

Let's see how this works. Normally, the blood sugar level should be from 80 to 100 milligrams; or, about one glucose drop for each 100 drops of blood...about two or three drops in your entire system.

You feel tired. You decide to reach for a sweet, or a glass of soda pop, or any soft drink. What happens? Minerals are flung into violent action, creating a severe yank of the insulin reaction. Minerals are forced to metabolize sugars and starches at a speedy rate. Just two hours after manufacture of glucose, the blood sugar has already been absorbed and "burned up." Minerals are depleted and so are you!

Coffee Breaks Are Anti-MDA

A certain manufacturing empire headquarters was enormous. In a mid-West suburb, the plant occupied the equivalent of 84 city blocks! It was a city unto itself. As part of a good will program, the manufacturers instituted the coffee break plan. Each morning at 10 and each afternoon at 2, employees could pause for 15 minutes, drink coffee from special in-plant carts, together with sugary doughnuts and cakes. It was assumed that this would invigorate the factory employees and desk workers.

Yet, it was found by foremen and supervisors that within 30 minutes after the coffee breaks, production fell off! The assembly line was slowed up; accountants and bookkeepers had to check and double check their figures. A few complained that the lines of columns would waver before their eyes!

A team of efficiency experts was called in. For three weeks, they watched the methods of all employees, marking down time levels, frequent pauses, etc. All the while the plant continued giving frequent, longer coffee breaks, and production kept falling off.

The vice president was nervous. "Well," he demanded of the efficiency experts who spread charts and graphs before him, "what does all this mean? How can you stop the slump? We've lost at least 50 thousand dollars in production delays!"

Each efficiency expert kept offering solutions about improved machinery, automation, rearrangement of equipment, and even replacing older workers with younger ones who, it was presumed, would have greater stamina.

One quiet member of the team kept to one side, astutely observing all. Just then, a knock at the door indicated it was another coffee break time. The vice president invited the team to drink coffee and munch cakes. All partook of this welcome break except the young man. He had brought a small thermos container with him.

The others watched him pour a wine colored liquid into a paper cup, then stir in a chocolate looking powder. He drank it, and looked calm, contented and relaxed.

"Some special type of potion?" growled the nervous vice president as he gulped his coffee and munched on a starchy looking cake.

"Not really. This is ordinary grape juice. The powder is something that gives it a zest and gives me pep. It's called carob powder." The young efficiency expert invited the others to sample the drink.

They remarked upon its tangy taste. When they asked why he shunned coffee, the young man explained, "Coffee makes me nervous and tired. In fact, I was just waiting to put in my observations about this fatigue problem in the plant. I think it's caused by these coffee and cake breaks."

The vice president listened as the young man explained about blood sugar and how coffee could cause a drop, as could sweets, and defeat the whole purpose of a "break."

They decided to change this one rule. Yes, they would have breaks, but they would offer sugar-free pop drinks, caffeine-free or coffee substitutes. Starch and sugar cakes and candies were taboo. Instead, natural fruit flavored cakes and candies without any artificial additives were the rule. Freshly squeezed fruit and vegetable juices were allowed. Considering the problem of time in squeezing juices on the spot, it was decided to install a large juice extracting device in the company cafeteria and someone would do this in advance. Fresh juices were put in cartons, labelled and given out to employees.

Carob candies were soon featured. The factory workers were amused but decided to go along with the new company policy. Daily, these breaks featured natural foods. Six days after this program was instituted, the production schedule was doubled and trebled. Nervous fatigue was ended. No one felt so tired again.

The efficiency team was fired because they had not come up with anything unusual. Their plans were useless. The vice president said they had had the answer right there and did not see it. The young efficiency expert promptly "resigned" from the company which sent out the team. It was an odd case where being smart and helpful actually backfired upon him. Yet, he had no cause for worry. He was immediately taken into the manufacturing plant as the newest and youngest assistant to the vice president who declared, "Any man who has common sense belongs on *my* team."

What Is Carob?

This food is mentioned in the Bible. There is a carob tree which produces pods. The tree's husk, incidentally, is the same bread eaten by John the Baptist in the wilderness and that is why it is known as "St. John's bread." It is said that the armies of Mohammed would live solely on "kharub." The ancient Greeks, Romans, Spaniards and British all knew of carob tree and ate wholesomely of its husks and powdered pods.

Powdered pods create a flour like substance that looks and tastes as delicious as chocolate. Yet it is a powerhouse of MDA and has none of the harsh effects of blood sugar yanking as chocolate. All health food stores sell carob.

Carob is a rich source of calcium, magnesium, potassium, sodium, silicon, iron, manganese, barium, boron as well as precious vitamins and minerals. All work together to feed a healthy energy.

Carob flour is used for baking and cooking purposes, too. This means you can use carob for health cakes, as a sweetening agent for a variety of edible meals. Carob flour is said to be the fruit of the carob tree, making it a wonderful replacement for chocolate and sugar. It also has a beneficial alkaline reaction in your system and *minerals need this environment to produce previous Mineral Dynamic Action!*

Grape Juice Energizer

WHAT ABOUT GRAPE JUICE? Minerals, such as calcium, phosphorus, iron, and copper, abound in the grape. There is a high supply of vitamins A and C which combine with these minerals to create a powerhouse of energy.

Here is a PEP DRINK to enjoy in place of a coffee break. Mix one heaping tablespoon of carob powder in a glass of grape juice. Stir vigorously. Drink slowly. You will discover that the mineral energy factors will truly put power into your body.

Reasons for Avoiding Coffee

You die-hards may insist upon coffee for instant energy. What's wrong with coffee? Dr. Carlton Fredericks, noted nutritionist-author and one-time professor at Fairleigh Dickinson University states:

> Of all the beverages, coffee is the worst one for a person with low blood sugar. Not only is coffee customarily sweetened with sugar but the caffeine present stimulates the liver into discharging still more sugar into the blood. However, these people often feel the need of a stimulant and choose coffee — which will lift them a trifle and then drop them with a thud. The low blood sugar type of person is a steady customer for soda pop, especially the cola beverages, from which they obtain caffeine and sugar in over-generous amounts!

Dr. Fredericks now warns:

> Without doubt, there have been fatal or maiming automobile accidents caused by low blood sugar; for then the condition is persistent, *it leads to abberrations in behavior, mistakes in judgment and complete alterations of personality.*
>
> Low blood sugar can cause rapid heart beat in the absence of organic disturbances. It can cause blackouts which resemble epilepsy. It can cause migraine headaches, extreme anxiety and nervousness, confusion — even coma!

Dr. Fredericks concludes by blaming personality changes upon a low blood sugar.

Personality Defects from Low Blood Sugar

A mineral-starved system leads to a low blood sugar crisis that can change a persons complete personality. Doctors at a New York hospital learned of this imbalance when they found that many nervous, high strung persons were influenced by a mineral-deficient condition of hypoglycemia. When these persons lost tempers, became irritable, "fit to be tied," their blood glucose dropped to a low level. When they were relaxed, properly nourished, the level was normalized.

Doctors at the Midwest Hospital treated some middle-aged persons who said they had dizzy spells, vertigo, profuse sweating, and trembling. When examined, it was found that not only did they have a low sugar level, but they suffered from mental frustration —

their mineral supplies were so deficient that the entire endocrine-hormonal system was out of balance.

A leading authority on the problem wrote that many victims of low blood sugar are noted for being conscientious and hard-driving. These are the go-getters who basically might feel insecure. Emotional upsets drain the mineral supply, drawing away these elements from the adrenal and pituitary glands. This means that minerals can transport *less* sugar into the bloodstream.

Tensions Due to Low Blood Sugar

Emotional tensions are blamed for three out of four cases of low blood sugar. Early symptoms include feeling weak, excessive perspiration, the heart beating at a furious rate, and a trembling sensation. The adrenal glands need more minerals to force the liver to pour forth more sugar into the depleted bloodstream.

Mental reactions of a mineral-starved condition related to low blood sugar include poor vision, light-headedness, inability to concentrate. More severe conditions include a blackout. A sudden collapse in blood sugar may be caused when a candy bar, doughnut or coffee has been utilized. In a severe form, your mineral-starved brain is without glucose. This may cause amnesia, temperamental outbursts, hallucinations, severe depression, and even stiffening or paralysis of your limbs.

The blood sugar supply to the central nervous system is particularly important, because abnormal fluctuations in the blood sugar level affect not only the function of the heart but also the central nervous system functions. Many of the symptoms experienced by heart patients are due directly to the effects of the fall in blood sugar on the cells of the brain and the spinal cord.

How To Make a Hot "MDA" Drink

You may be interested to know of a special hot drink that will put bounce into your blood sugar, give you wonderful energy and the *Mineral Dynamic Action* that you so crave.

Into one cup of boiled water, piping hot, spoon two tablespoons of Barbados Molasses together with a pinch of cinnamon. Stir vigorously until dissolved and then drink in place of coffee.

Barbados, a tropical isle in the West Indies, grows fields and fields of sugar cane from which this old-fashioned molasses is made. This particular molasses is superior in minerals because the soil of the West Indies is rich in sea minerals and sea air. It may be said to be the richest mineral-soil in the world. Anything growing from such soil is sure to be a prime treasure of minerals.

Cinnamon contains flavor and adds a zest to this MDA drink. You may obtain Barbados Molasses at most health stores. Cinnamon is found in just about any retail grocery outlet. Try this drink a few times a day and you'll discover the secret of treasured vitality.

Your Mineral Rich Energy Diet

The well-known doctor, E. M. Abrahamson, comments on a diet high in minerals that need to work with proteins and essential fatty acids. He has found that hypoglycemia is often the cause of allergies, asthma, personality defects asneuroses, epilepsy, and alcoholism because of its influence on the nervous system.

It is suggested that you avoid artificial foods. Eliminate such refined sugar foods as soft drinks, ice cream, cakes, pastries, candies. Cut down (or cut out) starchy foods made from white flour. Eat natural foods that have not been tampered with for a great source of minerals and protein. Here is a diet plan designed to give you the desired Mineral Dynamic Action:

ON ARISING: Medium orange, half grapefruit or 4 ounces of fruit juice.

BREAKFAST: Fruit or 4 ounces of juice, 1 egg with or without meat patty; only 1 slice of whole grain bread with plenty of butter; milk or coffee substitute.

LUNCH: Meat, fish, cheese or eggs; salad (large serving of lettuce, tomato or Waldorf salad with mayonnaise or French dressing); vegetables if desired; only 1 slice of whole grain bread or toast with plenty of butter; dessert and beverage.

3 HOURS AFTER LUNCH: 8 ounces of milk.

1 HOUR BEFORE DINNER: 4 ounces of juice.

DINNER: Soup, if desired (not thickened with flour); vegetables, liberal portion of meat, fish or poultry; only one slice of whole grain bread if desired; dessert; beverage.

2 or 3 HOURS AFTER DINNER: 4 ounces of milk or a small handful of unsalted nuts.

ALLOWABLE VEGETABLES: Asparagus, avocado, beets, broccoli, Brussels sprouts, cabbage, carrots, cauliflower, celery, corn, cucumbers, eggplant, lima beans, onions, peas, radishes, sauerkraut, squash, string beans, tomatoes, turnips.

ALLOWABLE FRUITS: Apples, apricots, berries, grapefruit, melons, oranges, peaches, pears, pineapple, tangerines. These can be cooked or raw, with or without cream but *without* sugar. Canned fruits should be packed in water, not syrup. Lettuce, mushrooms and nuts may be eaten as freely as desired.

JUICES: Any unsweetened fruit or vegetable juice except prune juice.

BEVERAGES: Weak tea (tea ball, not brewed); decaffeinated coffee and any coffee substitutes.

DESSERTS: Fruits, unsweetened gelatin, junket (made from tablets, not mix).

AVOID ABSOLUTELY THESE FOODS:

Sugar, candy and other sweets, such as cake, pie, pastries, sweet custards, puddings and ice cream.

Caffeine: this includes ordinary coffee, strong brewed tea and all beverages (soft drinks included) containing caffeine.

Potatoes, rice, raisins, plums, figs, dates and bananas. Spaghetti, macaroni and noodles.

Wines, cordials, cocktails and beer (if you must — an absolute minimum).

This recommended diet plan is a pattern that is designed to introduce a healthful and ample supply of minerals in your system. These internal body workers have the power to give energy and zest — so feed them the proper working materials.

A SUMMARY OF AIDS FOR DEVELOPING MINERAL DYNAMIC ACTION (MDA) FOR ENERGY AS PRESENTED IN CHAPTER SEVEN

1. Low blood sugar, also known as hypoglycemia, is a condition caused by a deficiency of minerals and protein. Both work together to create body energy.

2. You need iron, copper, phosphorus, calcium and magnesium, together with zinc, found in fresh fruits and vegetables and dairy products, for creating a strong energy power.

3. Sugar, starch, and coffee are harmful because of the seesaw yanking of the blood sugar level. Avoid these.

4. Carob is a natural sweet powder made from the famed Carob tree, used for food in the days of the Bible. Carob foods have a chocolate taste, but are free of artificial sugar. Use carob powder to make bread, cake, candies and for sweetening.

5. Tension drains minerals that are needed to raise blood sugar level. During times of severe stress-situations, eat many fresh fruits and vegetables as well as lean meats, liver, and unpasteurized cheeses, for more mineral intake.

6. Try the hot "MDA" drink in place of coffee and discover the joys of vigorous energy.

7. Try to adopt the precepts of the special mineral rich energy diet at the end of the chapter.

Eat properly and it will make you wise.

                    John Lyly

EIGHT

How to Wake Up Your Brain Power with Mineral Action

You are on a major highway in the traffic jam. You approach a multi-lane intersection. Suddenly, from out of nowhere, a huge trailor-truck swings toward you. In a split second, you twist the wheel, and swerve, saving the lives of yourself and companions.

It is Saturday night and you join a few friends for a little social get-together. Someone makes a joke — it's on you. Everyone looks at you and you start blushing.

You are a corporation executive. A group of important financiers are studying the blueprint you have prepared and they come up with some baffling questions. You tensely answer each one to the best of your ability.

At long last, you have washed and dried the dishes. You stack them up, then carry a waist-to-chin high supply to the cupboard at the other end of the kitchen. From somewhere your little boy scampers under your feet, chasing after a stray kitten. By a miracle, you do not topple over boy and kitten but manage to retain your balance (if not your temper).

How were all these seeming miracles accomplished? The answer is — via your brain! It is the power of your brain that enables you to make lightning swift decisions that change from instant to instant; you can direct your muscles, arms, legs and thoughts, all via brain power.

What Is the Brain?

Everyone has a brain, despite television and comic jokes. The *power* of your brain may vary from the power of someone else's, but you have one, just the same.

The brain is the most valuable section of your entire nervous system. It consists of about 16 billion cells. It has three basic parts: (1) the cerebrum or frontal part; (2) the cerebellum or hind part; (3) the medulla oblongata by which it is joined to the spinal cord and hence to all of your body nerves.

A man's brain weighs about 48 ounces. A female's brain is slightly less in weight, but since it is relative to body weight, there is no difference.

When something happens to any part of your body that necessitates mental and/or physical activity, a nerve impulse travels to your brain. That is, an internal electrical current moves along a well-defined path to a certain part of your brain. This impulse may just dissolve along the way — your brain may squelch it or put it into action. This depends upon your brain.

For example, the blushing herein referred to, is caused by the vasoconstrictor center of your brain whose activity is temporarily closed by your feeling of embarrassment; this causes the small facial blood vessels to dilate with blood. This is known as a "reflex" action which means that it takes without your consent or conscious knowledge. So, you can do nothing to stop it. If you've ever wanted to learn how not to blush, stop trying. You have no control of this brain action.

This indicates the amazing power and complexity of the brain which has a psychic (mental) component that is often out of your control.

In your brain are other life producing centers. You have the respiratory center that controls breathing. You have the olfactory center that regulates your sense of smell; the auditory center registers your reactions to sound; the visual center is for sight; the taste center for taste. You have a valuable motor center that controls physical movements. You even have centers for speech and creative arts, such as writing, music, painting. You have centers for mechanical aptitude and a center for household management!

How the Brain Rules the Body

Each single body movement depends upon a center of your brain. The vaso-constrictor center keeps the blood vessel walls contracting. You have centers that enable you to chew, swallow, cough, sneeze, wink. Another center in your brain regulates the flow of digestive juices or enzymes that are needed to act upon foods.

You need a healthy brain to enable you to perform autonomic (automatic) actions, such as breathing, blinking, etc. You are always performing these movements even though you are not conscious of them. There are myriads of such autonomic activities that are regulated by your brain. Putting it simply, the very actions of walking, talking, being alive, depend upon a healthy brain!

Famed author Napoleon Hill also says that the brain rules life. He refers to the brain as a giant built-in "broadcasting" station. Yet, according to Mr. Hill, man, with his boasted culture and little education knows but little concerning the physical brain and its vast network of intricate machinery through which the power of thought is translated into its material equivalent. But he is now entering an age which shall yield enlightenment on the subject.

Men of science have begun to turn their attention to the study of this stupendous thing called a brain, and while they are still in the kindergarten stage of their studies, they have uncovered enough knowledge to know that the central switchboard of the human brain, the number of lines which connect the brain cells one with another, equal the figure one, followed by 15 million ciphers.

Mineral Feeding Your 15 Million Brain Cells

Each time you want to perform a specific action, mental or physical, your impulse travels along a route to your brain. The center that is charged with the responsibility of enabling you to carry out that action is filled with these brain cells.

These cells are literally soaked and drenching wet with the mineral it needs for its very life. This mineral phosphorus, is found in the fluids and soft tissues (blood and cells) of your brain. A vital constituent, it requires both calcium and Vitamin D in order to function properly.

Your brain consists of about 80 to 85 per cent water. The solid portion of your brain consists of phosphorized fats. These mineral-rich ingredients increase in proportion as your nervous system grows older and your brain becomes more learned.

You may have heard of fish being "brain food." Considering the high percentage of phosphorus in fish as well as other valuable minerals, such as iron, iodine, sulphur, and zinc, it may be that these nutrients can improve the working power of the brain.

Where to find phosphorus

Since you need a balance of calcium and phosphorus, look to bone meal capsules or flour (sold at health stores). You may also find phosphorus in almonds, wheat bran (1215 milligrams in just five cups), hard cheese, dried kidney or lima beans, wheat germ (1050 milligrams in 12 tablespoons), Brazil nuts, cashew nuts, Swiss cheese, powdered soya milk (712 milligrams in 12 tablespoons), and whole mature soybeans.

Tension starves the brain

A young student, beset with family troubles, financial adverses, is forced to participate in a gambling racket that "fixes" college games. He is found out and disgraced. Depressed and despondent, he takes his own life. This tragic story appeared in many newspapers throughout the country. When an autopsy was performed, it was learned that he had an "underpar" brain. The cells, undoubtedly, had been starved for phosphorus and minerals, hence this could have easily led to his mental aberration.

A tense person uses up much mineral supply. Tension leads to fatigue which further depletes the body. A tired person has to push himself harder, causing even greater drain upon valuable body resources. A tired person's brain is charged with extra-activity to order him to continue on and on.

Dr. Edward Spencer Cowles calls this a condition of low nerve-cell energy. The billions of brain cells grow weak because of *demineralization*. He draws a comparison between the human nervous-brain system and a river dam. He says that all along the nervous system are erected small "dams." One giant dam is found in the brain: this brain dam holds back and keeps in check the flow of nerve and thought impulses that would otherwise pour in upon the consciousness. The lower the small dams are placed the more water rushes over.

This is applied to our nerve cells. The lower the energy source of the nerve cells, the greater the flood of impulses (desired or undesired) that gush over to the brain. Consequently, the less energy existing in a nerve cell, the more it becomes irritated. This leads to a fatigued brain and nervous system since both systems consist of billions of these cells.

Phosphorus is just one of the precious minerals needed by a brain for its power and vigor. Others are iron, iodine, silicon, sulphur, magnesium, and manganese. All work together in harmony with vitamins and amino acids to create a strong brain.

How to Feed Iron to Your Brain

Iron is the precious mineral that helps your bloodstream carry oxygen through four arteries into the brain. If you are iron-deficient, it means your brain may starve because of insufficient oxygen. An oxygen-starved brain results in weakness and even unconsciousness. A temporary blackout is often called a concussion.

You need to take a healthy iron tonic regularly and here's how to do it.

Visit any health food store and request *unsulphured* apricots; if unavailable, ask for dried peaches and raisins. Place a portion of this fruit in the bottom of a bowl. Cover with lukewarm water. (That is, boiled water that has been cooled to lukewarm temperature.) Stir slightly. Let remain overnight. The next morning, stir the mixture again. Now, pour the water into a tall glass, add two tablespoons of Barbados Molasses and drink. Do this every morning. As for the fruit, you will find it has regained its original size and is so delicious as a dessert that you will never want to go back to the artificially dried fruit again. The iron and mineral content of these dried fruits are valuable for enabling your bloodstream to send oxygen to the brain.

Benefits of a Mineral-Rich Breakfast

Mrs. Sawyer was a busy mother of four. Mr. Sawyer was her "fifth" child as she jokingly stated. But since she had to do everything herself, she often sent them to school with just a few crackers and milk in their stomachs. One day, her oldest boy collapsed while playing a game during recess. Three days later her husband fell down while he was leaving the commuter train. Only after extensive tests were made was it learned that both had a very low mineral supply in the bloodstream and *"brain fatigue."*

Mrs. Sawyer decided that breakfast could be *the* most important meal of the day and got up 30 minutes earlier every morning so her brood could be adequately fed.

"Come to think of it," she reflects, "I skipped many breakfasts myself and found myself weak by mid-morning. I just couldn't think straight."

In order to maintain optimal mental functioning, your brain needs a good mineralized breakfast. It uses sugars, and if it doesn't have an adequate amount it begins to show evidence of mental inefficiency.

Frederick J. Stare, Professor of Nutrition at Harvard University, School of Public Health, also advocates a good breakfast. He points out that not only will it make your brain work better, but also will close the hunger mechanism so that breakfast cannot cause weight increase.

A sample of a mineral-rich breakfast for the brain is cited in the following paragraphs.

1. One glass fruit juice (orange juice, or preferably, a whole orange).

2. Hot cereal, such as oatmeal or whole-grain cereal, with milk or half-and-half cream.

3. Eggs poached, boiled or scrambled in olive (peanut or soy) oil.

4. Toast with butter and a hot drink, such as Postum or Ovaltine.

Three Miracle Brain Foods

It has been found that a few foods are so rich in minerals needed by your brain, they should be a "must" in your quest for super mental power. You can find any of these foods at health stores or at special diet shops.

Lecithin

Here is a bland, granular powder that is made from soy beans. A natural phosphatide, it is an essential component of all the living cells and tissues in your brain. Rich in B-complex factors, it unites with iron, iodine, calcium, and phosphorus to give power and vigor to your mental capacities. When utilized by your system, the minerals in lecithin serve to metabolize fats and aid in the conversion of Vitamin A into a utilized nutrient form by your brain.

Lecithin may be used in tablet form or in granular form which can be mixed with fruit and vegetable juices or sprinkled on salads. Try two tablespoons of lecithin with freshly squeezed tomato or other juice every single morning. This will give you the brain power that you will discover to be equal to that of a wizard!

Kelp

If the Orientals are known for superior wisdom, credit should be due to their intake of seaweed foods as well as seafoods themselves. In particular, consider kelp, which is a food made by dehydrating all types of seaweeds. Harvested from the deep sea waters where a treasure of minerals exist, kelp is one of the best sources of iodine, iron, potassium, chlorine. Kelp has a good supply of phosphorus, too. All of these minerals join to build greater brain power.

We all know that sea water is a veritable trove of precious minerals, so whatever grows in the sea will absorb the same vital brain foods.

Dr. W. A. P. Black, as related in the *Proceedings of the Nutrition Society* of England (Vol. 12, p. 32), researched the values of seaweed and kelp to find these sea foods to be of inestimable value, like any buried treasure beneath the sea. "It can be said that seaweed contains all the elements that have so far been shown to play an important part in the physiological processes of man. In a balanced diet, therefore, they would appear to be an excellent mineral supplement."

Use powdered kelp as a flavoring agent for soups, salads, meats, baked dishes, etc. Take kelp tablets regularly to obtain precious iron, phosphorus, and potassium needed by your brain.

Desiccated liver

Liver is a prime source of calcium and phosphorus. It also contains iron, the important component of hemoglobin which is the oxygen carrying pigment of your red blood cells. The hemoglobin transports oxygen as well as nutrients to your brain. Liver also contains copper needed to work with iron and amino acids in the manufacture of brain-required oxygen. Another mineral, zinc, is also plentiful in liver. All ten essential amino acids, the building blocks of life, abound in liver.

Desiccated liver is dehydrated raw liver which is dried in a vacuum at a very low temperature to preserve the valuable minerals which may be lost if raw liver is cooked for the table. Desiccated liver is not a liver extract. It is the whole liver with no nutrients removed; the special drying process preserves nutrients and brings the final desiccated liver (powder or tablets) down to about 25 per cent of the original weight of the raw liver.

Take desiccated liver in capsule form or use the granules for sprinkling over soups, salads and baked casserole dishes.

Special Brain Tonic

In one tall glass, put two tablespoons of lecithin granules, a pinch of sea salt or kelp, two tablespoons of desiccated liver capsules. Pour in freshly squeezed carrot juice. Fill to the top and stir vigorously. If you have a blender or electric shaker, so much the better. When all items have been blended together, drink slowly. This "brain tonic" should be taken daily at noontime, as it contains the treasure of minerals needed by your entire system to so supercharge the system, that you and your friends will be astounded at the power of mental energy you display.

MAIN POINTS TO THINK ABOUT
AS PRESENTED IN CHAPTER EIGHT

1. Your brain, weighing 48 ounces, containing 16 billion cells, rules every voluntary and involuntary action of your mind and body.
2. Millions of brain cells are "soaked" with phosphorus, a mineral that keeps the entire organ alive. Other minerals enter into the picture of powerful brain health.
3. Tension can starve your brain; minerals are needed to meet the challenge of an overworked brain.
4. Iron is a valuable oxygen-carrying mineral as it lets your brain breathe, so to speak.
5. Your brain needs breakfast. Start the day right with a solid, mineral rich-breakfast. Follow the suggested special diet plan.
6. There are three special miracle brain foods that you *must* have for top level mental powers — lecithin, kelp, desiccated liver. Try these in a variety of ways and see the wonderful benefits.
7. Daily, at noontime, take the special brain tonic.

The life of the flesh is in the blood.

Leviticus 17:11

NINE

How to Make Your Blood Stream a River of Eternal Youth

Arlene was on the way to becoming a successful wallflower. In her middle 20's, she had an interesting position as private secretary to an executive in a leading steel corporation. Considering her eligibility, it would appear that Arlene would be much sought after at company dances, social events, picnics, outings.

"The truth is," moaned Arlene, "they take me out once or twice and never call back again. I try to smile, be cheerful and show interest in my date. What could be wrong with me?"

The listener was a girl working in the same company as an advertising artist. She had more than her share of dates; in fact, out of pity for Arlene, she had arranged double dates for the girl, but these had also resulted in unhappy "one shots." The advertising gal said, "You know, Arlene, personality-plus reflects in your face. You have to *look* personality, so to speak."

Arlene thought she understood. "But I've gone to charm school. I wear the right color combinations, even the cosmetic colors I use in lipstick, rouge, foundation makeup, and eyeshadow all blend in the way the book says, but I'm still far from being popular."

The friend handed her a small mirror. "Take a good look at yourself. But first, wipe away that excess makeup. What do you see? The truth, now."

Arlene did as suggested and stared at the ghostlike reflection. "The truth about what I see? My skin is pale. My eyes look dull.

My hair is brittle. You know, I'm not as colorful as I thought I was."

The friend saw that Arlene could make a good self-analysis. The first step toward popularity improvement had been made. "You get enough sleep so I would guess that your problem is an unhealthy or impoverished bloodstream. You need minerals to so enrich these internal rivers that you'll not only feel good, but also look youthful and colorful. I guess that's why you're not asked out on many dates. You do look faded." She reached out and held Arlene's hands in her own. There was a noticeable shudder. "Oh," she grimaced. "Your hands are ice cold — and clammy, too."

Arlene felt a bit abashed. "I once overheard a few of the salesmen talking about that, too. I had danced with them a few weeks before. I thought I had poor blood circulation. But what can I do?"

The friend suggested she pep up her mineral intake, particularly iron. "Go strong on iron and here's a tip. Beat the yolk of an egg into a glass of freshly squeezed orange juice. Drink one glass before each meal, three times daily. Try it for seven days and then see what happens. And, you might also include lean, broiled liver with raw onion slices at least twice a week. Beef or calf's liver are excellent sources of iron. That's just the start, Arlene. Suppose we get together in one week and see what happens."

Arlene did as directed and one week later when she faced her friend, she looked brighter, healthier and felt better. "How are my hands now?"

Her friend squeezed the warm hands. "They feel so good, I doubt if any of the boys at the company dances will want to give them up so easily."

Arlene continued on her blood improvement program, soon becoming energetic, popular, and even engaged!

Value of Mineral-Rich Bloodstream

An iron-rich bloodstream will give a rosy complexion, glowing cheeks and lips, ear tips with a delicate strawberry tinge. When all the minerals nourish these "rivers of youth" flow through your blood vessels, you have a zest for life. Not only do you feel healthy and happy, but also you think better and your memory is wonderful.

Your bloodstream often influences the power of your personality. Billions of your internal body cells, from your brain to the tips of your toes depend upon the bloodstream for nourishment, oxygen (the breath of life), and for removing waste products, such as carbon dioxide.

What is blood?

The blood is made up of a straw-colored fluid called plasma and contains both red and white cells. The red blood cells are born and developed in the bone marrow of the long bones at the speedy rate of about *one million a minute*. These cells function in a round trip manner, carrying life-giving oxygen to the billions of cells in your body and picking up carbon dioxide at the same time.

Red blood cells are round and have a slight depression in the middle. They carry hemoglobin — a red coloring ingredient created by minerals which is needed to carry out the oxygen delivering job. Hemoglobin depends upon iron and copper for its very life. If you are deficient in these minerals, the red blood cells "lose weight" and color, becoming thin, pale and anemic, and so do you!

You have about 6 quarts of blood containing 30 trillion red blood cells. (Adult females have 27 trillion red blood cells.) These are tiny concave red discs about 1/3,000 of an inch wide and only 1/15,000 of an inch thick. Put them all together, end to end, and they reach 116,000 miles or halfway to the moon! Put all of these blood cells on a flat surface, spread out, and they cover four-fifths of an acre!

Except for tiny spaces between your capillary cellular walls, your blood flows through a sealed conduit of vessels that add up to thousands of miles, if placed end to end. A mineral-nourished blood flow travels through the arteries at a rate of over 40 miles an hour! Just one line of 3,000 red blood cells would measure slightly less than one inch! About 40 red cells could be hidden under the period at the end of this sentence.

Power of white cells

While less common in the bloodstream, your white cells add up to the millions. You have about one white cell for every 700 red cells.

There are a few kinds of white cells, but the most valuable is the granular leukocyte. This develops in your bone marrow together with your red blood cells.

The granular leukocytes need minerals for sustenance and life. *When these are given sufficient iron, iodine, copper, and phosphorus, they can then rally to defend your body against bacterial infectious invasions which include allergies, winter colds, coughs, chronic sniffles, sinus, etc.*

The magic power of minerals becomes awesome when nourishing the valuable granular leukocytes as a means of building resistance against a horde of infectious summer and winter ailments.

When these while cells receive proper mineralization, they have the magic power to squeeze through the tiny openings in the walls of the capillaries; they capture infectious bacteria, absorb and digest them. You can see the winning results of the fight when you see pus — a thick yellowish fluid made of lymph, bacteria, and dead white cells. Minerals are needed by these white cells to battle against infection. If you have a weak defense line of white cells, the condition may progress into leukemia or blood cancer.

Signs of Mineral-Poor Blood Health

Are you afflicted with tiredness, sinusitis, frequent colds, breathlessness, rapid heartbeat, bronchitis, headaches, joint pains or a myriad of similar other symptoms? These symptoms may be related to your blood condition. Among early warnings signs of a mineral-poor bloodstream are numbness of extremities and tingling of the fingers.

A healthy mineral-rich bloodstream should show the following top-level readings in a blood count:

	Red Blood Cells Per Cubic Millimeter	Hemoglobin %	Grams %
MEN	5,000,000	105-110	17.0
WOMEN	4,500,000	95	14.5

(one millimeter equals one drop of blood)

A leading medical authority says every 24 hours your heart pumps 4,000 gallons of blood through your body. Red blood cells leaving your fingertip at this instant will make a complete circuit through your heart, lungs and blood vessels and return in about one minute. In the lungs it discharges carbon dioxide; in the kidneys, urinary wastes; in the liver, other waste products. Eventually it gives up its own life, becomes fragmented, and is carried by the bloodstream to the liver where part of its iron is recovered to build new blood cells and the rest is excreted through the bile into the intestines.

Power of Minerals in the Blood

Of all the minerals, iron is the most powerful in helping to nourish a bloodstream.

Sources of iron include organ and muscle meats, egg yolks, whole grain products, sun-dried fruits, legumes (beans, peas, lentils), and cooked greens.

After iron is absorbed from the digestive tract, some is stored in the liver for future needs. This explains why animal liver is a dynamic powerhouse of available iron.

Desiccated liver is a vacuum-dried powder with all connective tissue and fat removed but with all precious minerals and iron still in abundance. This is a miracle source of blood-building iron. You can take just six or eight tablets daily or sprinkle in powdered form over salads, soups, stews, and enrich your entire bloodstream.

A prominent medical practitioner states that muscle cells carry a kind of hemoglobin; in fact, all living cells of our bodies contain at least some iron. The body requires traces of copper in order to make hemoglobin, although hemoglobin itself contains no copper. The body is miserly with its iron. This is to our advantage since some of our foods provide too much iron. As red cells wear out, the body carefully pick out the iron and saves it for reuse in making new hemoglobin.

So you can see how the minerals copper and iron work together to produce a healthy bloodstream. Vitamins and amino acids also spark the action of these minerals.

Mineral-Deficient Dangers

A mineral-poor bloodstream represents a health hazard both mental and physical. Anemia, even to a relatively minor degree, constitutes a serious handicap to health in later maturity. A severe iron deficiency leads to this condition often referred to as "thin", "tired" or "poor" blood. The symptoms include pallid skin, loss of appetite, fatigue, shortness of breath, heart palpitations and overall weakness. A severe case of pernicious anemia may affect the nerves of the spinal cord, threatening the health of the whole body.

So you can see how minerals can become the greatest treasure to be sought since they can supercharge the entire bloodstream with the effect of a built-in fountain of youth!

Mineral-poor blood may lead to sensitivity. You can be bothered with colds, allergies, and slow-healing wounds. The 15 million Americans who suffer from asthma, migraine, hay fever, and skin ailments will find that if the health of the blood is improved, there can also be an improvement in the allergy.

Also, personality disorders, such as excessive nervousness or a grouchy disposition, may also be alleviated by *mineralizing the blood*. The nervous system of the body must have a mineral-rich blood supply or it screams!

Avoid "Fluff" Foods

A 36-year old bachelor wondered why he kept losing jobs, as well as girl friends. He was told that he always snapped at people. He not only suffered from a personality defect, but also a mineral deficiency. He ate in restaurants, frequently alone, and as with most lone eaters, the temptation was to eat filling, but not nourishing, items. He attended a health resort and after three weeks of corrective diets his personality changed. No longer mineral-starved, he became agreeable and pleasant with both friends and co-workers. Also, the continuance of his job was assured.

What are anti-mineral foods? Doctors will say that Americans eat too many "fluff" foods, such as sweets, white breads, pastries, crackers, macaroni, spaghetti, cookies, sweet rolls, French pastries, cake, pie and soda fountain delicacies (malted milks, ice cream sodas, popsickles) as well as fattening foods.

These foods tend to rob your system of valuable nutrients, particularly minerals, and also displace blood building foods in your diet. Sweets, by the way, cause a depletion of the B-complex vitamins which are needed by minerals to nourish the bloodstream.

Sweets cause fatigue

Excessive sweets cause a vitamin and mineral depletion. Sugar cannot become metabolized and turns into pyruvic acid, rather than carbon dioxide and water which minerals need. This acid is closely related to lactic acid in that it creates fatigue and tiredness. So, go easy on sweets, eliminate the "fluff" foods.

What Causes Anemia?

Severe mineral deficiency leads to anemia because of its relation to insufficient oxygen reaching your brain and other valuable body organs. You may become a melancholia victim. Other symptoms include prematurely greying hair that is also lusterless and dry, wrinkled skin, dried and flattened fingernails, an inflamed sore tongue and mouth. The skin of the anemic person is sad — pasty white and bluish. The eyeballs also are a sickening blue-white.

Often, anemia is traced to blood loss via hemorrhage, by diseases. There are some drugs or toxic agents which destroy red blood cells and interfere with iron utilization. Sulfamilamide is known for this anti-mineral action.

Benefits of Blackstrap Molasses

Possibly the richest iron source is blackstrap molasses. Just one tablespoon contains 9.6 milligrams of this valuable mineral food. (The National Research Council recommends 12 milligrams daily for adults as a minimum.)

Molasses is a back-to-Nature food product taken from raw sugar cane from which all possible crystallizable sugar has been removed. Yearly, America imports over 300 million gallons of molasses. Of this supply, 100 million gallons are fed to cattle. Consequences? Our cattle have healthier blood than we humans!

Inasmuch as blackstrap molasses is a wonderful mineral source, a prominent nutritionist suggests four and one half tablespoons daily on bread and butter or stirred into milk. You can use it with honey as a topping for desserts. He points toward whole grain foods as other iron sources. Two slices of 100 per cent whole wheat bread contains 1.4 milligrams of iron. Just one serving of rolled oats (two-thirds cup cooked) contains a bit more iron that an egg — 1.6 milligrams to be exact.

Barbados Molasses

Comparatively little is known about the dynamic mineral treasure found in Barbados Molasses. One of the most powerful sources of all minerals, especially blood-building iron, it is made from the sugar cane grown on the Caribbean island of Barbados.

The mineral-rich waters which nourish the sugar cane fields may be regarded as the purest and most sparkling in the world. Obtained from underground wells, the water is naturally filtered through 300 feet of coral and is free from contamination.

Also it has been estimated that 25 per cent of the island's rainwater percolates through the coral till it reaches an impervious stratum along which it slowly flows down until it reaches sea-level. When it reaches the sea it does not mix with the salt water, but takes the form of a lens over it. On the east coast, where no coral exists, there are small perennial streams. Underground there are also streams and lakes resting on a bed of impervious clay. Considering the acknowledged superior mineral quality of fresh, pure well and spring water, we can appreciate the valuable nutrients in Barbadian water which, by the way, has always been the envy of other Caribbean islands.

This same pure water is used on Barbadian crops as well as sugar cane, and is why Barbados Molasses is one of the world's richest supplies of iron and other minerals. For a truly dynamic and magic power of blood building food, try this molasses, sold in all health stores and many grocery outlets.

Other Mineral Sources

For necessary mineral intake your diet should include green vegetables, such as mustard and turnip greens, kale, collards, broccoli and Brussels sprouts.

In your selection of meats emphasize calf's liver which is delicious when broiled with sliced onions. It is also an iron rich food. As good mineral sources include lamb, egg yolks, kidneys, dark poultry meats, hearts, or lean beef. Remember apricots, millet and sunflower seeds, peaches, prunes, lettuce, artichokes, dried peas and beans, whole grain cereals, raisins, beet tops, apples, radishes, leeks, corn, grapes, berries, pineapple, oranges, lemons, lentils, pumpkin, walnuts, whole rye, currants, pears, onions, and pomegranates.

Germinated Wheat

Take a supply of wheat and put in a cup; keep it both moist and warm so it can germinate. When the sprouts are about a quarter of an inch long, eat the wheat *raw*. That's right, when eaten raw, germinated wheat contains a powerhouse of iron as well as other valuable minerals. You will discover the change in your appearance and your personality if you eat about one cup of this germinated raw wheat, every day, for a period of just three weeks. Inquire at your bakery for raw wheat or ask at a health store.

7 Ways to Build Healthy Mineral-Rich Blood

1. *Diet* — Feed iron to your bone marrow, liver and other blood making parts of the body. See diet at end of this chapter.

2. *Obtain enough rest* — Fatigue, over-tiredness, overwork prevents a healthy blood cell manufacture. Sleep is needed to help your body repair and rebuild valuable red and white blood cells. A mineral depletion follows fatigue and lowered physical resistance. Get at least eight hours of sleep every night.

3. *Exercise* — An active body is a healthy body. Stretch arms and legs. Blood health is sparked by physical movements. A 30 minute walk daily is helpful to keep the flow of minerals in the blood at a healthy rate.

4. *Water* — Plasma, the fluid part of your blood, contains 92 per cent water. Blood cells float in a lake of water inside the bloodstream. Since more than 75 per cent of your body consists of water, you can see how precious water becomes as a media for carrying blood, hormones, and minerals. A dehydrated body invites

infectious bacteria. Keep your blood cells in a watery environment. Drink six glasses of water daily.

5. *Sunshine* — When sunshine strikes the skin, it activates such blood building processes as manufacture of Vitamin D for the bone marrow. Get an hour's sunshine every day. Even in wintertime, you can go out of doors for at least 45 minutes at high noon when the sun is at its maximum.

6. *Fresh air* — Deep breathing stimulates circulation; your blood cells need oxygen so iron can "breath" and function. Fresh country air is best, of course. Try to find some place where you can enjoy at least one hour of deep breathing of delicious pure and fresh air.

7. *Blackstrap molasses* — Here's a wonderful *Mineral-Blood Beverage:* combine four ounces of freshly squeezed apricot juice, two ounces of freshly squeezed pear juice, two ounces of concord grape juice. Add four tablespoons of Barbados Molasses. Stir vigorously or mix in a electric blender. Drink immediately. For top notch results drink this special beverage before breakfast and as a night cap. Try this *Hemoglobin Tonic:* Into one cup of fresh yogurt (rich in calcium needed by bone marrow for manufacturing of red blood cells) stir four tablespoons of Barbados Molasses. Eat with a spoon every single day at noon. Add unsulphured raisins for extra flavor. These items are found in any grocery store or health store.

Your Blood Building Diet

BEFORE BREAKFAST: 2 glasses of water, 30 minutes before breakfast.

BREAKFAST :
2 poached eggs on 100 per cent whole wheat toast
1 cup oatmeal with raisins and wheat germ
1 orange, eaten whole
5 stewed prunes
1 cup boiled water with 4 tablespoons of blackstrap molasses

LUNCHEON:
½ cup beans
1 cup cooked green vegetable
1 baked potato with skin
2 slices 100 per cent whole wheat bread with peanut butter

1 glass soya milk
Raw vegetable salad
Small dish of raw, unsulphured, raisins

DINNER:

1 serving apricots or peaches
2 slices whole wheat toast
1½ ounces cottage cheese
Portion broiled calve's liver
Mushroom and onion soup
Cup of herb tea

IN REVIEW: ESSENTIALS OF CHAPTER NINE

1. Your bloodstream must have adequate mineralization for health and vigor.

2. Minerals in your blood will give you a youthful, colorful skin, build a white blood cell supply to protect you against bacterial invasions of allergies, winter colds, coughs, chronic sniffles, sinus, etc.

3. Iron is a prime mineral needed to feed red blood cells and build hemoglobin supply. Try desiccated liver as a top notch source of this precious blood building mineral.

4. Severe mineral depletion may lead to anemia and impair health of mind and body.

5. Avoid "fluff" foods, such as starched and bleached bread products, sweets, cakes, candies. These are destructive to minerals.

6. Barbados Molasses is a "secret" treasure of iron and other valuable minerals.

7. Eat one cup of germinated wheat daily as a remarkable blood-building food.

8. Follow the seven step plan for building healthy blood.

To be strong is to be happy.

Longfellow

TEN

How to Cheer Up
with Mineral Power

One of the greatest gifts is that of a cheerful and pleasant disposition. Call it personality, attitude, outlook, optimism, positive thinking, it adds up to the same thing: *good cheer*.

If you are mentally and physically tired, if body resources are "starved" for precious nutrients, you have a tendency to snap at family members and business associates. You soon develop an unsavory reputation for being a grouch. This may not be intentional but a product of a demineralized personality.

The noted photographer, Erwin Blumenfeld, known for having captured beautiful women on film, declares, "A woman must have two things to be beautiful. The first is personality. That is the only thing that counts in life. You can't fake it. The other necessity for beauty is enthusiasm. The capacity to fight with joy for something. Women must be educated away from conformity, and into the personal adventure."

Personality becomes more than something skin-deep. It is a power that comes from within. A feeling of glowing health will put a fresh bloom to a face, transform each day into one that is filled with adventure and excitement. Good health, as we have seen so far, comes from proper nourishment. This is the foundation and it includes minerals.

The case of the gloomy teacher

Grace was in her middle 40's. She had managed to combine

marriage, motherhood and a career as teacher in a well-known private school. Yet, she was dissatisfied. She felt nervous, given to fits of depression and occasionally, she would fall into a grouchy mood that was impossible to shake off.

"My department head called me in the other day," she gloomily confessed. "He said that I'm too grouchy, too cross with the students. He reminded me — as if I need anyone to remind me — that their parents are paying top money for a private school education. They expect teachers to be cheerful."

Her friend asked, "Well, aren't they right?"

Grace snapped back: "Whose side are you on anyway?"

"Nobody's side," was the instant response. "But you'd better relax, take it easy and do a little self-analysis, Grace. You're as taut as a stretched violin string. Pulled too far, you will burst into shreds. Played properly, you can give good music."

It was then that Grace "broke down" and admitted she was anything but the agreeable, sweet girl voted "Miss Cheer" in her college graduation Yearbook. "The pressures are great and my family comes first. Maybe I've been neglecting myself."

Her friend then said, "Like most active people, Grace, your career and home run neck in neck for attention. You've been able to take care of both, but what about yourself? I have a feeling you're becoming undernourished."

Grace discussed her eating habits and while she was getting a balanced diet with enough fresh fruits and vegetables to maintain a good internal power, she required even more. "What do you suggest?"

The friend, an astute home economics consultant, said, "We had a convention of food processors just a while ago and it was mentioned that a combination of ordinary foods can work wonders in making a person feel happy and really redo the entire personality."

How to Make a Personality Punch

The friend wrote down the recipe for making a special punch.

PERSONALITY PUNCH

This contained highly concentrated sources of such minerals as cobalt, magnesium, potassium, calcium.

Into a glass, pour freshly made soya milk, two tablespoons of lecithin granules, four tablespoons of brewer's yeast flakes, four tablespoons of powdered sunflower seeds. Stir vigorously or in a blender. Drink three times daily — before each of your three meals.

The magic power of minerals in these ingredients will so revitalize your personality that you will say, as did Grace, after just four weeks of this simple remedy, "Wow — I feel like a brand new person — that's what everybody else is saying about me." Gone are the moods, the depressions, the gloom, the melancholy.

Why is this so? These foods are rich in the following minerals: cobalt to help vitamin B_{12} in building a rich hemoglobin count; magnesium to act upon vitamin B_6 to treat insomnia, convulsions, nervousness, and tremors; potassium to unite with vitamin E to normalize the pace of your heartbeat.

Do you feel like retiring from the human race, including your family? Perhaps something has wrecked your chemical mineral processes. Many person are fairly vitamin conscious nowadays due to advertising, but minerals are unknown as to health benefits. And, your personality can seriously suffer from the lack of proper minerals. Their importance is clearly shown in the following report on mineral treatment:

A 75-year-old woman, who was considered hopeless by competent medical authorities, and who had been bedridden for two years, was suffering from severe depression, visual hallucinations, and extreme mental confusion. After a month's therapy she was able to leave her bed and start gardening with energy. The depression and mental confusion disappeared.

Undoubtedly, the unification of all basic minerals and vitamins had brought about this wonderful personality cure.

Child depression

Let us not neglect children who are often so mineral-starved they react with grouchy moods or fits of depression. Symptoms of youthful depression may appear in nightmares, sleep-walking, bed-wetting, absentmindedness, mischievous actions, laziness, dullness, indifference, lack of initiative and the inability to make decisions. Excessive dawdling should be looked upon as a possible symptom of deficient minerals.

Sugar vs. Minerals

White sugar and foods enriched or flavored with this artificial substance *act destructively upon minerals*. Many of the precious minerals *must have* the B-complex vitamins for power. Yet, sugar destroys the precious B-complex group and thereby weakens or nullifies mineral power. An interesting report on this was made by a dentist regarding a nine-year-old patient.

> He would return to my office every three months with from three to five new cavities to be filled. This continued over a long period of time, resulting in a filling in every tooth including the permanent ones.
>
> At first each appointment with him was the same — kicking, biting and screaming. I would have rewarded the child with anything to avoid this display. Since I had to preserve my hands (which to me are very valuable), my glasses, ear drums and nervous system, in desperation I prescribed a sugar-and-white-flour-free diet for the boy, mostly for my own protection.
>
> Six months later there were no new cavities and only one cavity a year later. I was amazed at the child's behavior while on this program. Here was a happy contented child, who six months before had been a pint sized tornado. His mother revealed some more facts which were amazing to me at the time.
>
> Before, he was having one cold after another and sore throats frequently; recently, he had only one cold and no sore throats. His mother had had to continually watch his bowels, now they moved normally without laxatives. The correlation between tooth decay, the common cold, sore throats, constipation and lack of interest in his school studies seemed important to me.
>
> It was obvious that the elimination of sugar in this boy's diet definitely was the factor contributing to the solution of the boy's mental and dental health.

The watchword here is — *no artificial sugar or foods containing artificial sugar*. To satisfy your sweet tooth, use rose hips powder, carob powder, honey, molasses, etc. Health stores sell these for use as flavoring agents. They also sell natural candies and cakes made with whole grain flour and carob.

Artificial or bleached white sugar has a destructive action upon B-complex vitamins and minerals.

A low or deficient mineral supply is also responsible for such personality defects as those reported by Dr. I. N. Kugelmass in the *American Journal of Digestive Diseases* (Vol. 11, pp. 368-373): fatigue, anxiety, irritation, forgetfulness, headaches, impaired judgment, bodily complaints, hypersensitivity, frustration and sleeplessness.

Calcium is needed

A calcium deficiency is almost always associated with moods and instability of the nervous system. A shortage of this mineral is noted during rapid adolescent growth, at menstrual periods, during pregnancy and lactation. So, remember to take calcium tablets if you don't get this mineral in your food.

Mineral Water and Your Emotions

Fresh mineral-rich water is a treasure of sparkling good cheer. Although water is not one of the mineral nutrients, we cannot utilize minerals without an adequate supply of water. Water is the body's major constituent, carries chemicals to all parts of the body and is the medium in which most reactions involving the nutrients in familiar foods takes place. Water is also important in the body's system for regulating temperature. The exact water requirement varies from person to person, but most of us need two to three quarts a day.

Dr. W. B. Cannon in *Wisdom of the Body,* tells us, "Water is the vehicle for food materials absorbed from the digestive canal; it is the medium in which chemical changes take place that underlie most of our obvious activities; it is essential in the regulation of body temperature, and it plays an important part in mechanical services such as the lubrication . . . of joint surfaces . . ."

Water carries minerals, via a well-watered bloodstream, to all body parts and can transform an exhausted, tired, nervous person into one that is refreshed, cheerful, happy.

Water and Your Personality

Rose's *Foundations of Nutrition* point out that when norma young men were water-deprived, they developed headaches, ner vousness, appetite loss, digestive upsets, inability to concentrate an soon turned into rascals and unpleasant characters. But, when wate intake was increased, their personalities changed for the better.

Benefits of Natural Spring Water

Since water dissolves and absorbs precious nutrients from th depths of the ocean (the greatest natural supply of minerals), it no only serves as a carrier for minerals, but has its own supply of thes valuable elements. The best water is that which is free from chlorine, fluorine and other additives. Natural pure spring water i a treasure trove of minerals.

Ask at your shopping center for natural spring water; they may be able to order some bottles for you. Look in the "yellow pages" o your classified telephone directory under "Water" to locate nearby outlets. Many will deliver bottles to your home or they can arrange for deliveries to be made via a neighborhood food store.

If you have access to pure well water, that is another little-known source of dynamic minerals. Bottled spring water is a "must" in your treasure hunt for minerals.

How to Make "Cheer Tonic"

If you have occasional bouts with moodiness or depression, here's a special Cheer Tonic that will banish the blues. Into a tall glass, put four heaping tablespoons of goat's milk powder (sold at many health stores). Combine with natural spring water. Stir vigorously. Add one tablespoon of Brewer's Yeast flakes. Stir thoroughly. Sip slowly. Take this Cheer Tonic when you feel the onset of an unhappy mood and you will be so mineralizing your system, you'll be able to weather the storm.

Four Keys for a Balanced Personality

There are four keys in development of a balanced personality. Let's take them individually and see how to apply them.

1. *Love.* A widowed neighbor had done a wonderful job in raising a large family. All the children were adjusted, happy and popular. I asked her about any secret formula. Her answer: "Well, I sort of pour so much love into them that it pours out." You express love by giving — and taking, too. Love is a spark that will warm, lighten, satisfy the dire need of everyone you meet, including yourself.

K. C. Ingram in *Winning Your Way With People,* tells us:

"The point is to treat people well, always. As a habit. Don't press for the reward. Special rewards come unexpectedly, from doing good deeds secretly. The man who doesn't care who gets the credit, does a lot of good for other people and himself. If you are at any time unhappy or bored, try doing something to help somebody. 'Cast thy bread upon the waters, for thou shalt find it after many days.'"

2. *Recreation-Play.* Recreation is what the word implies: *to recreate,* to make over, to rejuvenate and build anew. It means to cast aside all the cares and enjoy yourself in something frivolous, silly, even foolish — but something that makes you feel great.

An important attorney takes vacations four times yearly and returns to his office as nervous and wrought up as always. Why? His recreation-play time was a form of work. He had to play the lowest golf score or feel defeat. He had to go through 12 sets of tennis until he almost passed out from heat prostration. But he would not surrender. If he caught the smallest fish, he'd sulk and brood and be a terror to live with. What was wrong? He transformed his recreation-play area into a courtroom. He had to win! This is not very relaxing. You need a type of recreation that rests your body and mind and makes you feel glad all over. It's recreation that amuses you, not makes you fuss and fume. As John Locke, the brilliant English philosopher (1632-1704) once wrote: "He that will make a good use of any part of his life must allow a large part of it for recreation."

3. *Work.* Yes, a good and happy day's work will make you feel better. If you are alone all the time, you start to brood, to lament, to contemplate and this makes you feel depressed and unhappy. Some women have gone into business, acted as babysitters, foster mothers of "housemothers" in institutions so as to give themselves something to do. This helps improve personality and overall mental

health. A job can often be your ticket to happiness, but it should be a job you enjoy or can learn to enjoy.

4. *Faith*. Either spiritual love, or love of God, or faith in fellow man — if you believe — you are happy! Remember Dr. Norman Vincent Peale's statement, "Prayer is the greatest power in the world. It is a pity that most people do not know how to use it." Often, a person without faith is a lonely person. He retreats from the world. This is a personality defect. Dr. John W. McKelvey, once stated, "I am convinced that loneliness is 90 per cent self-pity. The victim shuts himself in, others out, Everybody avoids him, for nobody loves a self-pitier."

> Dr. Ingrams advises;
>
> We will save ourselves many disappointments if we do not expect people to be reasonable. One way to learn to like people is to cultivate the habit of telling them the good things we may hear about them. It is quite as blessed to give as to receive a good word.
>
> People are full of human fallibilities — every one of us. If we are tolerant of other people's mistakes, they will overlook our mistakes. People are also full of admirable qualities. If we look for such qualities in others, people will look for and find good qualities in us. *To keep life worth living, we must keep faith in human nature.*

Happiness is a by-product of living. There is no singular or simple formula to ensure happiness and good cheer. Rather, joy of mind and body is a fusion of sound mental and physical health.

Money not solution

A successful businessman has taken up yachting. He bought a six-place cabin cruiser. His home overlooks a beautiful harbor. No doubt, it is possible that he would enjoy happiness, but this is not true. The point here is that he is too wrapped up in himself. He rarely permits others to share the yacht, except hired servants or a few selected friends. Money, in this case, did not buy him happiness.

Money does help, *but a selfish use of money will not bring a permanent type of happiness.*

You may recall the life of Dr. Wilfred Grenfell, the famed medical missionary who practiced along the coast of Labrador and spent his entire life mingling with and ministering to the fisherman and their families.

Dr. Grenfell abandoned wealth and professional fame as he might have enjoyed in his homeland; he was brought up near Chester, England. His father was headmaster of a school for boys and independently wealthy. The school was located on the banks of the river Dee near where it flows into the Irish Sea. It is beautiful, idyllic and peaceful. Young Wilfred, however, gave up this life of luxury and comfort in favor of another. By healing the indigent and rescuing the near-fatal, Dr. Grenfell performed a service that brought him more complete happiness.

SUMMARY OF AIDS IN CHAPTER TEN FOR BANISHING BLUES

1. Minerals help in overcoming personality and mental defects that are seen in most average people.
2. Mental depression, hallucinations and confusion can also be eased by adequate mineral intake.
3. During spells of gloominess, the body demands more calcium, phosphorus, potassium, magnesium. Try a mineral supplement tablet (sold at all health stores and most pharmacies).
4. Avoid white sugar in any form; this non-food destroys B-complex vitamins needed by your minerals.
5. Try the "Personality Punch" made of natural foods. This will supercharge your whole Being until you'll feel happy and cheerful.
6. Drink bottled natural spring water for a true Fountain of Youth feeling.
7. Four keys unlock the secrets of a balanced personality: love, recreation-play, work, faith. Learn how to use these keys and discover a new world of magic personality-plus!

8. Happiness consists of good mineral nourishment and solid mental satisfaction. Blend both together and discover a new world — a real treasure chest of health and joy!

9. Aptly applied, the secrets in this chapter can help you say goodbye to gloom!

A happy life consists of tranquility of mind.

Cicero

ELEVEN

Stress and Tension Relief Through Minerals

It's no fun being rich, if you can't relax and enjoy it!

At this point in your treasure hunt, you are already making plans for having a great time. Good! Life was meant to be enjoyed. But suppose, after you acquire the treasure, you find you just can't let loose. Suppose you lie awake all night, tense and overwrought with all sort of anxieties. What good is it to have this treasure if you aren't at peace with your own self? You are now going to learn how to discover the secrets of stress and tension relief. If you shrug your head and say that it won't work for you, then your negative attitude cancels your ticket on this treasure hunt. Forget all about it.

But, if you are willing to seek a small cache of secret mineral nuggets that may help banish stress and tension, and you are willing to try to use these nuggets properly, then let's continue on our treasure hunt.

Nature of stress

The famed expert on stress and tension, Dr. Hans Selye, author of *Stress of Life,* tells us, "No one can live without experiencing some degree of stress all the time. You may think that only serious disease or intensive physical or mental injury can cause stress. This is false. Crossing a busy intersection, exposure to a draft, or even sheer joy are enough to activate the body's stress mechanism to some extent. Stress is the spice of life, for any emotion, any activity causes stress.''

The secret is *your reaction to that stress!* As we shall soon discover, a *solid mineral fortification* builds resistance against the ailments caused by stress. What are the dangers of mineral-poor resistance?

Stress-caused ailments

Dr. Selye points out that mental tensions, frustrations, the sense of insecurity and aimlessness, are among the most important stresses and very common causes of physical disease. How often are migraine headaches, gastric and duodenal ulcers, coronary thrombosis, arthritis, hypertension, insanity, suicide or just hopeless unhappiness, actually caused by failure to find a satisfactory guide for conduct?

Dr. Selye then defines stress as resulting from infections, intoxications, wounds, nervous strain, heat, cold, muscular fatigue, x-radiation, poor oxygen, bleeding, allergic reactions, and reactions to drugs, etc.

Early Symptoms of Stress

There are three kinds of stress. A specialist in stomach and intestinal disorders says that (1) stress and nervous tension may come from excitement, anxiety, resentment or frustration; the degree of stress depends upon your personality; (2) physical stress includes fatigue, insomnia, burns, exposure to extreme heat or cold; (3) gastrointestinal stress may be caused by irregular meals, badly cooked foods, alcholic excess, irritation from chemical processing of food, certain physical characteristics of edibles and laxatives, too.

Early symptoms of stress are: belching and gas, heartburn, a lump in the throat, poor appetite, nausea, ordinary indigestion, constipation, diarrhea, ulcerative colitis, *pruritus ani* (itching rectum) and the all too familiar stomach and duodenal ulcer condition.

How The Body Prepares You for Stress

When you face any mental or physical task, your body rallies to prepare you for the stress or tension accompanying that action. We already know that fright, anger, pain, etc., alert the adrenal glands to ready you for the circumstance. Your blood pressure goes up, your heart beats faster, and your blood sugar level is higher. Minerals, such as calcium, magnesium, phosphorus join with Vitamins A and D to cause an increase of blood flow from your digestive organs to other body parts. Metabolism is raised so you have a greater increase of muscular power and resistance to fatigue.

The same aforementioned minerals spark the adrenals so that you will be able to make faster decisions. You can also run, fight, and think with greater speed.

All body minerals now rally to perform a life-giving task: to stimulate your pituitary gland at the base of your brain to tell your adrenal gland to issue hormones. The pituitary gland does this when minerals help it to issue the hormone adrenocorticotrophic (ACTH). Minerals demand more of this hormone (ACTH) which stimulates the adrenal cortex to produce cortisone which then activates even more hormones.

Note carefully: A deficiency of minerals means that your pituitary cannot issue enough ACTH and this means you are ill-equipped to meet a stress situation. You feel a rapid pulse, shortness of breath, heart palpitation, a funny feeling in the pit of your stomach, dizziness and trembling. You *must* have enough minerals to issue ACTH or you fall vulnerable to the effects of a stress situation.

Furthermore, since the adrenal and pituitary glands must have strong mineralization, it is essential that you obtain plenty of these precious nutrients so that manufacture of valuable ACTH can be accomplished.

Worry and tension

Anxiety or worry is a great problem situation in our modern time. Your mind can so stir up your physical condition that just sitting and brooding can cause a depletion of ACTH and render you susceptible to a lot of ailments. Yes, worry *can* kill. Do you know where the word *worry* comes from? It is taken from an old Anglo-Saxon verb *wyrgan,* meaning *to choke.* That is just what worrying does to you. It strangles and chokes you. It fills you with bottled up anxiety.

When anxiety cannot find an outlet, it turns inward, demands more ACTH which, in turn, renders you mentally and physically ill. There is hardly any cell, tissue or organ in your body that is not affected to the injurious influence of worry and tension. Later in this chapter you will be told just how to meet worry and conquer it, before it conquers you.

Eventual Harm of Stress and Tension

In cases of prolonged stress or anxiety, the continuous extra production of hormones over a long period of time may exact a heavy toll on your ability to adapt. When you develop a faulty adaptive response to stress, when there are derangements in the secretions of these hormones, it leads to what Dr. Selye calls "diseases of adaptation," such as chronic high blood pressure, ulcers, colitis and heart diseases. Dr. Selye says that emotional stimuli causes inflammation of the external sheath of the arteries leading to heart pains. Prolonged strain raises blood pressure, reduces blood flow to and from the kidneys, causes an overall breakdown, including mineral reserves.

Your Tired Nerves

The ability to meet stress and tension requires you to have strong, not tired, nerves. Healthy nerves help you remain calm, quiet, happy and strong. Tired nerves mean you have lost the ability to meet tension. Your "general adaptation syndrome" is poor.

What are nerves and how do they work?

Stick your finger in a pot of boiling water and the reaction of heat is conveyed in a split second to your spinal cord. A *sensory nerve impulse* carries the message: "It's hot!" Instantly, a *motor nerve impulse* commands your finger, "Get out!" This is called a *reflex arc.* You jerk away your finger before you even realize the water is so hot. This reflex nervous system rules all of your thoughts and automatic actions.

The seat of your whole nervous system is your brain and spinal cord. From there, smaller nerves branch throughout your body. A nerve cell looks like an octopus with tentacles that receive and carry away impulses. Your body has millions of these nerve cells — your brain, alone, has 12 *billion* of them. These nerves run throughout your whole body, often paralleling each other, forming nerve pathways similar to telephone wires running underground. The parts of the body we commonly call nerves are actually bundles of nerve fibers. Some are so thin that a one-inch thick bundle may contain 25,000 fibers.

A nerve impulse travels along a human nerve fiber at the speed of about 100 yards a second or almost 200 miles an hour. As this impulse travels, a chain reaction occurs. One nerve cell triggers the next cell along the route.

Minerals are responsible to help or retard the journey of the nerve impulse. These minerals secrete internal substances at the synapse — the intertwining of the terminal branches where impulses pass from one nerve to the other. Without minerals, such as calcium, phosphorus, magnesium, zinc, etc., the synapses are denied valuable internal substances and this slows up the impulse. This may be the cause for Grandpa's being "slow" or the inability to react properly to certain stress situations.

Minerals work to provide nerve cells with their own source of electricity. Nerves need only a period of 1/1000th of a second to rest between the transmission of nerve impulses, but nerves must have the basic minerals for this rest and self-recharging power. Without these minerals, there is a general slowing down and dwindling of the "general adaptation" powers.

Minerals feed electricity to your nerves. A mineral deficiency means a short circuit in your nervous system. The very tiny nerve cells, neurons, must have minerals in order to transmit powerful electrical impulses to other nerve cells. These nerves rule other functions, such as thinking, remembering, learning, sight, smell, touch, hearing, taste, consciousness, etc.

Mineral nourishment for nerves

Nerves require nourishment just as do other body parts. Oxygen carried via the bloodstream and requiring iron and copper, is needed by the nerves as well as calcium and phosphorus. If you deny your nerves adequate minerals, they grow tired and weak, and you develop into a typical case of "nerves." Prolonged starvation of nerve tissue may cause an irreparable damage.

A calcium deficiency may cause nerve convulsions, as well as cramps in hands and feet. A magnesium deficiency makes your nerves taut and tight. Also remember the valuable B-complex vitamins and protein which work together with these minerals.

Catharyn Elwood, famed author-lecturer, says in *Feel Like A Million:*

> The study of geriatrics has pointed out that those in the last half of life are deplorably deficient in calcium, iron, iodine, Vitamin D and the B-complex. These are our most important feeding values for nerve stability.
>
> For nerves to relax and to send your impulses, you need calcium. No calcium can be absorbed unless phosphorus, Vitamin F (unsaturated fatty acids) and the enzyme phosphatase and Vitamin D are also on the job. See that you get at least two grams of calcium and never less than one hour of sunbathing or 800 to 4000 units of Vitamin D daily. Use safe raw milk and unrefined vegetable oils. Magnesium is another mineral which acts as a sedative to the nerves. It is abundant in leafy greens. When you don't get enough, your nerves are highstrung and you are easily excited and irritated.

How a college student crammed without strain

The students at a large Eastern university were in the midst of gruelling exams. Several were not doing so well and feared failure. Joel, an average student, may have burned the midnight oil in cramming Mathematics and English Literature with as much fervor as his dormitory buddies, yet he seemed to come out ahead.

"Come on, Joel," asked a chemistry major, "let us in on your secret. Do you cheat?"

Joel felt offended. "Say, I never did a dishonest thing in my life. Maybe I'm an undiscovered genius or something."

The others pressed him for any "secret formula" he had come upon but Joel kept insisting it was very natural, nothing unusual.

That was all he said. One student, his roommate, kept an eagle eye on Joel. He noticed that the "genius" occasionally received a package from home. In it was an ordinary metal container filled with a white powder. Joel mixed this with water and drank it regularly.

Only when they all cornered him, did Joel agree to let them in on the secret of this special "brain potion." It turned out that the powder was a form of *pulverized coconut*. That was all. Joel mixed the coconut powder with water and drank it in place of milk. Coconut milk, he pointed out, was something his grandfather discovered when he had made a trip to the tropical isles way back when. "Grandpa takes it all the time — he's brighter than most of us."

This started a trend and soon, after the boys did a little research, everyone was drinking coconut milk. It so revitalized them that they passed their tests with flying colors. What did they find out about the seemingly ordinary coconut from which milk was made?

It has a rich store of protein, natural sugars, *phosphorus, magnesium, potassium as well as iron and manganese.* All of the coconut inside the tough outer shell is a seed — the largest seed there is. The coconut grows on beaches close to the sea so it has a treasure of many minerals that are lacking in land-grown seeds and foods. Most of the precious minerals are concentrated in the brown skin that clings tightly to the white meat so this should be eaten. The coconut "meat" is one of our greatest sources of valuable minerals. In its unripe or custard-like state it forms a perfect food.

When sprouted, the "milk" of the coconut is transformed into a snow-white, sponge-like ball that has a naturally sweet taste and is brimming with the precious minerals.

Thus, Joel started what a few college quipsters hastily dubbed a "FAN" club. That is, FEED A NERVE club. You do this by drinking lots of fresh coconut milk available in cans at health stores, or by buying a coconut at almost any produce outlet, cracking it and drinking the milk in the center. Or, buy powdered coconut and make your own milk. This is your only requirement to belong to the "FAN" club.

How coconut works on nerves

The secret here is in what is known as the *myalin sheath.* Each nerve fiber in your body is covered with a fatty material called *myalin*. Its purpose is similar to that of insulation on an electric wire. Myalin, a white, fatty substance, is desperately in need of certain minerals, notably those in coconut milk and in those proportions and combinations with vitamins as placed there by Nature. Destruction of the myalin sheath in your body may lead to multiple sclerosis. A depletion of this fatty substance causes nervous tension and varied associated ailments.

Joel was wise — that is, his grandfather had tipped him off on the values of this brain or nerve food. (A healthy brain needs a healthy nervous system.) Grandpa, undoubtedly, learned of this secret of the tropics and passed it on to his grandson.

You, too, can join the "FAN" club and begin by drinking lots of coconut milk. No need to wait until you're nervous and wrought up. Build prevention with the magic power of minerals in the milk of the tropical coconut. Your myalin sheaths will welcome this nerve food.

Uses of Lecithin

Before the turn of the century, a noted European physiologist, Dr. Geheimrath Rouleaux, was aware that still another food is needed by your nerves. That food is *lecithin* — a phosphatide and a valuable constituent of all living cells, both animal and vegetable.

Lecithin is made from defatted soybeans; it makes up 17 per cent of your nervous system and as your body is faced with tension, lecithin declines. So, you should add it to your diet, even as a supplement.

Lecithin exists in all body cells; it is the nucleus of these cells and is found in abundance in your nerve and brain cells. *The myalin sheath which cushions your nerves against the ravages of tension is surrounded with lecithin*. The nerve fibers need lecithin for nourishment. A deficiency results in depletion of this fatty sheath and you suffer from nervous irritability, fatigue, brain exhaustion and a complete breakdown.

Did you know that your nerve cells are rich in lecithin when you awaken, yet the supply is slowly reduced during the day by ordinary stress and tension?

The dictionary says this of the miracle nerve food: "lecithin, from Greek *lekithos,* yolk of an egg, a nitrogenous, fatty substance found in nerve tissue, blood, milk, egg yolk and some vegetables."

Originally, egg yolk was known for having a tremendous supply of lecithin. It still does; but today, we can get a more concentrated amount in capsule form — convenient when traveling or working — and in granules so you sprinkle it over salads, soups, in sandwiches, or dissolve in juices and other liquids. All health stores have lecithin.

Lecithin, therefore, is another food for your nerves. Try it daily to be a member in good standing with the "FAN" club.

A doctor, N. A. Ferri, once said, "Lecithin is essential not only for the tissue integrity of the nervous and glandular system in all living cells but has been regarded as also the most effective generator and regenerator of great physical, mental and glandular activity. *Shattered nerves, depleted brain power, waning activity of vital glands,* find in lecithin the most active of all restorers."

Remember Calcium

A busy housewife keeps a jar of calcium tablets she purchased at a health store. (Also available at pharmacies.) She finds that taking two at a time with each of her three daily meals helps her meet tense household problems. With a brood of seven and a husband ("often, he's more trouble than the youngsters"), she needs nerve strength.

Nerve cells of the aged or exhausted are shrunken in outline. The nuclei look faded; granules are clumped together and the connective tissues are weak. These calcium starved nerve cells are degenerated and cannot send out the direct impulses to help control stress and tension. So, remember calcium in your "FAN" club duties.

11 Ways to Reduce Tension

Let us face reality. Tension is here to stay. Modern life is complex, rife with conflicting demands. We are constantly faced with instant actions and immediate decisions. Often, stress and tension are more pronounced when we have been made particularly sensitive — an unhappy childhood, feelings of insecurity, constant noise. So, we are going to have much tension. What can we do?

Adjust our attitudes to reduce the effects these stress-tension situations will have on us. Here are 11 ways that *you* (yes, very definitely, you!) can ease mounting and, often, destructive tensions:

1. *Talk out your worries.* Don't bottle everything up. Put your confidence in a trusted friend: relation, clergyman, doctor, teacher or counselor. Talking things over will relieve strain and enable you to view your worry in a better light and help you find a solution.

2. *Get away from it all.* That's it, escape! Flee! But only for a while. Lose yourself in a movie, a book, even a day's outing. This change of scene and pace helps give you breath and balance. Don't just stand there and suffer. Rather, get away from it all with the forethought you'll come back and deal with the problem in a more composed and relaxed condition.

3. *Work off your temper.* When your anger or temper rises, go into some physical activity, such as gardening, garage cleaning, home workship, cooking, cleaning, repairing. Walking, swimming, and hiking also will help unleash your temper. Working the anger out of your system helps cool you off. The next day, you'll be better able to cope with the problem.

4. *Give in and surrender.* Stand firm and believe in what you know is right, but be calm and recognize that you *could* be wrong. Yield. The others will, too. Everyone relaxes. Now the stress-tension is eased and you can work together to a sensible solution.

5. *Help another person.* Constant worrying is often traced to self-absorption. Get yourself out of your thoughts. Do this by helping others. This takes the steam out of stress. It makes you feel useful, too.

6. *Do one thing at a time.* That work load on the desk or in the kitchen sink looks like a mountain. Tell yourself it is only temporary. Tackle the most urgent tasks first, then go to the next ones. But, do one at a time.

7. *Avoid the "Superman" compulsion.* Some people want too much from themselves; they are perfectionists. They become stressful. Sure, try for perfection but bear in mind that you may fail. Do your best even with those tasks which you cannot do so well. No one asks you to achieve the impossible.

8. *Be slow on criticism.* Rather than being overly critical, look for the good points. Each has his virtues and shortcomings. Help

others and yourself in developing good points for mutual satisfaction.

9. *Give others a needed break.* Must you be first in line? Must you always be a winner? If that is your attitude, life is a continual race and this leads to severe tension. Competition is contagious, but so is cooperation. Give the other fellow a break and make things easier for yourself. When the other fellow feels you are not a threat to him, he automatically ceases being a threat to you.

10. *Be available.* Are you rejected or neglected? This may be in your mind. Maybe you are shrinking away from society. Make yourself available for acceptable recreational functions. Be part of the mainstream of life.

11. *Have a scheduled recreation.* Driving yourself too hard leads to nervous collapse. Have a regular scheduled recreation day or weekend. At least one day in a week should be devoted to any hobby or activity that gives you pleasure and joy. Famed Dr. Sara M. Jordan once said, "It is wonderful to see how the greatest stress can be endured by the human body if periods of relaxation are interspersed at enough intervals."

There is hope for stress and tension problems with corrected nutrition, including minerals, and physical remedies. Dr. Selye's own prescription for avoiding diseases of stressful emotions is: "The greatest practical lesson is to realize the deep-rooted biologic necessity for completion — the fulfillment of all our smallest needs and greatest aspirations — in harmony with our heredity make-up. We all had this priceless talent for pure enjoyment when young, but as time went by most of us have lost this gift. The true artist, the true scientist never loses this faculty. It is the essence of their being."

YOUR PLAN FOR FREEDOM FROM TENSION AS DESCRIBED IN CHAPTER ELEVEN

1. Stress-tension is part of daily life. If your reaction is negative and mineral-starved, you may become ill.

2. Typical stress-caused illnesses include headaches, ulcers, coronary thrombosis, arthritis, insanity, suicide, etc.

3. Thinking people are often under greater strain, especially if they endure months of unrelieved tensions.

4. Enjoy leisure and get away from it all to relax your mind and nerves.

5. When faced with stress, your body needs minerals to produce ACTH to meet demands of tension.

6. Billions of body nerves need minerals for action and strength.

7. Coconut milk is a powerhouse of mineral strength needed by your nerves.

8. To join the "FAN" club, remember daily coconut milk, lecithin for the myalin sheath, calcium for the nerve cells.

9. Try the 11-step plan designed to ease tense situations and enable you to better cope with daily problems, and take your mineral diet seriously.

Health is not valued till sickness comes.
                    Thomas **Fuller**

TWELVE

Good News for Victims of Prostate Gland Trouble

Gerald Asbury was a crew manager for a famous housewares chain. He had spent more than two decades on the road and was now an office executive. Yet, he was still required to take a few trips, now and then.

"Can't do it," he lamented to his golf partner when they were on the course. "In fact, I'm so bothered by getting up nightly, going to the bathroom, I hardly stray far from the office or home." He nodded toward the building on the greens. "See, I can't even get away from that. My prostate started bothering me a few years ago. Maybe I'll have an operation."

The partner agreed and said, "Sometimes, cancer can be caused by an infected prostate gland. But you know, Gerry, I heard that certain types of foods help a prostate gland condition."

Gerald Asbury scoffed. Yet he made a slight decision to find out more. He asked a co-worker who had a son studying chemistry to find out whether a gland could be treated by certain nutrients.

In due time, he received a packet of tearsheets and photostats from a medical library, courtesy of the chemistry student. Gerald Asbury tried some of the ideas, but was impatient. He eventually entered a hospital and had his prostate gland removed.

After his convalescence, he asked his wife what happened to the information he had put into a folder. Thinking he did not need the booklets anymore, she had given them to Mr. Brown, their next-door neighbor.

Mr. Brown was grateful when he came to visit Gerald. "Those ideas were pretty good," he referred to the medical researches. "In fact, I had some prostate gland trouble and followed the health tips. Wasn't bothered again."

"But why didn't it work for me?" wondered Gerald.

"Guess you didn't give it time," was the laconic, yet wise, response.

What Is the Prostate Gland?

The prostate is a gland in the male located immediately in front of the rectum, just below the bladder and encircling the urethra where it exits from the bladder. It is part of the male reproductive system, manufacturing a fluid that makes up the largest part of the semen. This prostatic fluid contains ingredients that nourish the delicate microscopic sperm cells whose health is essential for fertility.

The size and shape of a chestnut, the gland is subjected to constant use during a male's lifetime. By middle-age, it may be "worn" to the extent that it could cause trouble. The gland swells up, cutting off to some extent the flow of urine. This causes a serious condition.

Trouble symptoms

Early symptoms include a feeling of congestion, later developing into difficulty in urinating. At first, there is no pain. As the gland compresses the bladder mouth more and more, urination becomes increasingly difficult and the male has a feeling of an incompletely emptied bladder. This is often the case. "Residual urine" may collect in the bladder and lead to infection or the formation of bladder stones.

Untreated, the condition may progress to bladder and kidney trouble. Complete obstruction of the bladder mouth may occur, often with such suddenness that there is danger and pain. A doctor must insert a catheter into the bladder to remove urine; this is only temporary relief.

Causes and treatments

Celibacy, profligacy or venereal infection have little to do with this problem. In middle-aged men, this condition just seems to occur. It is estimated that one out of every 12 men who reach the age of 60 will suffer prostate enlargement. Neither drugs nor treatment can prevent enlargement of the gland. Diathermy is used to relieve congestion and X-ray offers minimal help. Hot tub baths help relieve symptoms, but these are not cures.

Removal of the gland appears to be the only treatment. As for the causes, these could be considered as part of the normal process of aging since all our glands mature along with the body.

However, considering that the prostate gland issues a substance that feeds the sperm cells, it appears that a *deficiency* of the proper nutrients and minerals that manufacture this hormone may be responsible for disorders of the gland.

The Magic Power of Zinc

Zinc is one of the minerals with magic powers. Since it exists in such tiny amounts, it is usually called a "trace" element. Yet, we know it is an important part of a body enzyme, "carbonic anhydrase," which conveys carbon dioxide in the blood and also influences the delicate acid-alkaline balance of the overall system.

Zinc has also been seen to help the body properly absorb the precious B-complex vitamins. Zinc also influences the entire hormonal system — all the glands, that is, including the prostate! According to a team of researchers, George R. Prout, M.D., Michael Sierp, M. D., and Willet F. Whitmore, M.D., when a prostate gland is seriously diseased with infection, it shows a low zinc supply.

How much zinc for prostate health?

According to Dr. Monier-Williams (*Trace Elements in Food*) the adult needs about 12 milligrams daily of zinc. Others have suggested more so a watchword would be to get zinc in natural foods.

Where to get zinc?

In the following chart the potency of this precious mineral in different foods is listed:

.25 to 2 p.p.m. (parts per million) — apples, oranges, lemons, figs, grapes, chestnuts, pulpy fruits, green vegetables, mineral waters, honey.

2 to 8 p.p.m. raspberries, loganberries, dates, unblanced green vegetables, most sea fish, lean beef, milk, polished rice, beets, bananas, celery, tomatoes, asparagus, carrots, radishes, potatoes, mushrooms, coffee, white flour and white bread.

20 to 50 p.p.m. some cereals, yeast, onions, brown rice, whole eggs, almonds, whole grain flour and bread, oatmeal, barleymeal, molasses, egg yolk, chicken, nuts, peas, beans, lentils, tea, dried yeast, mussels.

Over 50 p.p.m. wheat germ, wheat bran, oysters, beef liver, gelatin.

A good zinc tonic

In a glass of apple juice, mix four tablespoons of wheat germ, two tablespoons of unflavored gelatin, one tablespoon of wheat bran. Mix in a blender or with a beater. Drink one glass daily.

Remember, too, to have liver once a week. Also, use food supplements, such as bone meal, kelp, brewer's yeast, which are rich in other minerals and B-complex vitamins that work with zinc. These supplements have much zinc, too.

Magnesium for Prostate

A remarkable book by Dr. Joseph Favier, *Mineral Equilibrium and Health,* reveals the secrets of magic minerals, especially magnesium, in relation to prostate gland trouble.

Dr. Favier tells how his physician friends took magnesium tablets. They had been bothered with getting up nightly because of prostate gland troubles. All of them, after taking these tablets, found their nocturnal urinating troubles diminished or gone.

Dr. Favier tells of his colleague, Dr. Chevassu, who cured ten (out of twelve) prostatic cases with magnesium tablets. One of the doctor's patients, age 77, had a very enlarged prostate and suffered from complete retention. He was given four tablets daily (2g 40) for nearly nine weeks. Before the end of this treatment, he was so remarkably relieved that an operation could be postponed.

Dr. Chevassu confided about another patient who was sent for a prostate removal operation. But the doctor decided this would be too dangerous. Instead, magnesium tablets were prescribed and soon the patient left the hospital without any operation! He still came back for more visits but has never had the need for further treatment. This patient continued to take magnesium.

This valuable mineral is available (at health stores and pharmacies) in tablet form. Considering that 75 per cent of the body's magnesium supply is in the bones, you need more for your organs. Remember bone meal, too.

Magnesium is found in wheat germ, honey, kohlrabi, almonds dried lima beans, beet greens, brazil nuts, cashew nuts, corn, endive, hazelnuts, peanuts, dried peas, pecans, brown rice, soy flour, walnuts, and pumpkin seeds.

Eating Pumpkin Seeds for Prostate Health

A European physican, W. Dervient, may some day be heralded as the "father of gland relief." He used a mineral-naturalistic approach to the problem of prostate gland disorder and reported actual cures of patients who ate ordinary pumpkin seeds.

Writing in *Heilkunde Heilwege* (a German journal, 1:59), Dr. Devrient states,

> Modern medicine has not been able to find any successful weapon against early attrition and deterioration of the prostate gland and we have no other recourse than to seek prevention in the realm of healing plants.
>
> There is in fact a till-now little noticed, disease-preventive plant whose rejuvenating powers for men are extolled with praise by popular medicine both in America and in Europe. Experience reveals that *men in those countries where the seeds of this plant are copiously eaten throughout a lifetime remain completely free of prostatic hypertrophy and all its consequences.*

Dr. Devrient then says that this "neglected curative plant contains active biocatalytic (reaction-causing) ingredients which I should like to call 'androgen-hormonal.' " That is, the ingredients in this plant supplant the decline in male hormones of the prostate that takes place in increasing age.

Dr. Devrient says the plant is the well-known pumpkin — *cucurbita pepo*. Its seeds are rich in the androgen-hormonal building agents that are needed by the prostate gland for maximum health.

Dr. Devrient gave the pumpkin seeds to his patients and was able to cure them of prostate disorder.

Tried Seeds On Himself. "My own personal observations in the course of the last eight years, however, have been decisive for me. At my own age of 70 years I am well able to be satisfied with the condition of my own prostate, on the basis of daily ingestion of pumpkin seeds, and with that of my health in general.

"The beneficial result can also be found among city patients who are prudent enough to eat pumpkin seeds every day and throughout their life. But one must continue proving this to the city-dweller. The peasants of the Balkans and of Eastern Europe knew of the healing effect of these seeds already from their forefathers."

Dr. Devrient discovered that the biocatalytic ingredients in pumpkin seeds exert an action upon the male hormonal system to preclude prostate gland trouble and avoid hormonal disturbance. Minerals in the pumpkin seed — zinc, magnesium, phosphorus — perform this miracle action.

In a few words, eat *raw pumpkin seeds daily*! Nearly all food stores carry them. Specify *unshelled* seeds. If they have already been shelled, it means a chemical action has burned away the shell and entered the seed, itself, destroying valuable mineral supply. So, shell them yourself and eat them. It's fun. It's delicious. It's healthy.

The Mysterious Vitamin "F"

So new, vitamin F is hardly known; yet, it is more familiar as "unsaturated fatty acid" and is found in vegetable oils, such as corn, peanut, soya, safflower, sunflower, etc. These oils, especially wheat germ oil, are rich in Vitamins A and E, both of which help minerals perform their life giving jobs.

A team of researchers reported that 19 cases of prostate disorders were cleared with unsaturated fatty acids given in capsule form. Further, all 19 cases could then pass their water; nocturia (getting up nightly) was eliminated in most of the men; there was a decrease of fatigue and leg pains and an increase in marital vigor; cystitis (bladder inflammation) cleared up. In all cases, the size of the swollen prostate was normalized.

Daily, the prostatic patients were given six five-grain tablets of vitamin F complex, a concentrate containing linoleic, linolenic and arachidonic acids, each tablet having a total of ten milligrams of these unsaturated fatty acids. The dosage was administered for a period of three days to produce systemic saturation. It was then reduced to four tablets daily for several weeks, and finally, a maintenance dose of one to two tablets daily.

You may be able to get this formula prepared for you at a pharmacy; ask your doctor if he will write you a prescription. One current formula maker of this exact tablet is Vitamin Products, Milwaukee, Wisconsin. It is sold under the trade name of *Cataplex F.* You may wish to write to this company for further information.

The ingredients of this unique formula exert such a powerful stimulus upon minerals that the actions are highly beneficial. It all shows how minerals, vitamins, proteins, enzymes, and so forth, all work in harmony like a beautiful symphony. Withdraw one and you have confusion.

FOR PROSTATE HEALTH, FOLLOW THESE POINTS IN CHAPTER TWELVE

1. Prostate trouble occurs to 1 out of every 12 men who reach the age of 60.
2. The magic power of zinc helps to influence the entire glandular system, including the prostate gland which is rich in this mineral.
3. Take the zinc tonic daily. Remember bone meal, kelp, brewer's yeast. Liver should be eaten once a week.
4. Magnesium tablets are also valuable for prostate gland help.
5. Raw, unshelled pumpkin seeds are invaluable to maintain the male androgen-hormonal balance. Eat a pound of seeds daily.

6. Unsaturated fatty acids are valuable as they work harmoniously with minerals. Use vegetable cooking oils and try taking these same unsaturated fatty acid nutrients in capsule form, sold at health stores or pharmacies.

7. Keep your mind young and your glands follow through!

THIRTEEN

No More Nerve-Racking Menopause with a Mineralized Diet

Nearly all women anticipate a great personality change when they reach their middle years. Many calm, tranquil women suddenly change into nervous, tense and wrought up personalities. Others find themselves unable to control actions, such as temper, grouchiness, carelessness. Added to this personality defect is a physical change. Slim wives and mothers who always prided themselves upon youthful appearances now grow fat, slovenly, unkempt. Life no longer seems worthwhile. This combined mental-physical change that alters the personality until it is no longer recognizable is caused by the *menopause,* also known as the "climacteric" or "change of life."

What is menopause?

The word menopause is taken from the Greek *men,* meaning "month" and *pauo* meaning "cause to cease." Menopause means a cessation of the female's monthly periods.

Speaking in simple terms, during the menopause ovulation stops — the ovaries no longer release the egg for possible fertilization. Depending upon the individual, it may stop suddenly or gradually.

Some may experience symptoms for a short time while many more may endure symptoms for as long as ten years!

The menopause is not imaginary, it is real! Often, it is uncomfortable to those who live with the woman. According to Erle Henriksen, M.D. (*American Journal of Obstetrics,* Vol. 65, pp. 1182-91), these hormonal changes produce pressure on the brain's nerve centers and create personality defects including tension, quick anger, insomnia, headaches, vague discomforts, foot swelling, etc. Dr. Henriksen remarks, "It takes extremely stable husbands and children to put up with the worst sufferers. Some husbands just run and hide. Others ask for divorce."

Twin Sisters with Opposite Personalities

Eva and Adeline were twin sisters; they originally possessed the same or "twin" personalities. Both were cheerful, radiant, full of pep and vigor. For years after they became wives, mothers and grandmothers, they were alarmingly identical.

Then they reached their 48th birthdays and the change took place. Eva remained youthful; her greying hair only emphasized her colorful skin, the sparkle in her eyes. As for Adeline, she was sallow, nervous, gloomy and felt that life was over.

"I don't even know if I had any change of life," said Eva. "I heard about it so many years ago and decided to help Nature. I take all sorts of thyroid gland tonics — iodine, iron, calcium and vitamins, too. I guess I sort of 'fed' myself missing hormones."

Adeline snapped back, "Well, you were always the healthier sister of the two of us."

This was not at all true. Both had enjoyed radiant health and vigor. Eve pointed this out. "You just let yourself go, Adeline. There is still time. Why not start taking minerals, as well as vitamins. They work together, you know."

It took a bit of doing before Adeline was convinced that nutrition might help restore the inner balance and normalize the hormonal upset. She took mineral supplements as well as kelp tablets (rich in gland required iron). In two months, she felt better. While she had not yet reverted back to her previous charming, youthful appearance, she began to look more like a twin sister rather than an older sister, as one unkind person cruelly jested.

How to feed your thyroid

Body metabolism is the burning up of food to produce energy and sustenance. The thyroid gland controls this process. If it works too fast, food is burned up faster than you can take it in and the person is always nervous, fretful and loses weight.

But, if the thyroid slows up and becomes underactive as often happens during the menopause because glandular functions slow up, it means that food cannot burn enough. The fire is low. Women feel sleepy, dull, grow tired, listless, and hair grows stringy. Accumulations of fat appear. A lazy gland is really at fault. Nature has created a deficiency of some hormones so you need to make up for the shortage.

The thyroid must have iodine which is found in all deep water fish. Include this in your diet and take iodine food supplements sold at any pharmacy or health store. Your thyroid gland is the one first hit by the menopause. Give it ammunition with iodine.

Calcium is important

The menopause means a lack of ovarian hormones and also a severe calcium deficiency. This means you must take more calcium. Try bone meal tablets or powder, but remember that you must also have both Vitamin D and the valuable unsaturated fatty acids in vegetable oils. These nutrients work with calcium for overall assimilation. Combined, they can dispel leg cramps and body pains during the menopause. The *major* mineral needed during menopause is calcium. Adelle Davis in *Let's Eat Right To Keep Fit* declares, "Hot flashes, night sweats, leg cramps, irritability, nervousness and mental depression...can be usually overcome in a single day by giving calcium." Include Vitamin D and fish oils for assimilation. Calcium tablets are sold at all pharmacies and health stores.

Power of Vitamin E

It is possible to *prevent* severe menopause symptoms if you give your minerals a super-charger boost. How? With Vitamin E. Numerous physicians have found that when they give their patients Vitamin E in capsule form, ranging from 10 to 25 milligrams daily, the hot flashes, back aches and personality defects could be relieved and even prevented if nutrient treatment was begun early enough.

Dr. E. V. Shute, a pioneer in Vitamin E therapy, reported that giving this vitamin to menopause patients in doses of 30 to 75 milligrams daily helped to decrease the intensity and severity of hot flashes and relieved characteristic headaches. Dr. Shute states, "Certainly there are no people who cannot take 50 milligrams of Vitamin E a day safely. There are virtually no people who cannot take 100 milligrams safely, unless a third condition exists, namely an allergy. Fifty to a hundred years ago the average person probably ate about 35 units of Vitamin E a day. Now with increasing deficiency it may take a large dose to prevent trouble."

According to Henry A. Gozan, M.D., in the *New York State Journal of Medicine* (5:15-1952), when he treated 35 menopausal women with 300 milligrams of Vitamin E daily, with good nutrition including mineral supplements, the results were amazing. Within two to four weeks, 19 improved or were completely relieved of mental and physical disturbances, and the remainder gradually improved. But remember, to either prevent the menopause or ease symptoms, you must have minerals, such as calcium, phosphorus and magnesium, to work in conjunction with Vitamin E.

A prominent nutritionist tells us, "Among my personal friends whose diets have been unusually adequate, I know of no woman whose menopause has set in before the age of 53 to 55. Furthermore, I suspect aging occurs rapidly at menopause when Vitamin E is undersupplied and, conversely, that women with delayed menopause stay psychologically young. One woman whose nutrition I have checked annually since 1936 is still menstruating at 62 years of age; she can pass for 40 any day."

Your glands should be nourished with minerals as well as precious Vitamins D and E and the unsaturated fatty acids. Where can you get Vitamin E? Of course, there are fish liver oils and capsules sold in pharmacies and health stores.

Raw wheat germ and unbleached wheat foods contain precious Vitamin E. Chemical processing will destroy this vitamin so obtain chemically unprocessed bread from any health store. Vitamin E is found in the oil that is pressed from the germ or living part of the wheat berry; it is present in freshly-ground, whole meal flour sold at any health store. Use it for baking.

Cornell Bread

A well known society queen has reigned undisputed for many years; the Social Register does not give her age but intimates place her at 68. She looks a young 48. Servants who have been with her many years have confided that they do not ever recall having noticed any menopausal symptoms. She is youthful, alert, pleasant and a vivacious person. She has been a guest on TV panel shows but is "rejected" for those Life Begins After 50 types of entertainment for the simple reason that she looks too young! Nobody would believe she was 50!

This society queen has never eaten ordinary bread. She eats and serves others a delicious home made bread that is now known as Cornell Bread. Its formula was made known by famed Dr. Clive M. McCay of Cornell University. It is brimming with minerals and precious Vitamin E, a combination that can probably end or ease the menopause for many women.

You can make your own bread mix as follows:

6 cups unbleached flour	¾ cup dry milk (non-fat)
½ cup soy flour (full fat)	3 tablespoons raw wheat germ.

Mix and sift together all these ingredients and you have Cornell flour.

Here is how to make a loaf of bread — exactly as it is prepared in the kitchen of this wealthy society queen:

1 package of yeast	2 tablespoons of buckwheat honey
2 cups of water	6 cups of Cornell flour
8 teaspoons of corn oil	1 heaping teaspoon of mineral-rich kelp.

Dissolve the yeast in ¼ cup of tepid water. Combine all liquids. Add to the blended dry ingredients. Sift in the Cornell Flour. With a rotary beater, make smooth. Allow to rise in oven until twice in bulk. Knead for ten minutes until bouncy. Shape into twin loaves; put in an oiled baking pan. Let rise until nearly twice in bulk. Remove from oven. Set oven heat at 375° F. Put bread in hot oven, bake for 45 minutes.

This mineral bread that is rich in associated vitamins will be a grateful blessing in disguise for those wanting to avoid or ease the menopause. Note that you should eat this bread at all times in place of ordinary bread. Be sure you have enough minerals so the nutrients in this bread can work effectively to help normalize your hormonal system.

Cambric Tea for Health

Remember when Grandmother would drink cambric tea? Wasn't Grandma a sweet, gentle person? Maybe the tea did it. You can make it today.

Take ¼ glass of soya milk, add to ¾ glass of boiling water and serve with three tablespoons of honey.

The minerals in this cambric tea are needed by your glands. Maybe Grandma hardly cared a whit about glands and did not know a hormone from a darning needle, but she had enough wisdom to know that this tea made her feel good and that was all that mattered.

Secret Oriental Foods for Health

Several missionary husband-and-wife teams traveled throughout East Asia, China and Japan and noticed that the middle-aged women appear to be remarkably free from the menopause effects. A few of the missionary doctors also observed that when the change of life occurred among the native patients they treated, except for an occasional tremor, other symptoms were absent. The same sweet, placid personality (so familiar to the benign Orientals) prevailed throughout the critical period and thereafter.

The doctors attempted to find out the secret. Just how did these Oriental women avoid the menopause effects? The doctors noted their food habits and discovered that two special homemade edibles were part of the staple diet. No one knows where or how the custom began, but it is an essential one. The missionary doctors then told me of two of these "secret" Oriental foods. Both of them are powerhouses of precious vitamins, minerals and other nutrients needed to nourish the glandular system during the menopause. You, too, can benefit by these delicious foods.

1. *Fresh Soya Milk*. Thousands of small factories in the Orient make fresh soya milk which is then sold on the street. You can make it in your own home. Here's how. Buy ¼ pound of the best, undamaged yellow soya beans. Cover with water to soak for eight hours or overnight. They swell, from this soaking, to triple their original weight. After thorough washing (in which a portion of the membranous skin is washed away), cover the beans with ¾ quart of water and — wet — grind them. You can use a mixer or blender.

This turns the soy beans and water into a milky solution. Take the milk with the (now) insoluble portions of soy beans, put into a linen bag and press out. That which is squeezed out is the soya milk. Cook in a pot for five or ten minutes. Use a large pot because the mineral-rich lecithin portion of the milk will foam to the top. Let it cool, then drink. This is a dynamic supply of all minerals, vitamins, as well as proteins, that are needed by the menopausal female.

What about the remaining small portion of residue *in* the linen bag? Use it as an addition to baked goods, puddings, etc. This still adds to your mineral intake.

2. *Secret "TOFU" Food*. Virtually unknown in the United States is the secret TOFU food that is consumed daily in the Orient. It is quite possible that the minerals in the TOFU act as buffering agents to meet the stresses of the menopause. If you eat TOFU early in life, it is reasonable to hope that you can so build up enough resistance that the change of life will pass over with few or no symptoms. It works in the Orient. Why not for Americans?

To make TOFU, after you have heated the above soya milk, add a precipitating substance. Vinegar is convenient and practical. Let this remain for about five minutes. This enables the small particles in the pot of soya milk to flocculate into a large mass of curd which slowly sinks to the bottom. Water which accumulates on the top is partly drawn off and discarded. A complete precipitation is seen when the milk changes into a yellowish clear liquid and solids form. Keep drawing off the water that accumulates on top and discard. When you have a large amount of curd, transfer into a cheesecloth place in a strainer or colander and drain off excess water.

TOFU is a form of soya cheese; tastes delicious and is nutritious, too. It is used in the Orient either as a straight cheese, or as an additive to soups, vegetables, broths, etc. You can dice tofu, and add to cut leeks, tomatoes or beets. Use four tablespoons of raw, cold-pressed wheat germ oil for a heavenly salad that belongs with every dinner for the female — and you males, too!

Incidentally, about ¼ pound of soya beans will make ½ pound of curd or TOFU. You can buy soya beans, as well as wheat germ oil, at most any grocery establishment or health store.

Women, take a tip from the Orient and help yourself be rid of the menopause effects. Minerals do the trick in these Oriental foods.

KEY POINTS ON HOW TO AVOID MENOPAUSE SIDE EFFECTS IN CHAPTER THIRTEEN

1. The menopause is a time of life in the 40's or 50's when the ovaries cease activities and the female hormonal system undergoes a change. Symptoms include hot flashes, palpitation of the heart, a feeling of fullness. Mental symptoms include nervous upset, irritability, quick temper, insomnia. Some women react so vividly they jeopardize their family, home, and themselves.

2. The thyroid gland helps overcome menopausal symptoms. Daily, feed your thyroid iodine in supplemental capsule form. Also, include deep water fish in your diet.

3. The calcium mineral works with Vitamin D and unsaturated fatty acids found in vegetable oils to combat menopausal cramps and pains, and mental depression. Take calcium tablets and remember to eat yogurt.

4. Vitamine E is seized upon by minerals as necessary food. If you want to obtain the maximum benefit from the magic power of minerals, feed them enough Vitamin E in capsule form and in raw wheat germ foods. In reported tests, 300 milligrams of Vitamin E daily helped ease menopausal symptoms. Without minerals, this vitamin is weakened or useless.

5. Use Cornell Bread whenever you have to eat any bread product. It's a powerhouse of minerals and vitamins.

6. Try Cambric Tea for a good mineral tonic needed in the menopause.

7. Take a tip from the Orient where the bad effects of menopause seem unknown. Drink soya milk and eat the secret TOFU that is a buried treasure of minerals.

A thing of beauty is a joy forever.

Keats

FOURTEEN

How to Get and Keep the Look of Youth with Minerals

"Keep your secret treasure," grumbled the young bookkeeper. "I can't buy myself a new face with it." She was already discouraged as she had been told that little could be done for her sagging face, crow's feet, skin blemishes. Although she was only 38, she already showed indications of developing an unsightly "crepe" skin.

"You can't buy yourself beauty, or happiness, for that matter," was my reply. "Neither can you buy health! The treasure hunt is for something that money can never buy simply because it is priceless."

"What kind of a treasure is that?" She was pessimistic, to say the least. "I want to look young. Not younger than my 38 years, but young, if you know what I mean."

I replied, "Yes, I understand what you mean, and I repeat that this treasure is priceless; it will not be sold for any consideration. It is yours, absolutely free! The treasure will help you enjoy a dynamic personality and vivid health."

"And just how is this magic power supposed to work? Do you have a special wand you wave? Or do you use a crystal ball? No, thank you. It's not the treasure that I can use." She was already so discouraged it was disappointing.

I then said, "The magic power lies in the minerals that can help make you cheerful, vibrant, bouncy, intelligent, happy. They can also so revitalize your system, you'll have a beautiful skin. You can't eat any gold coins you find in a pirate treasure. Sure, you can buy all sort of things with the coins, but they may not make you young. Minerals in foods *can* do this 'fountain of youth' trick. So, that means that minerals are a greater treasury discovery than gold coins."

"If that's so," she showed interest, "let me go along on the treasure hunt and see if it can reward me with a beautiful skin."

What Is Your Skin?

Actually, your skin is a reflection of your health. Call it "lovely to look at," or "peaches and cream," or "milk and honey," the skin is the body's envelope. Keep the envelope in good shape and it's young.

Let's look at your skin. Now, that's quite a look! Use both eyes. Actually, your skin is your largest body organ. It covers an area of about 17 square feet on an average adult and weighs close to six pounds, twice the weight of your liver or brain. Your skin gets one-third of all blood circulating in your system. It has from two to three million sweat glands, particularly in the armpits, hands, feet and forehead. The average adult has over 3,000 square inches of surface area. Thickness may vary from about 1/50 of an inch on your eyelids to as much as 1/3 of an inch on your palms and foot soles.

Your skin protects you against bacterial invasion, against injury to delicate tissues inside your body, against harsh sunshine rays and loss of needed moisture.

Your skin serves as an organ of perception for the complete nervous system. When *one* square inch of skin is examined under a microscope, it shows 72 feet of nerves, hundreds of pain, pressure, heat and cold receptors.

Your skin also regulates temperature. The same *one* square inch of skin has about 15 feet of blood vessels. These dilate (grow larger) when you have to lose heat and constrict (grow narrow) when you have to prevent heat loss, such as in winter.

Little wonder that Logan Clendening, M.D., in *The Human Body,* speaks of the skin as "one of the most interesting and mystic structures...that outer rampart which separates us from the rest of the universe, the sack which contains that juice or essence which is me, or which is you, a moat defensive against insects, poisons, germs. The very storms of the soul are recorded upon it."

What's Under Your Skin

Actually, your skin consists of three tissue layers: epidermis, dermis and subcutaneous. The *epidermis,* or outer skin has two layers — the horny top layer of dry dead cells constantly being shed and the growing layer in which minerals work to replace dead cells with new cells. Minerals in the deeper layers of the epidermis help form new cells.

The *dermis* layer, also called the "true skin" has the nerves, sweat glands, blood vessels, nerve receptors, hair follicles, and oil glands. The top of the dermis consists of a layer of tiny cone-shaped objects called *papillae.* Over 150 million papillae are scattered over the entire body. More are found in sensitive regions as your finger and toe tips. (That's why foot tickling creates a nerve response.) Nerve fibers and special nerve endings are found in many papillae and this gives you a sense of "feel" and touch as well as response to being touched.

The *subcutaneous* layer contains fat lobules, blood vessels. Minerals make this layer smooth and a springy base for your skin. It links the dermis (middle layer) with tissue covering the bones and muscles.

Since the skin reacts to mental and physical situations, you need solid mineralization. Skin health is an inside job — minerals do the work.

Skin and Personality

Magic minerals are needed to strengthen personality traits. For example, you have two million sweat glands in your entire skin. Placed end to end, they'd make a six-mile tube. These sweat glands give off heat, sweat and waste products. The amount of perspiration, from one to 20 quarts each day, depends upon mental and physical exertion. This perspiration contains potassium, iron, sulphur, phosphorus as well as salt and vitamins B and C. These minerals must be replaced if you expect to stay healthy and want to avoid fatigue and other deficiency ailments.

A nervous or tense person can develop skin disorders and premature aging. If a personality is mineral-weak, the "magic powers" are simultaneously weak and reflect upon the skin. D. Cappon, M.D., in the *Canadian Medical Association Journal* tells of a man who developed a case of hives each day at 5:00 P.M. when he had to be locked in his quarters.

In another case, a manufacturer saw his factory burn to the ground and he developed a severe case of hives. Then, there is the case of a woman who was irritated by her husband in public places and felt frustrated because she could not rebuff him. She developed hives instead.

Dr. Cappon feels that psoriasis (scaly skin) is a symptom of a personality weakness. In treating patients, a waxing and waning of eruptions could be directly associated with variations in the emotions. As for acne or pimples, he found that skin outbreaks could be traced to the emotional state of the patient. Warts, too, are largely mentally-induced.

Tension and nervousness cause sweating which, in turn, cause loss of precious minerals. Buffer yourself against potential skin ailments by getting plenty of the precious nutrients.

Mineral food tip

Noted Catharyn Elwood in *Feel Like A Million* has this mineral food tip: "Many minerals must be included before your skin will look rosy and alive. The enviable healthy, ruddy glow which is seen so rarely today comes only when iron-rich red blood courses through capillaries and blood vessels.

'To build up and keep your iron intake high, use blackstrap molasses, leafy greens and apricots generously. If you lack iodine in your foods, your circulation will be slow and sluggish. Even if your blood be richly red, if it does not circulate freely and bathe the skin cells they will be pale and lifeless. Use dried sea greens." You can get dried sea greens or kelp at any health store.

Why should women in the Mediterranean countries (and also South and Latin America) have a priority on beautiful skin? One traveller remarked, "The women never seem to age in those countries. "What's the secret? In a word — *minerals*. They use olive oil, a prime source of unsaturated fatty acids and other valuable nutrients which *combine* with minerals to create a healthy and youthful skin. Use olive oil as well as any other vegetable cooking oil for all dishes.

One well-known Italian songstress uses olive oil in still another manner. She pours pure olive oil in a small, wide-mouthed jar. Two hours before going to sleep, she dips her fingertips into this oil, *lightly* lubricates her entire skin, and that's all! The minerals go to work as they soak through the skin pores. Before retiring, she tissues off the oil so the pillows won't stain. The reward? A soft face that is like rose dew — youthful and healthy!

Olive oil and millet lotion

Take two tablespoons of millet meal, two tablespoons of honey, two teaspoons of pure olive oil, and blend into a smooth paste. If you desire, add one tablespoon of almond meal. Apply this paste over your face and throat. Let remain for 45 minutes to an hour. Wipe off with cleansing tissues. Dash on cold water. The minerals in these foods are remarkably beneficial and will do wonders for a tired or aging skin.

Ask for these foods at any produce or grocery outlet, or health store.

A prominent doctor feels that you can "nourish" the skin by using any *edible* fats. These replenish lost skin oils. He recommends using salad oil as a skin cream. An excellent type to us is cold-pressed soy oil, rich in those minerals found to occur naturally in skin tissue. Nearly any large supermarket or health store has cold-pressed soy oil.

Lemon rinse

Your skin is generally slightly acid. Most soaps are highly alkaline and take off the acid mantle or coating. To retain this acid coating, rinse your face and hands in a basin of water to which the juice of a lemon has been added. A good tip is to keep a sliced lemon in a dish in your bathroom; squeeze a few drops over your hands after washing. Or, use special lemon-enriched soaps that many pharmacies sell.

Skin beauty minerals

The prime skin mineral is sulphur which helps maintain normal perspiration balance. Sulphur unites with proteins to feed the miles of blood vessels in your skin. Remember to eat cabbage, Brussels sprouts and the famous sulphur-and-molasses spring tonic.

Manganese is another vital mineral which works with iodine, copper and cobalt in building a healthy, firm and resilient skin and helps build resistance to infection. Green leaves and beets are rich in this mineral. Unmilled grains are powerhouses of maganese. Use them for baking. Ask at a health store for any unmilled grains in flour form or cereals. Delicious with a scoop of yogurt.

Why Does Your Skin Age?

A deficiency of sulphur, manganese, calcium, copper and other minerals tends to dry the skin. Elasticity disappears. A mineral-rich skin is a moist skin and research has revealed that a moist skin has better pliability. Water retained in your skin, *held there by minerals,* keeps you looking young. It is the mineral-starved skin that becomes dried of its moisture and turns hard, brittle.

Minerals work to help your skin absorb some body moisture so as to be pliable and youthful. Minerals help to prevent surface loss of moisture if you live in a hot, dry climate.

Home face-lifting exercises

If you want to prevent wrinkling, "crow's feet," here are some tips. Put some wheat germ oil around your eyes and the rest of your face and throat. Look at yourself in the mirror. Lift your chin. Open your mouth just one inch. Smile upward as powerfully as you can. Your facial and neck muscles become rigid. Relax. Repeat. Continue tensing your facial muscles into an upward smile with as much force as you can until you feel your face turning warm. It will take time. But continue with this smiling exercise. The exercise tends to pull up your facial muscles, counteracting the sagging or drooping pull of gravity.

The more you do these exercises, the more results you will obtain. *Minerals in the facial muscles become liberated and stirred up into nourishing the entire skin surface. Minerals must be given movement, and exercise gives them that driving power.*

This home face-lifting exercise will firm flabby muscles and tissues, strengthen your uplift muscles, upholster and cushion your face and cheeks, work to improve muscle tone, and give a rounded fullness to your face. *Just five minutes daily helps ease weariness and paleness from your skin.*

How to combat that unsightly "cow's brisket"

Age appears first in the neck. A double chin or horrible "cow's brisket" dangling under a chin is a forerunner of complete facial collapse. To combat it, when you do the above-described exercise, *tense your neck muscles at the same time.*

When you finish, do this exercise: push forward that lower jaw; open and close your mouth against resistance, working your jaws speedily. Drop your head back as far as possible. Repeat the pushing and open-close-of-mouth exercises. Now, turn your head toward your right shoulder and then toward your left shoulder.

Continue on for just seven minutes daily.

How to get rid of those wrinkles

"The true secret of restoring to the skin the smoothness of youth is friction," says Sanford Bennett in *Old Age, Its Cause and Prevention.* "The skin can be polished and the wrinkles rubbed out like any other piece of leather, and the palms of the hands and the tips of the fingers are the very best tools to use for that purpose. Use a lubricant of some kind to prevent chafing. To keep the skin in place while you rub, stretch the skin between the first and second fingers of one hand and rub with the fingers or palm of the other. Don't be too energetic at first."

Mr. Bennett advises an egg-white mask for erasing wrinkles. Use a rotary beater to whip an egg white to a light froth. Apply to your face with a shaving brush coating heavily the wrinkled areas. Let remain until dry, about five minutes. Rinse off with warm water. Do this regularly. Minerals in egg white become absorbed into the wrinkled skin and help nourish until smooth.

Here's another anti-wrinkle tip for youthful skin. Put mineral-ich cold-pressed vegetable or seed oil on the "crow's feet" or vrinkled portions of your face. Remember to cover the scowl-frown vrinkles between you eyebrows, the tiny wrinkles near the eyelids and the dark circles under your eyes. While you oil your face, tense and contract the muscles.

It should look like a combined wink and smile. Do this for one side of your face at a time. Do this 20 to 30 time for each eye, per minute. As you gain dexterity, you should be able to do this exercise a few hundred times daily. It is said to help erase disfiguring vrinkles and keep you looking young.

Mineral Suggestions For Skin Beauty

Sunflower seeds are wonderful for a combination of vitamins, minerals, unsaturated fatty acids, amino acids that combine to nourish your skin. Shell them yourself and eat raw sunflower seeds just like peanuts or popcorn or any between-meal snack. They're delicious and healthy, so keep them handy when watching TV.

Drink a glass of apricot juice daily. Use whole grain products. Raw onions are rich in iron. Take kelp and seaweed for iodine.

Personality-Caused Wrinkles

A Parisian portrait painter came to New York in the hopes of finding some youthful faces he could put on canvas. He walked the streets, looked at hundreds of models, but did not start painting. 'Everyone here looks gloomy, unhappy. Their faces are so strained, so wrinkled. How can I paint them?"

He made a discovery that is already well known. Most folks look strained, tense, disagreeable. Maybe the pressures of modern times and competition have made us constantly on the defensive. We have to take care lest someone else gets our parking space; don't talk freely to strangers or they will do you ill. Be careful of what you say or gossips will ruin your reputation. Watch that new man in the company because he's after your job.

These attitudes affect (rather, they infect) personality health, giving a wrinkled appearance on the face. Small wonder that the

Parisian portrait painter was disappointed. Unfortunately, he did not see his own face. He, too, looked strained!

Relax your face muscles. Tell your personality to be pleasant, happy. After all, a happy face is a healthy face and a healthy face is a young face! Minerals can help greatly in this regard!

Home Remedies For Skin Health

At any pharmacist, buy glycerine and rose water. To one cup, add five tablespoons of freshly squeezed beefsteak tomato juice. The natural mild acidity in tomato juice and its valuable sulphur, copper, iron, etc., work to keep a healthy skin. Use this combination as a night cream.

Try Swiss Milk Soap sold at better types of pharmacies. This soap has a PH-7 factor which gives it the same ratio of acidity to alkalinity as the human skin. A rare combination that is needed by skin minerals.

Rub freshly squeezed cucumber juice over your skin and let dry. Or, rub a cucumber (cut midway) over your skin and let the manganese rich ingredients become absorbed by your skin pores. It is said that Sarah Bernhardt, the Divine Actress, used this for her own beauty. Legend has it that Cleopatra kept her fabled youthful beauty by rubbing cucumbers over herself.

Ask a pharmacist for a liquefied elder flower. Mix a small quantity with cucumber juice and use it to revive your freshness of your skin and ease wrinkles. You might also ask a Homoeopathic Pharmacist (listed in the yellow pages of your telephone book) for the same elder flower liquid.

Keep your skin in the prime of youth by using a complexion brush. Most beauty supply outlets have a rubber brush made of tiny soft rubber bristles by the score. It helps massage your face and neck, speeds up circulation, and puts color in your cheeks.

Hazelnuts are rich in minerals and unsaturated fatty acids. Mash hazelnuts into a fine paste and use as a handcream (or facial cream) to restore smoothness.

Want to be immune to disfiguring mosquito bites? To begin, you must have a good mineral reserve. Then B-complex vitamins can combine with minerals to make you resist most insect bites. The vitamin apparently confers immunity by rendering the subject

npalatable to the insect! You can get B-1 complex tablets at any
pharmacy or health store.

HOW TO GET AND KEEP THAT YOUNG LOOK AS EXPLAINED IN CHAPTER FOURTEEN

1. A mineral-starved skin can give you wrinkles, a baggy look, and make you much older than you really are.
2. A nervous personality can cause skin infections, acne, eczema, even warts. Minerals help strengthen personality traits and build resistance to skin infections.
3. Eat blackstrap molasses, leafy greens, apricots, dried sea greens, for good mineral supply. Make these staple foods part of your daily food fare.
4. Use ordinary olive oil as an emollient for the skin. Just lubricate your entire skin and let remain for two hours.
5. Try olive oil and millet as a face mask to ease wrinkles or aging skin.
6. A slightly acid rinse of water and lemon juice helps counteract effects of alkalinity in soap.
7. A youthful skin must have internal moisture; minerals work to keep moisture within the skin.
8. Try the home face-lifting exercises for wrinkles, "crow's feet," "cow's brisket," etc.
9. Eat some sunflower seeds daily.
10. Try the healthy mineral-rich home remedies for skin beauty as described in this chapter.

He who has good health is young.

H. G. Bohn

FIFTEEN

How Minerals Help You
to Grow Hair

It has often been lamented, "I'd give a buried treasure to anyone who would show me how to grow back my lost hair."

This promise is uttered not only by men but by more and more balding women. The unhappy truth is that we have close to 15 million hairless women, and their ranks are growing. Hair loss and premature greying can be destructive of a personality. The person who shows bald spots feels old, past the prime of life, sometimes depressed. Hair loss can also mean job loss.

One young salesman found himself out of one job after another. He had a youthful physique and healthy appearance. He was well-suited for his job as salesman of modernistic Ivy League types of clothes to the young set. He created a good identification. But then, he started losing his hair until he had just a fringe around the back of his head.

"I must have aged 25 years, looking 50, although I'm only 24." He looked glum as he slunk down in his seat. "Some of those kids called me the nastiest names when they saw my shiny pate." What made it worse was that some of them were actually older than this salesman, but Nature favored them with thick hair and they appeared younger!

Many of you yearn for a nice head of hair because you know it will make you look young, virile, attractive. You would give anything to get that coveted hair. So would just about any other person in the world who has thinning hair. Maybe this treasure hunt will give you the greatest gift of all, second only to health — hair! Let's continue on our journey and discover a little-known truth: *minerals can help grow hair!*

What Is Hair?

The scalp is a complex organ; it contains between 150,000 and 200,000 hair follicles with an equal number of pigment (coloring agents) and sebaceous (oil screting agents) glands and many thousand sweat glands. You have at least a half million organs and glands in your scalp that serve the purpose of growing hair. So you can understand the value of having a well-nourished scalp — proper mineralization of the half million hair organs and glands. Starve these glands and hair loss results.

Each hair is an independent organ just as each eye. The health of each hair varies; some weak, some strong. When starved for minerals, the weak hair falls "ill" and then falls out. This accounts for thinning hair before baldness.

There are six parts of the complete hair organ:

(1) *The pigment gland* receives such minerals as copper, iron, iodine, calcium, silicon, which it uses to color the hair to which it is attached. Pull one hair from your head and note the tiny white tip at the end of the hair which has broken off below the pigment gland and not yet colored. This pigment gland must have minerals, else it dies and hair grows white.

(2) *The sebaceous glands* lubricate your scalp and hair with a substance called sebum. This is an oil-rich substance, yellowish, with the ability to absorb and retain large amounts of water. The sebum fills skin tissue, keeping it plump and firm. A sebum deficiency means a dry scalp that becomes drawn, wrinkled, scaly. Without sebum, hair becomes brittle and may break or split. The sebaceous glands also require the precious unsaturated fatty acids in foods that combine with many minerals to issue this necessary sebum.

(3) *The papilla* is a tiny bulb-shaped organ; it is the hair bud. The shape of the bulb determines the characteristic of your hair. A

round bulb grows straight hair; an oval-shaped bulb grows wavy hair; a flat bulb grows kinky hair. The papilla hair buds are present at birth. Lose a papilla and that hair is gone forever like a tooth. You have from 150,000 to 200,000 hairs in your scalp — each papilla grows a couple of hairs. Each papilla is self-reliant and requires its independent nourishment of the valuable minerals that you get from natural foods. Iodine and iron help your glands nourish the papilla hair buds.

(4) *The papilla nerve* regulates the hair organ. This is a pain nerve; when you pull a hair, you feel a pain sensation. This nerve is like other body nerves and needs nourishment for strength. Read Chapter Eleven to see how minerals can build strong nerves. Apply the same rules to hair nerves.

(5) *The hair canal* through which the hair grows gives the hair its direction or grain. Nature put hair on your scalp to protect it. These hair canals point out from the crown all around the head, similar to shingles on a dome roof. This gives heavy padding to protect you from heavy blows. It also insulates you from the sun rays, cold, rain, and other elements. The hair canal must have minerals in order to keep flexible and to create a healthy environment through which hair grows.

(6) *The arrector pili* acts as a draw string around the mouth of the hair canal. During tension, this arrector pili muscle becomes so tight, it can make hair stand on end. It reacts to cold, heat, fright, etc. Again we see how tension must be eased with minerals. If the arrector pili muscle is constantly tense, it chokes the hair canal, starves the entire hair organ and loss is inevitable. You can "relax" your scalp with proper minerals. Calcium and phosphorus balance is a must. Remember the valuable bone meal tablets and flour for a treasure of these minerals, and Vitamins A and D that put them to work.

The Effect of Diet on Hair Health

A cosmetologist, Katherine Pugh, author of *Baldness: Is It Necessary,* reports:

> When children and young adults, and their parents (both of them) before them, learn to select their food more intelligently

and become responsible for their own health by making every mouthful of food count, and ask themselves — does this food contain enough protein, minerals, such as silicon, sulphur, iron, etc., and all the other elements necessary for my hair and health or, am I eating just empty calories that will not sustain growth or repair, or build glands, but instead just put weight on me?

According to a study by Dr. Pauline B. Mack of Texas Woman's University an inadequate mineral intake is responsible for hair loss and other signs of so-called aging, as young as the 40's. Dr. Mack found that these problems were reversed when such persons were given supplements of mineral rich wheat germ and brewer's yeast. In addition, the problems of failing eyesight, brittle bones, anemia, senile blindness and poor memory were also relieved with these mineral foods.

Scalp tissue must have proper mineral nourishment to do its job of growing and maintaining a healthy head of hair. Denied natural nourishment means the scalp tissues break down and hair loss is the end result.

Of course, other reasons for hair loss include illness, glandular malfunction, scalp infection, tension, poor blood circulation. Had these conditions been treated and relieved with use of minerals, hair might still be growing for some unfortunate people. As for heredity, this is also related to diet. Dr. Melvin E. Page, in *Body Chemistry in Health and Disease*, states, that birth defects are traced to improper dietary habits of the mother; hair weakness or poor scalp health is another birth defect that a mother passes on to a child.

If one is born with a thick shock of hair and keeps it until adulthood and then somewhere along the way loses it, it is his own doing, his own neglect of proper diet, including minerals.

Circulation, Tension, Exercise

Minerals carried by the bloodstream via the circulatory system will nourish the hair roots. Circulation alone does not do the job; the bloodstream must have iron, iodine, sulphur, silicon, etc., together with other nutrients, such as vitamins, proteins, enzymes, needed to work together in hair nourishment.

Poor circulation is often traced to tension. A person who is high strung, nervous, experiences a tightening of the blood vessels leading to the scalp. Prolonged tension means that minerals cannot squeeze through the tight vessels and hair roots become starved.

Sometimes, fear, strain, will swell the nerves, putting pressure on the blood vessels leading to the head, and all over the body, causing poor circulation. If this is prolonged, the tiny vessels, especially those in the temples, may dry up completely. When this happens, no nourishment can reach the hair roots in that region and the mineral starved hair roots will wither and die.

Arthritis or tightness in your neck and spine will also tighten blood vessels to the head. The same applies to tight collars, hats, scarves or neckties, etc.

Exercise is also needed to keep the miles and miles of arteries in supple condition. In movement, there is life — for your hair, too. Exercise helps the body manufacture needed hormones which are needed for hair growth. Here, again, we see how a nervous, tense person who hardly gets enough exercise, can cause hair loss by his unhealthy personality!

The well-known nutritionist, Dr. Alfred W. McCann, pleads for the retention of precious minerals in bran and wheat germ grain and flour in the diet. The woman who values the thin and lusterless hair that remains to her, and the bald-headed man who wishes he had some hair to value, even thin and lusterless, will look dejected upon the discarded silicon, and the anemic creature who seeks in vain for solace in beef iron and wine will pray for the miller who throws all this elemental food to the hogs. *The hair not only of human beings, but of all animals, requires silicon.*

Where can this hair-growing silicon mineral be obtained? Remember steel-cut oatmeal and unbleached whole wheat products. Ask at your grocery or at most health stores.

A young man suffered from a boyhood bone infection. He prematurely aged so at only 19, his hair began to gray, his skin wrinkled, his voice was feeble. He displayed all symptoms of very advanced age.

His doctor decided to try nutritional therapy. He gave the boy enormous amounts of every known mineral, together with large supplies of mineral-rich brewer's yeast and whole wheat germ. He lso prescribed fresh liver juice. In two months, the boy underwent a omplete rejuvenation including his hair.

The magic power of minerals not only helped restore natural hair olor but prevented further hair loss and then regrew lost hair. Three magic mineral foods did the trick — brewer's yeast, whole wheat germ and liver juice. Of course, we have desiccated liver ablets that are more palatable than raw liver juice. Health stores ell these hair promoting foods.

Carrot Juice Grows Hair

The famed H. E. Kirschner, M.D., may go down in history as the hair-growing doctor. He grew hair for bald people by means of minerals and special freshly squeezed vegetable juices. No drugs. No injections. No medicines. Just *Nature!* He treated ailing persons with huge supplies of freshly squeezed raw fruit vegetable uices. Some included liquified peaches, lettuce juice (Romaine), celery, pears, dates and honey. His patients not only were remarkably rejuvenated, but enjoyed freedom from fatigue, colds, convulsions, tensions, etc.

Carrot juice was Dr. Kirschner's major treatment. Fresh carrot juice contains all known minerals for the body. One pint has more constructive value than 25 pounds of calcium tablets. Raw carrot juice is rich in potassium, creates an alkaline balance, and works on the entire endocrine glandular system to issue valuable hormones needed by your scalp. Carrot juice also builds a nourishing bloodstream and strengthens the nervous system. Its treasure of potassium, iron, phosphorus, and natural chlorine make it a real miracle food, one that we have known about all our lives, but never really used much.

If you have a juicer, then extract home made juices from fresh carrots. Drink at least six or ten glasses daily. Mix with raw celery and cucumber juice for added power. Carrot juice has a prime supply of sulphur and silicon and when mixed with cucumber juice seems to have a better effect.

Actress Regains Youth

In another case, a young actress who had formerly been seen on magazine covers and in films, described herself as "dumpy" and having a "complexion like the bottom of a dried river." She had no eyelashes and her hair was "a matted mass of colorless twine."

Rather than looking like 25, she appeared more like "a tired woman of 50." She placed herself under the care of a doctor who treated her with a special diet. She drank vegetable juices daily. No white bread or starch was permitted. Carrot juice was a must. In a short time, she rallied. Her skin improved, her complexion was marvelous, and her hair was glowing. She had healthy eyebrows and lashes. This may read like a detective thriller, except there is no thrill about ill health! The thrill is in the discovery that the minerals in raw juices can solve the crime of premature aging and hair loss.

He grew back lost hair

Katie Pugh, author-nutritionist, tells the story of a man, past middle-age, who started growing his own lost hair! At about 29, he noted thinning hair; his remaining hair turned salt and pepper gray. Soon, he began to lose most of his hair. What remained turned completely white.

The frantic man spent time and money on ointments, heat lamps, massage, etc. You name it, he tried it. All failed. Then he worked with Miss Pugh in trying a mineral plan. Slowly, he gave up highly processed foods for natural foods. He gave up coffee and white sugar as well as bread. He used honey, fruit and all natural mineral foods.

He started out by eating sunflower seeds, about one-half cup for breakfast. Then he tried sunflower seed meal, (ground at time of using), along with pumpkin seed meal and other natural foods. In a few months he noticed dark hair at the temples, with the result that to date the hair is nearly half black. After about 18 months, the once shiny pate developed fuzz which could hardly be detected by the naked eye.

After 18 months more, hair at the forehead, usually regarded the hardest place to get it to grow, filled in slowly. All this took a period of four and one half years. Miss Pugh feels progress would have been more rapid if he could have obtained other mineralized foods (as I cover in this book) in greater quantity. (Ask your state agricultural society for an outlet of organic grown fruits, vegetables, whole grain products. You may wish to write to *Organic Gardening*

Magazine, Emmaus, Pennsylvania for a list of nationwide sources of supply).

Eliminate all devitalized foods from your diet plan. Daily, eat one cup of sunflower seeds. Use sunflower seed and pumpkin seed meal in flour baked foods prepared at home.

Another man, young and bald, had the shiny pate type with just fringe around the edges and dropped deep back. He started replacing commercial foods with natural, mineral-rich and *un*processed foods. Bit by bit, his hair slowly began to regrow! Soon, he had a very good growth that could be considered a miracle. It was the magic power of minerals.

This man used no tonics, wore no hats, and never had any scalp diseases. His hair had turned gray, but when it started to grow back, the color became dark. Soon, he had only flecks of gray in the original hair and the regrown hair. This all happened within weeks and by a diet rich in mineral supplements as well as completely consisting of natural foods!

Raw Seeds For Minerals Intake

Raw seeds, grains and nuts are the best sources for minerals needed by your hair. If the seed does not germinate, the plant does not grow. Therefore, these same raw grains (wheat, oats, barley, etc.), seeds (sesame, sunflower, flaxeed, pumpkin), and nuts (walnut, pecan, almond, brazil nut) contribute growth factors or germination to furnish the body with building elements, including those for hair.

When seeds are eaten *raw,* they contain the minerals, hormones, enzymes and vitamins that processed foods do not contain. They also have natural vegetable and grain fat (oils) and protein that are all needed for growing healthy hair. A recommended eating plan is as follows:

Diet For Growing Hair

1. Eat organically grown seeds, nuts and grains. Visit any health store to get a supply. Eat at least one cup daily. Don't get the idea that this, alone, will give you a heavy shock of hair. It's not that simple. You must have a *complete* mineralization.

2. Eat *fresh* fruits and *fresh* leafy and root vegetables as well as freshly made juices. This is valuable and should be part of your daily fare. Eat and drink these mineral foods as much as possible. Select organically grown fruits and vegetables.

3. Take mineral capsules or food supplements as desiccated liver capsules and powders.

How to Handle Dandruff

It is believed that excess hard or saturated fats and bleached flour and sugar cannot be absorbed fully by the body. These unnatural foods are rejected in digestion and may be responsible for extra scalp secretion. Dandruff is said to be caused by the activity of the glands that secrete sebum. Normally, the body issues a quantity of the sebum each day and half goes to the scalp. An excess of sebum is released and causes minute flecks of dead skin on the scalp. These flecks are constantly being replaced by new skin. Yet, the particles of dead skin are glued together and result in the larger, visible crusts known as dandruff.

One authority reports that 1 tablespoon of corn oil, taken morning and evening with meals, might cure dandruff within four to eight weeks.

Here is a simple suggestion for a dandruff lotion. These ingredients are available at any pharmacist. Buy and mix yourself or ask him to do it for you. 2 drams lactic acid; 2 drams castor oil; 3½ ounces alcohol. Mix together and use as a shampoo twice a week.

If you have a dry and scaling scalp, apply an ointment made of ½ dram of precipitated sulphur in 1 ounce of benzoinated lard. Rub into the scalp, then shampoo.

Mineral Feeding Your Hair

In addition to chlorine, zinc and silicon, you should include iodine capsules for hair care. When insufficient iodine is provided the thyroid gland cannot produce its hormone and this leads to brittle, lifeless hair that falls out too rapidly.

Each single hair is made of protein. Your hair must have the sulphur-supplying amino acids found in egg yolk. It is a well known trick among horse fanciers to give a show horse plenty of eggs so he can acquire the beautiful sheen so greatly admired in a prize animal. We all know of egg shampoos as a way of improving hair health. Feed your hair with egg yolk by eating this food regularly. Several eggs a week in any preferred form, except frying, will give you the valuable sulphur you need to create amino acids for your hair health.

Massage your scalp

Your scalp needs exercise, too. Put all spread-apart fingertips against your scalp. Make tiny, speedy circles. When you feel the warmth, move your fingertips to another region. Keep on until the entire scalp is treated with this massage. Move your scalp surface around. It feels wonderful and helps your hair grow, too.

Shampoo Tips

A Cornell University study found that too much shampooing creates a mineral loss, such as calcium, phosphorus, iron and nitrogen, from the hair. This means you should not shampoo too much.

If your scalp itches between shampoos, apply witch hazel to small cotton balls and clean your hair that way. After a shampoo, rinse your hair; brunettes, use vinegar; blondes use lemon juice. Why? Normal healthy skin is acid and most shampoos are alkaline. The vinegar or lemon juice as a last rinse helps restore the normal acid condition to the skin. After the vinegar or lemon juice rinse, use clear water to rinse off.

Use a mild, bland herbal shampoo. Ask any pharmacist or health store for one. You may dilute with water. Herbal shampoos leave skin refreshed and clean.

Rain water is the ideal water. Hard water from the tap has chemicals. If you can get rain water, use it. If not, after a shampoo, rinse, rinse, rinse to get all traces of shampoo out of your hair.

Keep your scalp clean. Get rid of oils, wax, dust, dirt, grime, dandruff, by using a boar bristle hair brush. Nylon bristles tear the hair shaft. After each brushing, wipe the bristles with a clean towel. The time-honored 100 strokes daily should be a "must" for those who want healthy hair.

Brushing stimulates the scalp, aids circulation by having a pulling effect, brings oil from the hair roots all the way down to the ends, promotes a lustrous look, helps brush out flakes of dandruff, dirt, dust, etc. Bending your head toward the floor while brushing will help bring blood to your head.

Hair creams

Pure, unrefined lanolin (made from the wool of sheep) seems to be the best. Use just a few fingertips to keep hair and scalp in natural lubrication. You may also use a few drops of cold-pressed, unrefined, fresh vegetable oil rubbed onto the hair. Use enough to get the vegetable minerals into action.

Remember that hair growth and regrowth is not an overnight affair. It may take months, a year, or even longer, before improvement is noted. A condition that took a lifetime to create cannot be eliminated in a matter of days or weeks.

This will take time and effort but is worthwhile. If you don't want to take the time to improve your health, then stop right now on this treasure hunt. But if you want to expend a little effort to win the rewards of youthful, mineral-rich health that will be a great treasure, then start mineralizing your body so you, too, may be able to grow healthy hair.

THE HAIR-RAISING POINTS IN CHAPTER FIFTEEN

1. You need a healthy head of hair to make you look and feel young. Hair loss is destructive to personality.
2. Just about all major components of hair depend upon a variety of minerals for nourishment and life.
3. Inadequate mineral intake is responsible for many cases of hair loss, greying, scalp infections, etc.
4. Brewer's yeast, wheat germ, natural foods help restore hair to patients who showed symptoms of so-called aging.
5. Mineral deficiencies lead to tension, improper circulation, sluggishness, and are responsible for hair loss.
6. Silicon, found in steel-cut oatmeal and unbleached whole wheat products, is valuable for hair growing.

7. Freshly squeezed carrot juice contains all the known minerals needed to grow hair. Combine with cucumber juice for added power.

8. A good diet plan to follow is to eliminate coffee, sugar, white flour products. Eat honey, fruit, natural foods. Eat one cup of sunflower seeds daily and use its meal and pumpkin seed meal in baked goods. All foods should be natural, *un*processed and organic.

9. Massage your scalp regularly, just as you exercise other body parts to keep them in shape. Do the same to your scalp to keep it alive, too. Use rain water, if you can get it. Otherwise, finish a shampoo with either a vinegar or lemon rinse.

10. Brush your scalp with a boar bristle hair brush.

11. Use unrefined lanolin as a hair cream or try a few drops of vegetable oil.

Water is the only drink for a wise man.

Thoreau

SIXTEEN

Water: Nature's
Treasure Chest of Minerals

The greatest source of minerals is in Nature and this tremendous vitality force is found in water. Here, all known (and many unknown, yet-to-be-discovered) minerals are in healthy abundance. Fresh, clear natural water is a "must" in building a healthy mind, body and personality, and creating a "mineral environment."

Minerals in water mean life! You can go without food for as long as five weeks or more, but without water you can survive for only a few days. Close to 65 per cent of your body weight is water. A 170 pound individual has about 110 pounds of water.

When you drink water, some of its minerals go to your stomach; others are absorbed directly into your bloodstream through digestive walls. More minerals are sent to your intestines where they help keep food in a liquid state while being absorbed. Later, these same minerals will be absorbed in the blood.

How Water Minerals Influence Health

Water is continually shifting about the body, so as to provide a carrier for digestive juices and other secretions, to transport nutriments and carry off waste products.

Here's how this works. Water minerals support all nutritive processes from digestion on through absorption and circulation.

through your body to assimilation and disassimilation to excretion. Water minerals regulate your body temperature. They are found in all tissue, cells, blood, lymph, glandular secretions. Also, water minerals keep body mucous membranes soft and prevent friction of their surfaces.

Water minerals and kidneys

Minerals in water help kidneys filter blood and eliminate waste substances of metabolism. You may accumulate systemic body wastes that cannot be removed without mineral action in water. These minerals also ease bladder trouble, soothe this gland, help to dilute and reduce excessively acid urine.

Water minerals and arthritis

Systemic wastes may accumulate in and around body joints, causing or aggravating arthritic symptoms which are often traces to improper kidney function. Minerals in water help rid the body of these harmful wastes, help reduce excess urine acids, and reduce arthritic symptoms.

Water minerals and ulcers

Tension, worries and stress overstimulate the mind, leading to an excess acid formation in the stomach. An accumulation of acid means you must have water minerals to dilute. Mentally upset persons are so obsessed with problems, the instinct of hunger and thirst is displaced. They have no time to drink enough water. All the while, acid glands secrete hot acids into the stomach. This acid passes over the delicate duodenum lining and is responsible for burning the lining and creating an ulcer. Minerals in water dilute the acid, weakening its harmful powers.

Water minerals and virus

Are you surprised to hear that water minerals can protect you against a virus infection? These minerals fortify your body by proper hydration against infectious bacteria accumulations. These same minerals nourish body tissues and cells to resist virus attacks.

Through tiny chinks in the cellular lining, viruses make entry and may cause a cold, flu or other infection. You need water minerals to build cellular resistance against virus attacks.

Water minerals and your personality

Thoreau, in his works, *Walden*, knew what he was saying when relating water to wisdom. Your 15 billion brain cells are 70 per cent water! When the body water level drops, mineral depletion leads to behavior and personality changes. A nervous, irritable person may be suffering from a "thirsty" brain that cries out for water minerals. These same minerals are needed by the sleep centers of your brain. A deficiency may lead to insomnia and nightly tossing and turning. Water relaxes the brain and reduces the mental stimulus to the acid-producing glands of the stomach. Water washes diluted stomach acid into the intestine, giving you a very pleasant feeling.

Try this water treatment right now: Put this book down. Go into another room, stretch your legs. Now drink a glass of freshly poured water. Return to this book. Don't you feel better? (I tried it just now...and I feel great!) One of the things you did was to get the minerals moving along in your body.

How to Drink Water Intelligently

Don't go off on a water drinking binge. Begin with eliminating foods that are highly salted, seasoned, spiced or greasy. These tend to cause abnormal thirst. Water drinking should be avoided with your meals. Food is washed down, rather than being properly chewed and insalivated. Let mouth glands secrete necessary liquids and enzymes needed for proper digestion.

You should daily drink from six to eight glasses of water *between* meals. Try two glasses when you awaken; two glasses between breakfast and your noon meal; two glasses between lunch and dinner. This makes a total of six glasses of fresh water, daily.

Fresh fruits and vegetables have water, too. Remember to drink lots of fresh juices. Since an adult body has about 45 quarts of water and loses up to four quarts daily, you can see how valuable water minerals can be. Incidentally, your body loses water minerals through the air you breath out — about a third of a quart a day. A tip for speakers and those who talk a lot is to drink plenty of water.

Effects of Water Mineral Loss

Olaf Mickelsen, Chief of the Laboratory of Nutrition and Endocrinology of the National Institutes of Health, writes:

> The longer an individual goes without water, the greater the number and severity of symptoms he shows. Weakness, lassitude, thirst and dryness of the mouth are the first signs of dehydration. Loss of weight and mental confusion set in later. The individual becomes uncooperative and sullen. The cheeks become pale, and the lips are dry and bluish. The skin loses its elasticity. The eyeballs have a sunken appearance. The volume of urine decreases and its specific gravity rises.
>
> At the end, the respiration ceases, even though the pulse and general circulation may be well maintained. The volume of blood is maintained at the expense of the water within the body cells. The central nervous system undergoes the same dehydration as the cells in the remainder of the body and is the first area to show functional changes. If the dehydration occurs in a very warm place, the person may develop heat cramps, heat exhaustion, or heat stroke before the preceding cycle has run its course.

Thus, you can see how minerals in water hold the power of life and death!

What water best to drink?

Of course, fresh spring water is the best. When water has been subjected to chlorination and fluoridation, much of the natural mineral supply is destroyed, not to mention the potential harm caused by these chemical additives. So, fresh, uncontaminated and chemical-free water is the best.

Drink bottled spring water or well water. Ask your local food outlet to stock some bottles for you. Or, look in the classified section of your local telephone book under Water and arrange to have home deliveries of bottled mineral spring water. Be sure to request natural water that has *not* been subjected to chemical action.

Most department stores (housewares division) sell water filters which can be snapped over your faucet tap. It screens out harmful chemical agents and is another way of obtaining pure water. The disadvantage here is that a filter may screen out chemicals, but if the water has been pretreated with these chemicals, the mineral supply is diminished.

The Ancient Mineral Bath

There was a time when physicians prescribed mineral baths and mud packs as treatment for many ailments. This led to the rise in health resorts known as spas. The upper classes of 18th and 19th century Europe and America would frequent the health spa, drink and bathe in mineral waters which gave a tonic effect that was considered a miracle. This was known as *balneology* (the use of mineral water) and *peloids* (mineral-rich mud packs and mud baths). *Balneotherapy* (bath treatment) is slowly gaining recognition as having a mineral power that can aid not only afflictions of muscles, nerves, bones, but also psychosomatic disorders. Mental disorders, diseases traced to delicate nerve endings, strokes, multiple sclerosis and other conditions may benefit by minerals in spa waters.

Balneology is not necessarily new. The ancient Greek physicians had recourse to the sulphur springs of Tiberius. Rome had its mineral-rich spa baths at Baiae, the ancient city, ten miles west of Naples. These people left a legacy of the importance of taking mineral baths.

The spa is also known as being a place of friendship. Old acquaintances are renewed and new friendships are begun on the verandas and promenades. The average spa provides scheduled massages, supervised rest periods, daily consumption of mineral waters and controlled diets.

Mineral waters are temperature-regulated; heat may run from 70° to 98° F. This warmth causes the opening of skin pores so bathing will enable minerals to become absorbed by the body.

As for peloids, these are usually collected from the beds of mineral springs of volcanic origin. There are also sea muds which come from shallow beds from inlets along the seashore; some mud baths are made from peat which is a vegetable mud formed by the decomposition of marsh vegetation. All of these are rich in minerals which can then be absorbed and assimilated by the skin.

Spa baths are helpful

It is true that a little vacation makes you feel better but mineral water and mud baths make you feel great! Walter S. McClellan, M.D., in the *Cyclopedia of Medicine* (Vol. 12) says that the minerals in the spa waters do benefit the body. "Basically, the principle of spa therapy is the treatment of the individual patient rather than the treatment of the specific disease. Influence of spa therapy must be considered as constitutional treatment."

Minerals help chronic ailments

Spas which have mineral waters containing carbon dioxide are good for chronic ailments. In Europe, such spas were helpful to patients who suffered from rheumatism, circulatory disorders, and heart conditions. Minerals in these waters exerted this magical power.

Researchers reported that 107 patients who suffered from coronary disease were given spa therapy and definite clinical improvement was noted in 96 of these patients. They had a decrease in severity of agina pectoris attacks.

Other researchers find that minerals in spa water and mineral water help to increase elimination through the intestinal tract, strengthen the kidneys, improve skin health, improve blood and lymph circulation. Also, minerals help break down adhesions and soften the thickenings in the muscles and peri-articular tissues.

Small wonder the patients with arthritis, gout, gastrointestinal disorders have always flocked to the waters at Karlsbad, Vichy, Montecatini and other noted spas on the Continent.

A medical journal reports that mineral waters relieve gastric disturbances, congestion of the intestinal tract, liver and gall bladder. These minerals clear the intestinal tract, correct constipation and promote well-being.

Also, patients who suffer from sinus, headaches, coughs, brochitis, seem to be relieved by "taking the vapors." They breath the vapors from the springs, rich in minerals in gaseous form, and experience relief in the respiratory tract.

Skin disorders, too, seem to clear up in response to bathing in mineral waters. Of course, a spa treatment includes a proper mineral-rich diet, exercise, and rest. Before any spa treatment is undertaken, obtain complete medical approval. Many spas, by the way, have doctors in attendance, too.

How to Find a Spa

Ask your local travel agent to give you folders about nearby spas. Some of the more well-known spas are these:

Saratoga Springs Spa Baths
Chamber of Commerce
358 Broadway
Saratoga Springs, New York

Hot Springs National Park
Chamber of Commerce,
Hot Springs, Arkansas

Eureka Springs Spa Baths
Chamber of Commerce
Eureka Springs, Arkansas

Sharon Springs Mountain Spa
Chamber of Commerce
Sharon Springs, New York

Take a Home Spa Bath

It is possible to take a spa bath right in your own tub. Ask your pharmacist for a package of mineral salts which you dissolve in a tub of comfortably hot water. Soak yourself for a half hour or more. While not as good as an actual spa, it can be effective.

And, remember to order bottled mineral waters or spring waters to drink and enjoy the power of these precious mind and body-building mineral nutrients.

HOW WATER CAN INVIGORATE THE ENTIRE SYSTEM ACCORDING TO CHAPTER SIXTEEN

1. Minerals in water are used by your bloodstream, digestive system, glandular system and all body parts.

2. Water minerals help ease problems of kidneys, bladder, arthritis, ulcer, infectious virus. Water minerals can nourish your brain and transform you from being irritable to being personality-powerful.

3. Drink at least six to eight glasses of fresh water daily.

4. Bottled spring, well or mineral water is the best since there is freedom from chemical treatment and additives. Order these from any supplier found in the yellow pages of your classified telephone directory.

5. If you can arrange it, take a vacation at a spa resort and enjoy bathing in spa waters, soaking in mud baths, drinking mineral-rich, pure spa waters. Or, use mineral salts in your bath for a second-best home spa treatment.

6. For a magic power of mineral action drink plenty of spring water.

The health of the people is really the foundation upon which all their happiness and all their powers as a state depend.

                                    Benjamin Disraeli

SEVENTEEN

How Exercise Can Put Dynamite into Your Sleeping Minerals

Ask yourself these three questions:

1. Do you feel tired out after working eight hours at your desk or machine?
2. Do you gasp for breath after walking up a flight of stairs or running a few yards to catch a bus?
3. Do you wake up in the morning feeling as tired as when you went to bed?

If you can *honestly* answer "no" to all three questions, it is possible that you are getting enough exercise. But it is more likely that you will *honestly* answer "yes" to one or more questions, or at least concede that on occasion, you do experience some of the aforementioned symptoms.

You may say that you are not as young as you were or that you need more rest. Perhaps this is true. But it is also possible that your body is signaling that it needs more exercise so that movement will put power and dynamite into the minerals that flow throughout your body and your mind.

Exercise and Mineral Power

Mention the word exercise and you think of physical fitness; most folks regard this as a matter of strength. This is true, too, but actually exercise is a reflection of your ability to work without undue fatigue, with enough energy left over to enjoy hobbies and recreational activities and sufficient strength to meet unexpected emergencies. It is the ability to get the optimum use out of your body. Physical fitness does not apply only to the muscular, athletic individual, but also to the activation of nutrients in your body, making them work.

Exercise stimulates body tone, sending minerals to your muscles, skin, organs, blood vessels and other body parts. Exercise causes minerals to help keep your body properly hydrated, to get rid of waste materials properly and to keep you operating at optimum level with little fatigue or loss of quality.

When minerals are stimulated by exercise, they work to help pass food along your digestive tract, enable you to breathe air into your lungs, to regulate blood vessel action when more pressure is needed in an emergency.

Minerals that are pepped up via exercise will speed up circulation to furnish more oxygen to the billions of your body cells, helping them remove waste material. The faster minerals bring oxygen to your cells, the better you feel. You "come alive." This increased mineral activity brings more blood to your brain, too, making you more alert which is a powerful personality gift!

The faster mineral action of the circulatory system also helps the functioning of the internal organs. Your heart becomes stronger and steadier. Your lungs are feed by minerals and are now capable of taking in more oxygen. Elimination of body wastes is properly regulated. *Without exercise, minerals may remain inert and lazy, and so will you!* In most cases, people grow tired because minerals cannot be sent moving to various body parts. This causes a gradual deterioration of the entire body and mind. So you can appreciate the value of movement by exercise.

Symptoms of Inactivity

Lack of sufficient exercise constitutes a serious deficiency comparable to vitamin deficiency warns Dr. Kraus, famed physiotherapeutic authority. "Physically inactive persons (those who do not exercise) age earlier, die younger, and are more prone to backaches, ulcers, lung cancer, appendicitis, prostatic disorders, psychiatric (mental) illness, cirrhosis of the liver and hemorrhoids. Death from coronary heart disease occurs twice as often among the physically inactive."

A noted medical writer tells us that muscles can starve through lack of exercise — witness hospital patients who eat perfectly balanced meals and get out of bed too weak to walk. The reason is that muscles are nourished by thousands of miles of hairlike capillaries, which transport food and carry off wastes.

In the sedentary adult, large numbers of these capillaries are collapsed, not functioning briskly nearly all the time. Exercise alone can open them up and provide better muscle nutrition.

Movement will spark the action of minerals to feed the billions of your capillaries as well as your one and only heart.

What Kind of Exercise to Take

"What kind of exercise is more important than how much," says Dr. Arthur Steinhaus, Dean and professor of Physiology at George Williams College. In a laboratory where I worked, it was discovered that a muscle can grow at only a certain rate — and a very small amount of the right exercise will start it growing at that rate. If you contract any one of your muscles to about two-thirds of its maximum power and hold that for six seconds once a day, that muscle will grow just as fast as it can grow.

For instance, just clench your fists and hold them for six seconds daily (or more often), and you will experience new strength in your arms. Do this for other body parts that need to be awakened.

Suppose you say you do not care to build muscles but want to exercise for your minerals. Here is an exercise that can be done while towelling yourself after a bath.

Loop the towel behind your neck. Then pull your chin in, pull forward on both ends of the towel and resist the towel with your neck as hard as you can for just six seconds. Do it only once. Now slide the towel down to the small of your back. While pulling forward on the towel, resist by contracting the muscles in your buttocks and your belly. Push back hard against the towel and count six. Now that's done. Loop the towel under your toes and pull up with both hands while your toes push down. Hold it for six seconds, then let go. Once for each foot and you're done for the day.

This free-hand type of exercise does not require any weights, can be followed by a housewife, a secretary, a businessman and just about any other person who wants to get more and more from the mineral treasure in his body.

Simple Walking Exercises.

The famed Mr. Roebuck of Sears and Roebuck, was interviewed on the occasion of his 90th birthday. Mr. Roebuck celebrated by taking a walk in Central Park. It was reported that he walked every day, selecting slightly uphill pathways. Did it help?

Mr. Roebuck replied to a reporter, "Son, I sold out to Mr. Sears who made ten million dollars and now he's dead. Mr. Sears sold out to Julius Rosenwald who made 300 million dollars and now he's dead. When writing about me, tell your readers that on his 90th birthday, Mr. Roebuck took his usual walk in Central Park."

Numerous accounts attribute longevity to walking. This movement *stimulates action of minerals in the entire circulatory system.* As an example, we refer to William Wordsworth the famed English poet laureate who walked 180,000 miles during his lifetime. He lived to be 80 during a time when people died young. Wordsworth frequently attributed his mental powers to his walking; no doubt, this movement caused minerals and oxygen to "soak" the brain, particularly nourish it, impart superior powers of thought.

Walking is best accomplished on a slightly uphill grade. Walking on level ground places less of a breathing demand and less stimulation to the minerals. Select pathways or roads that are slightly inclined upward. Mountain climbing is a good exercise but you have to know what you are doing. You can climb little hills and pathways in parks and recreation areas and derive good mineral activation.

Try running

"Hold it a minute," said a tired production man in a small suburban Pennsylvania plant. "Are you telling me, at my age, which is 49, to start running so my minerals will get stimulated? Suppose I collapse? I'm not used to running, let alone any exercises."

I replied, "Before you do any exercise, ask your doctor's approval. Just as you do not plunge into an ocean until you know how to swim and dive, neither do you do running exercises until you've built yourself up to them."

A weekly magazine related the story of 65-year-old Mr. Meadows, who celebrated his birthday by running ten miles on an indoor track. What's so unusual about that? Well, Mr. Meadows had been a heart attack victim some years before.

This man, like others, was under the direction of a physical director of the Cleveland YMCA's Businessmen's Club. Others were given gradually accelerated paces that started from fast walking to little sprints. One member started by *walking* the width of the pool just once. *Gradually,* the lengths and speeds are increased.

The story ended with this warning, "The lesson is clear. You must walk (or swim) before you can run. But first consult your family doctor. If he approves, walk one block vigorously each day for a week. Add an extra block each week. When you can walk a mile without tiring — and your doctor consents — you can begin jogging. Try 100 paces the first week, and build up gradually."

How to Exercise in Your Bathtub

You can exercise with ease, safety and comfort right in your bathtub. These exercises were developed by a 76-year-old Englishman, T. R. Togna, who found that blood pressure, plus rate of oxygen intake, varied during an exercise session in a bathtub full of water.

Apparently, minerals helped reduce excess pressure and also improve metabolism. The secret here is that the body weighs less under water. If you are 150 pounds, you may weigh only ten pounds when submerged in water. Therefore, exercise in a bathtub can be done with ease. Minerals can thus work better. The best way to do it is as follows:

Fill the tub with water that reaches just six inches from the top after you are in the tub. Lie down, rest your head on the tub. Stretch out your legs full length. Double your right hand into a fist in front of your chest while you bend your right knee and bring it up out of the water. Now lower your right leg and stretch your right arm out on top of the water while you bring up your left leg. This is much like bicycling in that your arms move in unison with your legs, except there is less fatigue because your water immersed body has little weight.

The next exercise is to bend your knees, massage them and your thighs just prior to lowering them in the water again.

Still another exercise is to lie down, with your hands below you, bracing your buttocks. Raise your trunk so you are suspended in the water. Do this exercise again with hands resting on your stomach. Massage your stomach while you raise and lower your trunk in the water.

Waist twisting, another exercise, is done in the same position as above, except that you pivot on your toes and swing your body from side to side while your head and feet remain stationary. When you become more adept at twisting from side to side, vary this exercise by bending one knee at a time and crossing it over the other knee. If you dissolve mineral salts into the bath, you will get added benefits from the exercises.

Tips to Observe

Your minerals run into a stagnant pool when body muscles remain in one position too long. If you bend over your work all day, whether it be reading, writing, typing, cooking, machinery, and so forth, stop frequently. Turn your head from side to side, gently and slowly. Or, stand up, bend over from the waist. Let your complete upper body hang limply like a rag doll. Your arms should dangle downward in the same rag doll fashion. Count to ten; straighten up. Feel that relaxation flowing through tired muscles? Minerals have started streaming through your circulatory system once more, free from that stagnant pool.

No Time for Exercises?

"We're very busy people," explained the housewife-mother who was married to a lawyer. "It's not only cooking, cleaning and keeping house, but acting as hostess to my husband's business associates. Then there are the children to take care of, too."

Her sister looked around at the very modern house. It was once written up in an interior decorating magazine as being virtually automatic in every sense of the way, complete with electric eyes to open and shut doors, timing devices that started and stopped cooking appliances, and various other electrical mechanisms that really made life very simple. "But you hardly have to do much. Everything is so mechanical."

"It has to be that way because I just don't have time for all details. But I still have to supervise and manage." She later hired a cook and cleaning woman.

Her husband spent most of his time reading up on cases, preparing legal briefs, arranging for court appearances. He pointed out, "Because of so much tension, I have to take advantage of every convenience. Maybe I don't get much exercise, but I just can't take time for doing that barbell stuff."

Everything ran smoothly until one day the wife collapsed while ordering groceries over the telephone for home delivery. A week later, while she was still undergoing tests in a hospital to determine the reason for her collapse, her husband suffered a heart attack in his office.

Luxury and convenience had made them both mineral-starved and predisposed them to ailments that might be permanent. It is true that life should be easy, but not so easy that you grow inert, lazy and like the aforementioned stagnant pool — a living death!

Simple 60-second exercises

Here are nine different types of 60-second exercises that can be followed at your deskside, while waiting for a bus or commuter train, while sitting before television. Just 60 seconds will help flush out impurities and stimulate internal mineral action.

1. Stretch while sitting at your desk, lying down on a couch, while standing at a filing cabinet or waiting for a bus. (Can you walk the distance, instead of ride? Do so!)

2. Straighten your spine. Lean against a wall in a supermarket or an office. Press hard and flat against that wall.

3. Roll your neck up, down, and around. You can do this while sitting or standing, whether washing dishes, in a theatre, at a club meeting or during a "break" at your office or factory job.

4. Suck in your stomach as far as possible while sitting at a desk, bending over a draftsman table, machine shop tool, digging in the bottom drawer of a filing cabinet. Hold for 60 seconds and then breathe out. Do this regularly.

5. Expand your chest. You can do this in conjunction with Exercise. 4. Try to really throw out your chest. Do this 60-second exercise at most any place where you stand, such as your office, home or on the street.

6. Flex your arms by pushing, pulling and reaching. No need to actually push, pull or reach for anything, but go through these motions.

7. Bend your legs. Squat, climb or walk. Bend at your knees. Feel those cracking sounds? Minerals have broken through the "walls of confinement" and now speed to all body parts to keep you fit and healthy.

8. Limber your toes and feet. At any time, wiggle your toes. Shake your feet at the ankle joints, in all directions. You can do this while sitting. If standing, just take one foot at a time.

9. Firm your muscles. Bounce, pinch, knead or pummel. Do this to yourself on all body parts. You'd be better able to do it in the privacy of your home as it would look peculiar to wait in line before a box office and pummel your arm with everyone looking up. This is a simple exercise that sends minerals rushing into your muscles, making them firm.

These nine exercises can be done just about anywhere at almost any time. Each exercise is performed for only 60 seconds. You can do them longer, if you prefer. You can practice all nine of them throughout the day at varying intervals. You will discover the magic power of minerals when execises act like dynamite in super-charging your entire mind and body with the action of minerals.

Seven Ways Exercises Help Mineral Power

Here are seven distinct ways in which exercises work to put genuine TNT power throughout your whole body:

1. Exercises send minerals into your circulatory system, thereby the heart helps to keep the bloodstream actively moving (muscular contraction squeezes the veins, which with their valves direct the mineral-rich blood back toward the heart).

2. Minerals, released from locked pockets, are sent to the lungs, which through good tone of the diaphragm, make it easier to bring oxygen into the body and pump carbon dioxide. Minerals are needed for this process and they have to be kept moving by exercises.

3. Exercises send vital minerals to your brain and also waves of oxygen and valuable blood.

4. Minerals are sent throughout the nervous system by exercises, helping to improve sleep and maintaining equanimity and mental stamina. Exercise so oxygenates your system, so drenches your billions of tissues with minerals, you can actually sleep better.

5. Exercise via mineral action may protect against peptic ulcers. Modern tensions cause stored-up emotions. Exercise is an outlet to help you "blow off steam" and reduce inner emotional tensions. Minerals, such as calcium and phosphorus, are excellent for building resistance to ulcers. Send these minerals into your digestive system via exercise.

6. Exercise helps minerals perform metabolism or burning of foods thereby controling your weight.

7. Exercise can help you live longer. The minerals released and sent into action in your body will help reduce the vulnerability to high blood pressure, coronary thrombosis and diabetes, to name just a few of our more tragic diseases.

Remember that fatigue is *not* the aim of exercise. Stop when you feel tired, rest and begin again, or wait for the next day. Watch your ability to recuperate from an exercise session. If your heart pounds for more than ten minutes and the feeling of weakness persists, you should slow down. Begin with the simplest exercise and continue to the more vigorous ones. Also, all exercises must be followed after your doctor has given his approval.

With vigorous exercise the blood supply visits man's tissues eight or nine times more frequently than a man at rest. The blood, instead of traveling at a rate of 55 feet a minute in the large arteries may move 450 feet a minute. This makes possible a more rapid and complete removal of waste from all parts of the body, and increases the amount of oxygen in parts of the body depending on it. Exercise taken simply and regularly tends to keep the arteries soft, warding off arteriosclerosis or other old age conditions.

Small wonder that the historian, George Macaulay Trevelyan who lived to be 90, once said, "I have two doctors — my left leg and my right leg." He must have been a good walker!

STEPS TO MOVE THOSE SLEEPING MINERALS BY EASY EXERCISES AS DESCRIBED IN CHAPTER SEVENTEEN

1. If you feel tired, breathless and achey, you need to take advantage of exercise. You may have plenty of treasured minerals in your system, but must put them to work by bodily movements.

2. A properly exercised body will cause minerals to be liberated from stagnant pools in your body, to be sent to your muscles, skin, organs, bloodstream, brain, etc. Exercise acts as the motor power for minerals.

3. Deprived of minerals because of inactivity means you may age earlier, suffer from backaches, repiratory disorders, prostatic disorders, mental upset and heart ailment.

4. Exercise does not mean lifting heavy barbells and weights. It can put TNT into minerals if you just clench your fists for six seconds daily. You can use the special fun-to-follow "towel exercise" described. For just five minutes, this exercise can really turn the tide and send a wave of minerals throughout your body and mind.

5. Walking is a simple exercise. People with a long life span are known for being devoted walkers. Try slightly uphill pathways to gain benefits of increased oxygenation and better mineral stimulation. Join a walking club in your vicinity. If there is none, try to form one. A few friends are needed.

6. Running is helpful. But first, try fast walking until you are adjusted to it. Then speed it up. Join a supervised health club for this exercise.

7. Try the simple bathtub exercises. Your body, submerged under water, weighs a fraction of its ordinary poundage, making it easier to exercise.

8. Turn your head frequently during the day, while watching TV, reading a book. Even do it now! Put down this book; turn your head in a circle for the count of ten.

9. Try any or all of the nine 60 second exercises throughout the day, whether in your home, at your office or plant, while waiting in an office or store or even while standing on line. Who says you have no time to exercise?

10. There are seven distinct benefits from exercising. Minerals need the TNT dynamite power given by bodily movement. It's up to you. Exercise can prevent premature old age. That's incentive enough for anyone to take advantage of the power exercise has upon minerals in your body and mind.

The best doctors in the world are Dr. Diet, Dr. Quiet, Dr. Merryman.

Jonathan Swift

EIGHTEEN

How to Banish Headache with Minerals

Your head is the "home of your brain." At times, there's nothing more you'd want to do than "leave home," especially when you have one of those splitting headaches. It is true that head disorders are rarely fatal, although they feel deadly and cause more misery than most any other part of the body. Your head is regarded a "port of entry" for infections and is the first to react when something goes awry with your body.

Headaches are not a new ailment

Legend has it that the Egyptian goddess Isis was bothered by headaches and was told by Ra, the sun god, to prepare a special recipe.

This recipe was found in a tomb in Thebes by archeologists in 1862. The remedy called for combining a few plants and herbs with poppy berries in a tonic to ease head pains. Poppy berry is opium from which is derived codeine, a modern "cure" for headaches. But like most of these remedies, it is dangerous, habit forming and masks the symptoms. You still have the headache, but don't feel it. The point is that you would much rather get rid of headaches and become immune to them. We're going to discover this choice nugget in the treasure.

What Is a Headache?

Your brain does not ache. Brain tissue does not transmit pain. You have a headache because you have a pain sensitivity in the membrane covering the brain and the membranes lining the skull. The blood vessels throb because they become dilated, distended and tend to distort sensitive structures and nerve endings. The skull is different from other body tissues; it does not yield and does not give way. Tensions and nervousness cause a reaction upon the membranes lining the skull and this leads to the symptoms of a head pain.

A migraine headache or one that is very severe and pounding is usually traced to irritation of the upper neck nerves which affect the cranial nerve fibers and cause the throbbing pain which later becomes a steady dull pain in the region of the temples. The irritation of the vaso-constrictor nerve fibers cause dilation of the blood vessels of that area and also, because of reflex action along the vagus nerves, may cause an upset stomach, a feeling of nausea and a fast heart beat.

According to Dr. Henry Ogden of Louisiana State University's Medical School, a survey was made of 5,000 persons and it was found that six out of every ten persons in the United States suffer from headaches. Also, more than 50 million aspirins daily are gulped by sufferers: an average of about 1,100 aspirins for each person, each year!

Incidentally, single persons have more headaches than married persons. The more educated you are, the more susceptible you will be to a headache. Farmers suffer least. Young persons have more than oldsters. Women are more headache-prone than men. Medical students suffer most, but patients in mental hospitals suffer the least or not at all!

Doctors say, "The headache is not a disease by itself but a symptom." This means that your body condition is in need of something. What? Let's look to minerals and see how they can build immunity, prevent and relieve headaches.

Minerals and Headaches

Among the varying symptoms and mineral-related effects of headaches are:

1. A calcium-phosphorus imbalance or a deficiency of copper or iron, may lead to swelling (dilation) of arteries in the head. This is the "blush" of the arteries inside or outside the skull. Cranial arteries are delicate and react to any shortage of these valuable minerals.

2. Insufficient magnesium, potassium or manganese may cause a feeling of "pulling" or traction on the pain-sensitive structures within the head. These structures beg for minerals by "pulling."

3. Potassium, silicon, fluorine and sulfur are needed by the billions of tissues that cover the brain. Denied these minerals, the tissues become inflamed and cause irritation to the pain-sensitive structures of your head.

4. The precious calcium-phosphorus balance must be maintained. If there is a shortage, it may lead to vaso-constriction (narrowing) of the head's blood vessels which marks the early stages of an approaching severe headache attack.

5. Iron and copper unite with vitamins and amino acids to feet the cervical nerve fibers that control the health of your head. If these fibers are denied sufficient nutrients, they react by sending signals through the head. This leads to another throbbing pain.

Note carefully: The magic power of minerals MUST possess the influential powers of vitamins, amino acids, water, oxygen, etc. All work together to create a healthy condition and a resistance to headaches.

Wonder Nutrients to Combat Headaches

Three nutrients work together to build immunity from headaches:

1. Vitamin B6, pyridoxine, prevents or alleviates the peripheral neuritis that may develop into a headache. It prevents irritability, muscular twitchings and convulsive seizures. This vitamin is found in wheat germ, whole grain foods and vegetables.

2. Vitamin E preserves oxygen in the blood which means greater efficiency as blood is pumped through the cranial blood vessels, bathing them with precious minerals to keep them flexible, healthy and less subjected to painful disturbances. This vitamin is found in raw wheat germ, whole grain foods as well as in capsule form available at most pharmacies and health stores.

3. Potassium is needed for the transmission of nerve impulses to the brain. This mineral combines with manganese to help the body utilize Vitamin B1 (thiamine) to nourish the nervous system. Potassium is found in citrus fruits and, especially, figs.

Make Your Own Mineral Tonic Against Headache

You can make this special mineral tonic right in your own home. A wise course is to drink this tonic every single day, ill or not. Fortify your body with the precious nutrients and minerals in this tonic and help build resistance to headaches. You can get the ingredients in a health store.

> 5 tablespoons raw wheat germ oil
> 2 tablespoons desiccated liver granules
> ½ cup freshly squeezed pineapple juice
> ½ cup natural fig juice

All of these items should be thoroughly blended together. Now add 4 tablespoons soya milk. Stir vigorously. Drink slowly. The minerals and vitamins in this special tonic all work together to feed your entire circulatory system and nourish your brain and the vascular network. These nutrients are natural antidotes for headaches. You can obtain the ingredients (raw wheat germ oil and desiccated liver granules) at any health store. The pineapple juice should be home squeezed from a fresh, raw pineapple. Natural fig juice is sold at almost any food outlet.

How To Make Anti-Headache Poultice

Edwin was a well respected and competent laboratory technician. He took his work seriously, constantly peering into microscopes, studying slides, researching among thousands of books. Needless to say, he was subjected to much mental tension and eyestrain. He could be a ripe victim for headaches.

"Not me," was his boast. "I should get lots of headaches just like any close-working man. That's true of engineers, mechanics, craftsmen, accountants, and even the expert shorthand secretary."

What was Edwin's secret? He had long ago come across a forgotten remedy that can ease headaches and even erase them from the very start. It was a mineral remedy to be externally used.

Edwin explained, "If I feel a headache coming on or if I have had a trying day, as soon as I go home, I make an onion or horseradish poultice. I dice onion and/or horseradish, then mash into a pulp. I apply this poultice to my neck, the calves and the soles of my feet. Inflammation is thus drawn away from the head and terminated. Onions and horseradish have plenty of minerals and these seep through the pores of my skin and cause this normalizing action."

That was Edwin's discovery. His job as a researcher and lab technician was maintained because he could be free from headaches.

Relief of headaches is often obtained from warm showers on the neck and spine; and if the headache be the result of a disturbance of the digestive organs, a warm shower on the stomach will usually disperse the trouble.

Onion, horseradish or cabbage leaf packs on the back of the neck will relieve a headache, too. Put the leaves or poultice in a small cotton bag and apply to the back of the neck. Let remain for 30 minutes to an hour.

Ways to Prevent Headaches

The following three methods can be used to prevent headaches.

1. Emotional Tension causes depletion of valuable minerals that cover the nerve endings. Self-examine your emotional state. Do you fly off the handle? Do you snap at people. Are you frustrated? Do you repress your hatred? Do you bottle up your resentment? Are you one of those people who argue all the time? These personality defects cause headaches. Strengthen your capacity to meet the rigors of daily life by taking a vitamin-mineral food supplement every single day. Subsitute dark honey for any sweetening agent. Honey is a rich source of potassium, calcium, and phosphorus. Your entire system will benefit with this mineral treasure source.

2. Correct your posture. Don't cramp yourself. Keep your neck flexible. Often, the neck arteries become choked if you hunch over a book or desk for hours at a time. Minerals become lodged in this choked region, denying your brain its due.

3. Take good care of your eyes. Constant close work may lead to headaches. If you watch TV or read for hours at a time, look up frequently. Stare at a far distant object for the count of 15, then

turn back to your task. Do it right now. Feel better? You may have prevented a headache this one time. Do it frequently.

Use of Mineral Vapors

Some time ago when I visited with a friend who was a very important insurance executive in Vermont, he told me that ever since he could remember, he found instant headache relief by taking "mineral vapors."

He went on to say, "It's one of the oldest folk remedies we know of around these rural parts. I put equal parts of apple cider vinegar and water in a small basin. I allow this to boil on top of the stove. When the fumes are comfortably strong and start to rise from the basin, I lean my head over.

"I do this for 80 breaths. Usually, you will find that the headache pains are eased by the time you reach 40. If the pains come back, keep inhaling again."

My question then was, "If the headache does recur, is it just as painful as before?"

He shook his head negatively. "It's less painful and eventually, it goes away. There are minerals such as potassium, sulfur, manganese, that saturate the tissues of the respiratory tract and circulatory system. It's a mineral-soaking method that really helps replace lost nutrients."

This same folk remedy is used in other rural areas of the country. The local people may not know much about minerals, themselves, but they do know that the magic ingredients in apple cider vinegar that are given off in vapors really relieve headaches. Let's take a tip from our country cousins and benefit with the mineral vapor treatment for headache relief:

HEADACHE-EASING TIPS IN SUMMARY FORM AS PRESENTED IN CHAPTER EIGHTEEN

1. Headaches are not new and have plagued mankind for thousands of years. Modern science has succeeded in masking the symptoms of a headache but you must still look to Nature for secrets of preventing this personality-wrecking ailment.

2. A headache is usually caused by a mineral deficiency in the blood vessels and membrane covering the brain.

3. To build resistance and possible immunity to headaches, remember to take copper, iron, calcium, phosphorus, magnesium, potassium, manganese and other precious minerals.

4. Try the mineral tonic described in this chapter as a wonderful preventative and home remedy. This tonic contains the remarkable minerals needed by the membranous blood vessels that are crying for nourishment, hence creating a headache.

5. Use an onion or horseradish poultice. Mash to a pulp, put in a small cotton sack and apply to your neck, calves and soles of your feet. This drains inflammation from your head and helps to terminate a headache. Minerals in these items do the magical trick.

6. A warm shower on the neck, spine or stomach helps relieve headaches. Cabbage leaf packs on the back of the neck is also suggested.

7. Watch your tension meter, correct your posture, don't strain your eyes.

8. A mineral vapor inhalant is a good idea. Heat equal portions of apple cider vinegar and water. When boiling, inhale for 80 breaths. Minerals thusly introduced in your respiratory and circulatory tracts will help replace a deficiency and ease headache symptoms. A thoroughly mineralized body may become immune to headaches.

Good health and good sense are the two blessings of life.

Menander

NINETEEN

How Minerals Help You Cope with Constipation

Each year, more than $100 million is spent upon purgatives and laxatives to help establish regularity. Often labeled the "American disease," constipation is a problem that is traced to improper living habits and a low mineral intake. It seems simple to gulp down some flavored concoction and, thereby, find temporary relief. But the more laxatives you consume, the more irregular you become. Laxatives have been seen to *cause* constipation, creating a vicious circle.

What Is Constipation?

This problem, also know as intestinal sluggishness or intestinal stasis is a condition in which there is prolonged retention of food residues in the bowels. These may turn putrid, ferment and create an unhygienic condition in your system. Constipation is one of the most frequent conditions which the physician is called upon to treat, yet there is probably no other common disorder which is so often badly managed.

Constipation is said to exist when an individual does not spontaneously evacuate the bowel at least once in 24 hours. Such a daily movement is generally accepted as normal and for the majority of persons a daily movement is apparently necessary for comfort and health. So, a rule of thumb is that regularity consists of movement at least once every 24 hours.

Potential Harm of Irregularity

It is estimated that there are over 36 "intestinal poisons," some of which are more toxic than others. These include skatole, indole, ammonia, methylgadinine, mytilotoxin, and sulphemoglobine. If these poisonous substances remain in your system, there is the health hazard that they may enter the bloodstream.

Early symptoms of irregularity include sallow skin color, nervous irritability, coated tongue, bad breath, body odor, headaches, bloating, feeling of heaviness (especially in the region of the stomach) and appetite loss.

Incidentally, the word "constipation" is derived from the Latin, meaning "crowded together." How true!

Six Reasons for Internal Irregularity

A famous health authority lists six basic reasons for constipation as:

1. Lack of food and the eating of highly refined food.
2. Lack of bulk.
3. Lack of *mineral-rich water* intake between meals.
4. Hasty eating without proper chewing of food.
5. Emotional upsets, such as worry, grief, fear, resentment and the strain of professional, business and social life.
6. Failure to repond to the urge for a bowel movement because of business or social appointments or because of false modesty.

Mineral Power in Water

Fresh water is one of Nature's greater sources of minerals that are needed for establishment of regularity. A famous doctor urges you to step up water intake to introduce precious minerals in your system and normalize the intestinal processes. "Since the body is composed largely of water, and since water is necessary for the normal functioning of the cells, tissues and organs, it is important that the supply be replenished regularly."

Normally, four to eight glasses are needed each day. Water is essential for digestion and putting into solution the food nutrients so that they may be absorbed and utilized by the body. Water is also necessary for softening the feces in the colon and in the elimination of body wastes through the kidneys, skin and lungs.

When you are mineral-deficient because of poor water supply, "the selectivity of the body is such that water is absorbed from the colon in order to supply these needs. This action dries the feces and results in constipation. Drink more water to meet your body's needs."

What are mineral-rich foods? Some recommended ones are fruits, whole-grain cereals, nuts and vegetables, especially the green leafy ones. *Avoid* fried foods, condiments, spices, tea and coffee, cola drinks, and processed foods. Devitalized foods lack sufficient cellulose or bulk-forming substances.

You can increase the cellulose with the roughage-rich sources found in fruits and fibrous vegetables such as celery, figs and carrots.

Natural Mineral Plan For Prompt Regularity

A well-known industrial executive has conquered the problem of constipation and risen to success. Why is this so? Because discomfort and sluggishness impaired his thinking processes. "I was nervous, fitful, on edge at business conferences. I just couldn't take laxatives and then attend an important meeting. So I tried a simple home remedy that worked."

Here is the natural mineral plan that established regularity for this executive. Immediately upon arising in the morning, eat two large fresh apples, skin and all. Chew well before swallowing. Follow this with two glasses of freshly poured cold tap water or bottled spring water. The minerals in the water will act upon the pectin and acid in the apples to create a highly stimulating action upon sluggish bowels. This is a dynamic treatment but a powerhouse of mineral action that is without comparison.

Mineral Soup For Regularity

A soup which helps to combat intestinal sluggishness can be made from freshly ground whole wheat grains with chopped onion and a crushed garlic clove. Cook these ingredients together and then add some finely chopped parsley and a spoonful of pure olive oil. Take this soup hot, in the morning, with crisp or whole meal bread.

Mineral Tea

Steep, as for tea, senna pod or senna leaf tea. Strain it and then add a sliced raw potato, including the skin, a teaspoon of bran, a teaspoon of linseeds and simmer for about a quarter of an hour. Then you can strain it and just drink the liquid. Later you will be able to take it unstrained. This type of tea or soup will help cope with the most stubborn cases of constipation.

Vitamins Work With Minerals

You need other nutrients to combine with minerals. Experiments with animals reported by Dr. Clive McKay of Cornell University showed that powdered brewer's yeast (rich in B-complex vitamins) and the pulp left from making tomato and citrus juices (vitamins C and P and minerals) may help many persons suffering from constipation. The tip here is to use tomato pulp or any citrus pulp for valuable vitamin-mineral intake. Just chew carefully and swallow the pulp. Remember to take several tablespoons of brewer's yeast, too.

Roughage Foods

Minerals work best when they have roughage or cellulose to act upon. Here are some foods which, by the way, are also mineral-rich and give you a double-barrel action: figs, dates, dried peas, nuts, navy beans and raw tomatoes. Bulky juice-rich foods are essential, including cantaloupes, tomatoes; also foods with edible skins, such as raisins, dried peas and beans. Tough foods, such as seeds and nuts, are also valuable.

How do minerals work on them? Minerals transform the bulk and juice foods into a high cellulose mass. Minerals in the unpeeled vegetable and rough nuts, raisins and dates create a rather prodding action by stimulating the intestinal wall in doing its muscular duty.

These minerals work to strengthen the weakened intestinal musculature as well as the sphincter muscles.

A simple dietary pattern to be followed daily is as follows:

Daily, have a serving of four vegetables, one of which may be potato. Daily have one whole grain cereal and at least one slice of whole wheat bread. Include prunes, bananas, and fresh apples as well as the usual servings of vegetables. Daily dishes of whole grain steel-cut oat cereals are excellent roughage. Select organically grown vegetables and cereals and whole grain bread products.

Which foods are to be avoided if you wish to establish and *maintain* intestinal regularity? Most doctors caution against all foods which are rich in animal fat (including gravies) and fried foods. Also to be avoided are foods highly spiced or seasoned with mustard, pepper, ketchup, horseradish. *Avoid all ice cold beverages because they tend to tighten the intestinal canal.* Drink liquids at room temperature or from the tap.

You need not suffer from this disease of civilization. Return to the nutritive laws of Nature with the glorious treasures of minerals and be rewarded with bountiful health and joyous internal regularity.

STIMULATING POINTS IN CHAPTER NINETEEN

1. Prolonged constipation may lead to internal toxication. Early symptoms include poor skin color, nervousness, coated tongue, bad breath and other offensive conditions. To delay is to worsen the condition.

2. Minerals in ordinary water or bottled spring water can create a miracle action to help you achieve internal regularity. Drink six glasses of fresh water daily. The water must be at room temperature — *not* ice cold which tightens the intestinal canal and leads to constipation.

3. For instant relief, when you awaken, eat two large fresh apples, skin and all. Chew well before swallowing. Now drink

two glasses of freshly poured cold tap water or bottle spring water. This double-barrel mineral action has no competition when it comes to effectiveness.

4. Mineral-rich soup is a fountain of goodness for constipation.

5. The simple senna pod or senna leaf tea recipe is a natural remedy for constipation.

6. Other vitamins are needed to work with minerals to ensure regularity. Remember Vitamins A, B-complex, C, etc.

7. Remember the roughage foods described in the chapter. Include these in your daily diet.

Every day, in every way, I am getting better and better.

Emil Coué

How Three Magic Mineral Sources Can Give You Added Mineral Power

We have come a long and rewarding way. The effort has been worthwhile because you are discovering how magic minerals have the power to control your body health and mental health or personality. Now we approach the last fork in the road and head down the pathway to discover three treasures that can help give you the vibrant health and sparkle you have always wanted, as well as the personality that will make you stand out. These treasures can even determine your success in business and social life. An alert mind is the prime requisite for those who want to climb higher and higher. Let us now climb a little hill and seek out these three golden nuggets in the treasure chest.

Bone Meal Means Better Minerals

Bone meal is made from the bones of selected cattle, ground as fine as flour and sold in health stores or pharmacies in flour form or capsules. This valuable treasure is a nearly complete mineral supplement because of its content of nutritionally important trace elements (minerals) as well as calcium and phosphorus, which are present in suitable proportions. The importance of traces of copper, manganese, nickel and fluorine in bone meal is generally conceded.

Bone marrow helps the body make use of calcium, too. Remember that calcium must have Vitamin D for utilization which means you should take fish and vegetable oils. Cod liver oil is an excellent source of Vitamin D and unsaturated fatty acids which combine with the calcium in bone meal and aid in overall body assimilation.

Miracle Magic of Bone Meal

Elizabeth M. Martin, M. D., writing in the *Canadian Medical Association Journal* tells of some dramatic results obtained by the clinical in-hospital use of bone meal.

The first was a 6-year old son of a hospital nurse. He had a cleft palate and hare lip, both of which were repaired before the age of two years. However, he still had grave defects in dentition. He was underweight and undernourished.

> He complained bitterly of pains in his legs — the so-called growing pains of children. He was given a brand of dicalcium phosphate with Vitamin D in 10-grain doses twice a day with some improvement in his symptoms but no weight gain. Also he had much restlessness with night terrors. We supposed from this that he was getting very little absorption of the calcium which he took.
>
> It occurred to us that if we gave bone meal to calves and young pigs and puppies to promote proper growth, why should not Nature's own combination of bone minerals be completely utilized by any animal body? Accordingly, we sifted and pulverized the available bone meal and filled 10-grain capsules by hand. In one week the chid was playing as hard as any of his schoolmates. He was getting three 10-grain capsules daily. He began to grow and gain weight, until he caught up to the normal average for his age. His teeth were very slow to appear, it being about a year before his central incisors came through, but they were sound when they did arrive.

Dr. Martin feels that when any child complains of "growing pains" or of kicking or screaming, it is a signal of a mineral deficiency. Dr. Martin treated 113 such youngsters with calcium. Symptoms eased. "Just as a matter of curiosity, when they were changed to bone meal, all symptoms disappeared." Apparently, minerals in bone meal are more influential than in calcium, alone.

Ease Pregnancy Problems

Dr. Martin treated a group of pregnant women who had cavities and dental problems while carrying their children. She gave them bone meal capsules (10 grain potency, three times a day) and in a short time, the pregnant women showed *no* dental problems.

Each one of these women also received Vitamins A and D; 7,500 units of A and 750 of D daily to ensure proper mineral metabolism. None of the women had aching legs or cramps in the legs at night nor cramps in the legs on delivery. All of the babies were healthy at birth, but those whose mothers had been given bone meal had such long silky hair and such long nails that the phenomenon was remarked upon by the nurses." Dr. Martin says that, "We use bone meal in place of any other form of calcium for all evidences of calcium deficiency in our patients, including muscular pains and cramps in the legs in both sedentary workers and laborers. All of these symptoms clear up promptly on 10 to 15 grains of bone meal daily.

Bone meal an ancient remedy

Bone meal is an ancient remedy. It is said that the Indians would cut bones, boil them and drink the liquid. Oliver LaFarge, the Indian expert, also wrote that beef bone was boiled in water together with corn with the result that much calcium was transferred to the corn and then eaten. In the Orient, bones of small fish are eaten regularly and the calcium is easily digested. Both fish-eating Indians and Eskimos eat the softened bones. The enviable health and stamina of these people serves as the best example. In ancient Tibet, the most cherished treasure received by a new mother was a little bag of powdered bone that would replace in the body of the mother the calcium and other minerals that had been depleted by the child's birth.

You need not go to all the effort of boiling bones; just ask at any health store or pharmacy for bone meal tablets. Bone meal flour is good for baking wherever flour is needed. Or, mix five heaping tablespoons of bonemeal with tomato juice and drink as a morning stimulater. Bone meal is not a medicine. *It is a food!* A treasure of a food!

Kelp: Treasure from the Sea

Peer into this treasure chest. As you open the lid and look down deep, you hear the roar of the ocean, the pound of the foaming surf, the scent of the fresh salt water. Nature abounds. What else do you see? A sparkling powder that is as precious as gold dust, except this powder has an even greater value than money. This treasure of kelp can be eaten and built into your mind and body to give you the superior personality and vigorous health that you are seeking.

Kelp is a form of powdered or dehydrated seaweed. It is a powerhouse of minerals, containing iodine, calcium, phosphorus, iron, copper, potassium, magnesium, sodium, manganese, sulphur. Kelp has close to two dozen of these precious minerals.

According to the Chinese *Book of Poetry,* written during the era of Confucius (551-478 B. C.), a housewife cooks and eats seaweed, thereby enjoying exotic beauty and munificent health. The Orient has always eaten seaweed; even today, it is part of the staple diet. In Japan, seaweed is part of the daily diet. They use brown seaweeds in flour form for making noodles, cakes, breads, etc. The ancients so prized seaweed for its health-giving treasures that they would offer this delicacy to the gods as a sacrificial food.

How kelp is made

Special boats go out into the ocean and harvest seaweed from the deep with a great hook. This hook pulls the plant up out of the sea and special cutters mow off the tops of the kelp plants which are then carried back to land to be put in a processing plant. Here, kelp is chopped fine, dried, sterilized and shredded. This means that there is no boiling, no draining of water. All the minerals placed in kelp by the depths of the ocean are still in the powder that you use. Kelp plants, themselves, are so healthy that when they are cut to a depth of four feet, they can again grow and reach the surface within 48 to 60 hours. Minerals work this magic.

Other values of kelp

These sea plants have rich sources of carbohydrates, proteins, unsaturated fatty acids, Vitamins A, B, and C. The sea water, a veritable treasure trove of minerals, soaks the kelp plant, drenches it with these precious substances, making it a true mineral treasure.

Dr. W. A. P. Black in the *Proceedings of the Nutrition Society* (Vol. 12, p. 32) tells us: "It can be said that seaweed contains all the elements that have so far been shown to play an important part in the physiological processes of man. In a balanced diet, therefore they would appear to be an excellent mineral supplement."

Iodine that is needed by the glands for personality-plus, is also found in rich supply in kelp. About 100 micrograms of iodine is generally a minimum necessity. Iodine from food not of the sea requires you to eat ten pounds of fresh fruits or vegetables, six pounds of meat, freshwater fish, fowl or two pounds of eggs, etc. Kelp contains about 200,000 micrograms per kilogram (about two pounds) and the dried kelp meal nearly ten times as much, or .1 per cent to .2 per cent iodine. Used as a condiment this would provide ten times as much iodine as American iodized salt.

Use kelp for seasoning. Some health stores sell seaweed in dried form to be munched on as a delicacy. Chop this dried seaweed and add to salads, chowder, soups, etc. But, make kelp part of your diet.

Desiccated Liver for Dynamic Vitality

Do you want to experience a great internal revolution? You can completely change your body and your mind until you are throbbing with youthful vitality. The mineral treasure is that of desiccated liver — made from fresh, animal livers, dried at temperatures that will not affect mineral properties, with external fat and connective tissues removed. This fat is a highly concentrated source of precious minerals.

Minerals in desiccated liver

Precious minerals include iron, needed for a healthy blood stream; copper, too, which utilizes iron and aids in its storage. Zinc is found in this miracle food. You know that zinc is needed to help food become absorbed from the digestive tract. Calcium and phosphorus for skin and bone health are also abundant in liver.

Other nutrients

Desiccated liver contains three times the Vitamin A content of other foods. This vitamin is needed to keep eyes, skin and teeth in good condition. Desiccated liver also has Vitamin D which promotes calcium assimilation and builds strong bones. Other valuable nutrients include amino acids, B-12 and the B-complex vitamins in varying potencies. Do remember that fat and fibrous materials are removed before liver is vacuum-processed into capsules or powder.

How to take liver

At any health store, obtain brewer's yeast, rice bran extract and desiccated liver capsules. Daily, take three teaspoonfuls of brewer's yeast flakes, three teaspoonfuls of rice bran extract and six desiccated liver capsules. Wash down with a glass of carrot juice for a powerhouse of assimilation.

Mineral tonic

Into a glass of freshly squeezed cabbage juice, place four heaping tablespoon of desiccated liver powder or granules. Add a pinch of kelp. Add three tablespoons of beet juice. Mix in a blender or stir vigorously. Drink this mineral tonic every morning, at noon and about two hours before dinnertime to help perk up appetite and stimulate flow of enzymatic fluids to aid in digestion.

Sleepy-time mineral tonic

Mix together these foods: one-half glass of mineral-rich spring water, one-half glass celery juice, four tablespoons bone meal powder, four tablespoons desiccated liver extract, pinch of kelp. Drink this relaxing mineral nightcap about two hours before bedtime. The minerals will have time to go swimming throughout your bloodstream, stimulating the flow of lactic acid that is conducive to sleep.

You have already discovered part of the treasure. The major portion is in store for you. Before we continue on the last lap of our journey, let us pause and reflect upon our possessions.

CAPSULES OF TREASURES AS DISCOVERED IN CHAPTER TWENTY

1. Bone meal in capsule, powder or flour form, is rich in precious minerals. It can tighten teeth, improve gum and mouth health, ease growing pains in youngsters, strengthen pregnant women.

2. As a food, take at least six tablets of bone meal daily. Use bone meal flour in recipes calling for any flour.

3. Kelp is a rich source of sea minerals, used since the days of Confucius. Its prime iodine content can influence your glandular system to help build a dynamic personality.

4. Use kelp powder in place of salt. Kelp is available in seaweed form, to be eaten as a delicacy or chopped with salads, chowders, soups, etc. Take at least six kelp tablets daily.

5. Desiccated liver has mineral properties to fill you with youthful vitality and energy. Take desiccated liver capsules with Brewer's yeast and rice bran extract. Your health store sells these foods.

6. Try the mineral tonic for overall mineral invigoration; try the sleepy-time tonic for a night of wonderful, relaxing sleep.

TWENTY-ONE

Mineral Healing Methods for Home Use

And so, we have come to the actual treasure. Open the chest. Behold the glorious gems of health; the marvelous trinkets of superior mentality; the wondrous mineral nuggets of vitality. See the diamonds of dynamic personality. These are all yours for the taking. You have come a long way. If you have maintained optimism, if you have remained steadfast in your determination to discover the true secrets of magic minerals that will give you a new wealth and a new personality, you richly deserve this great treasure. Now, let us see how Nature, which placed this treasure in its hiding place, can help reward you. Surely, there can be no greater reward than that of mental and physical happiness. Here are some of the different types of jewel-like nuggets.

SCRATCHES AND WOUNDS
If you have small cuts on your skin, rinse first with a liquified whey lotion. Cover with soft curd or fresh cottage cheese and let remain for three hours. For a deeper cut, soak wheat kernels or bran with soya milk and mix into a paste. Apply to the cut and let remain for two days or until fully healed.

TIRED, INFLAMED EYES
After long sunshine or otherwise bright exposure (or after prolonged reading or TV watching), here is how to relieve tired

eyes. Beat the white of an egg until slightly fluffy. Soak gauze in mixture and apply to the eyes. Repeat this poultice for a few hours. Relief is amazingly powerful.

SNIFFLES AND WINTER COLDS

When you first experience sneezing, coughing, sniffles follow this home health healing remedy. Immerse a slice of a fresh raw onion in a cup of boiled water for only five seconds! Remove onion. Now, sip this water slowly, a few spoonfuls every 30 minutes. This relieves throat ailments. For a congested, stuffed nose, slice an onion in half and sniff. The volatile oils and minerals will permeate and clear the stuffed condition.

ACHING FEET AND LEGS

Boil six small potatoes in a kettle of water. When done, remove potatoes. When water is tolerably hot, immerse your feet for just 15 minutes. Now remove, wrap your feet in cloths or bandages which have been sprinkled with hot kelp or sea salt. The minerals in kelp will seep through the pores of your feet and legs, easing the muscular ache.

CHEST PAINS

Chew dried raisins and currants all day as they are rich in iron. Boil the woody, interior dividing walls of walnuts in a pan for ten minutes. Drink this tea and discover how it acts like Nature's balm for chest pains.

HEARTBURN

Grate, finely, one raw potato. Fold pulp into a cheesecloth. Squeeze out all raw potato juice. Add one glass of slightly boiled spring water. Drink when you begin to experience this burning sensation.

GASTRIC ULCER CONDITIONS

Before each of your three daily meals (or as many as you eat) drink one glass of freshly squeezed raw cabbage juice. *After* each of your daily meals, drink one glass of freshly squeezed raw potato juice. Minerals in these vegetables exert a beneficial influence on stomach disorders.

POOR LIVER FUNCTION

Radishes are prime mineral sources. But use them sparingly in this manner: daily, drink no more than two tablespoons of raw radish juice. Combine with freshly squeezed carrot juice for better assimilation.

GALL BLADDER PAINS

Try this compress: soak cheese cloth in cold soya milk and apply to region of the gall bladder — a pear-shaped pouch on the undersurface of the liver in the right upper part of the stomach. Renew compress every 45 minutes since the influence is lowered when it becomes too warm.

STOMACH UPSETS

Make a poultice by soaking cloth into a cup of diced, pulpy onion. Or, wrap the same pulpy onion in a cloth. Press upon the part of your stomach where pain is severe and let remain for 15 minutes. Renew poultices until pain is gone.

CONSTIPATION PROBLEMS

Soak six prunes in boiled water for 30 minutes. Remove prunes and drink water when you awaken. Another remedy is to mash together equal amounts of figs and raisins into a paste. Stir into a glass of apple juice and drink before breakfast.

DIARRHEA

Eat raw oatflakes and nothing else for a full day. If you are thirsty, drink lime juice with water.

HEADACHES

Make a poultice of a pulped onion or horseradish (or combination of both) and apply to the back of your neck, your calves and soles of your feet. Slowly, the pain should ease. Renew regularly. Here's another treasure: rub a menthol stick across your forehead a few times when you feel a headache coming on. Ask a pharmacist for pure imported natural crystalline menthol. It is highly aromatic and soothing.

NEURALGIA OR FACIAL PAINS

Soak a cloth in boiled alfalfa and apply to the affected portions. Alfalfa seeds are sold at most health stores or large food outlets. Just boil the seeds and use the water for soaking the cloth as a compress.

SKIN IRRITATIONS

Apply slices of raw potato to the portion of the skin that irritates you or has acne or other ailments. You might also make the potato into a pulp and use as a poultice.

ARTHRITIS-RHEUMATISM

Before breakfast, each morning, drink half a glass of raw potato juice. You may add half a glass of tepid spring water.

Throughout the day, drink the water in which potatoes have been boiled. For especially painful joints, make a poultice of pulped cabbage, sauerkraut and raw carrots. Eat daily. This is a rich source of valuable minerals, and calcium especially.

CALCIUM DEFICIENCY

This leads to porous bones, brittle skelton that becomes easily injured during minor bumpings, bruises. You can obtain calcium tablets and bone meal tablets at most health stores or pharmacies. Here is a natural remedy: grate together red and white cabbage, sauerkraut and raw carrots. Eat daily. This is a rich source of valuable minerals, and calcium especially.

ANGINA PECTORIS

This refers to any repeated, suffocating chest or breast pain. The famed Father Sebastian Kneipp, who in 1886 wrote *My Water Cure,* brought relief to many of his followers of such chest pains by this natural method. Bath the arms in hot water as this helps draw away excess blood from the heart. If you add a full glass of lemon juice to this water, it imparts a remarkable relief. An older health healer is to boil ordinary apple cider vinegar. Soak towels into this substance, then put on both arms as poultices. This heat, together with the mineral acids of the apple cider, helps to improve heart circulation, aids the nervous system and brings relief for heart pain.

INSOMNIA

Mix together equal portions of lemon juice, oat juice (boil whole grain oats and strain out the juice) and six tablespoons of raw honey. Drink three hours before hitting the pillow for refreshing sleep.

JAUNDICE

Drink one quart of fresh carrot juice daily. Jaundice is believed to be caused by a congestion and infectious blockage of the gall bladder duct. You should apply a compress of cabbage leaves to the gall bladder. Another tip is to include artichokes, radishes and chicory in your daily salad.

SALLOW OR "AGED" SKIN

Apply whey directly to the skin. Whey is a natural fermented milk product. Its minerals stimulate skin circulation and help destroy infectious bacteria. Use whey (sold at health stores) in place of facial creams until youthfulness is restored.

GOUT

This is an arthritic infection traced to a mineral imbalance and high acid diet. To neutralize excess acidity, try raw potato juice. Add the same juice to soups, chowders, vegetable juices, sauces.

WEAK FEELING OR FATIGUE

Horses are strong. They eat lots of oats. Why not try to become as strong as a horse by following his eating patterns — to a certain extent, that is. Raw oats may be unpalatable. Mash oats, cover with boiled water for ten minutes. Strain. Sweeten liquid with raw brown sugar or honey, add a few raisins or seasonal berries and you have an anti-fatigue food. It's a powerhouse of instant energy. It is also believed that the juice from oats helps to soothe the inflamed mucous membranes of the intestinal and digestive systems in combination with certain minerals.

NERVOUS DISORDERS

Often, the back of the neck becomes "choked" by tension and minerals cannot flow to your brain and other body parts. To relieve, apply an onion compress to the back of your neck until you feel relieved. Incidentally, if you feel nervous and must walk and jitter, apply an onion slice to the calves of your legs and feel relief flow through your limbs.

SCIATIC PAINS

Sciatica is a form of neuralgia or neuritis affecting and causing pain along the course of the sciatic nerve (longest body nerve) which runs down the back of the thigh and into the leg. Tenderness is felt in the thigh and leg. Cold, damp water or pressure on the nerve only intensifies pain. Did you know that the ancients found relief with garlic milk? Here's how you can try it. Mash or crush several garlic cloves. Add to uncooked soya milk. Boil for five minutes. Drink one quart daily. Minerals in garlic and the soya milk form a chain reaction to each sciatic pains.

BRUISES, BLEMISHES

Mix grated fresh horseradish with sufficient alcohol to make a thick paste. Apply to affected parts as a tincture.

BRONCHIAL AND RESPIRATORY DISORDERS

Grate horseradish, add six tablespoons of raw brown sugar. Squeeze through strainer. Cook this residue with some water.

Sip slowly. This is potent so use it sparingly, yet regularly, particularly with mealtime vegetable salads.

COUGH PROBLEMS

Try radish juice. Grate organically grown radishes and sweeten with natural honey. Eat with a spoon in this pulpy form.

We have come to the summit of our journey in search of the secret treasure of minerals. We have found this treasure. We have been told, by Nature, how to use the various parts of the treasure to enjoy health, success and personality vitalism. The treasure is yours, but you must use it wisely. Live according to the ways of Nature. Stray not from her pathway. Remain upon the natural road that leads to the Golden Garden of Nature.

Here, where the secret treasure lies, is a scene suffused with the golden glow of health. It is a dream-like vision of meadows, calm water lapped in a green hollow, a lovely shore that is still and peaceful.

The dreamy azure blue of the skies, the dappled shade of fragrant woods, the sparkle of waves in the sun, all beckon the searcher of health. Come forth, claim your treasure, then emerge in good health.

Our long voyage of discovery is over and our ship has drooped her weary sails in port at last. Once more we take the route back home. It is evening; we climb the long slope up to the hills, from whence we came. We look back and see the sky ablaze with sunset, its golden glory resting like the aureole of a sailing bird, touching with a crest of fire the lid of the golden treasure chest of minerals.

The vision, once glimpsed, can never be forgotten but we turn from it and make our way along the mountain side, till we come to the outer limits. We now look down on the lake in its deep hollow, now fast disappearing in the evening shadows. The woods are still green, and as the sunset fades above them, there comes to us, borne on the swell of the fragrant wind, these parting words:

GOOD AFTERNOON TO SOME OF YOU,
GOOD EVENING TO MORE OF YOU,
GOOD HEALTH TO ALL OF YOU!

Your Mineral Cookbook

*The discovery of a new dish does more for human
happiness than the discovery of a new star.*
                                    Brillat-Savarin

TWENTY-TWO

Your Mineral Cookbook:
How to Preserve Minerals
in Cooking Foods

When purchasing foods, whether they be fruits, vegetables or
meats, select items that have been raised upon organically fertilized
soils. The richest minerals are found in soils that have been spared
chemical drenching and harsh, artificial sprays. Write to your State
Agricultural Commission and ask for names of farms selling
organically raised edibles. Many of these farms sell through the
mails. There may be outlets in your own locality. Ask any local
health store.

Three Ways to Preserve Minerals While Cooking Foods

1. *Avoid excessive heat* — High temperatures will reduce mineral supply. You should cook your foods but not overcook. This
means your foods should be tenderized by cooking.

2. *Use little or no water* — Some minerals dissolve in water. This
not only devitalizes the food but upsets its nutrient balance, making
it indigestible. Use a waterless cooker, explained below.

3. *Beware of oxidation* — Air is destructive to minerals. Use lids
that seal. Keep fruits and vegetables in closed storage regions, away
from sunshine and air exposure. Calcium, sulphur, iodine and iron
are some minerals which evaporate when exposed to air.

Waterless Cooking

A "must" for preserving minerals in foods that have to be cooked is the well-known waterless cooker. You can buy one at any housewares outlet. Minerals are saved with a waterless cooker because this method uses low heat. It tenderizes foods in a waterless semi-vacuum seal, preserving the natural mineral balance, retaining the delicious, delicate, natural flavors. Select a stainless steel cooker. A good one has a three ply metal. The center ply is the heat conductor which keeps the temperature *low* and makes it possible to cook *waterless*.

Most such cookware have a little valve on top which tells you when the heat is too high so you need not burn the food and avoid mineral loss. When foods are *tenderized* (not over-boiled) at a low temperature, the precious minerals are retained.

Ask for an electric all stainless steel skillet which you use to brown or cook in a small amount of oil; you can cover this skillet and cook without water, such as roasting. You can use it for stewing or simmering (to cook in a liquid just below the boiling point, maintained accurately by a controlled temperature.)

The all electric skillet may be used to cook by dry heat on range top or counter to bake muffins, breads, cakes, pies, small yeast buns. You also use the skillet for casserole dishes. To clean, just remove the termperature control. Immerse the skillet in hot water for easy cleaning.

Vegetable Cookery

Your vegetables should be eaten raw, wherever possible. There is no comparison for mineral power in a fresh raw salad from your garden or from one that is organically fertilized. If you must cook vegetables, here are some tips. When vegetables have to be stored prior to use, wash, dry and then store in a cool place. *Do not peel.* The minerals in most root vegetables are concentrated beneath the skin and discarded when you peel. Whenever possible, leave on the skin. You may peel when the vegetable skin is tough, bitter or too uneven to be completely cleaned.

To insure mineral power and flavor, cook vegetables for the shortest time necessary. This helps preserve the natural colors.

When a vegetable is cooked quickly, little natural plant acid is freed and the bright color is maintained. So is the mineral supply.

To boil vegetables, first preheat a kettle of water to the bubbly point. Drop in the vegetable and let boil until tender. Be careful not to overboil.

About Meats, Poultry, Fish

These foods have much iron, phosphorus, calcium as well as vitamins and certain proteins which combine with minerals to create internal absorption. Liver is well known for its dynamite-iron content. To preserve nutrients in meats, poultry, fish, cook at low temperatures. Soaking or cooking meat in liquids will cause depletion of minerals. A simple rule would be: *Cook in less time, cook in low heat, cook in little water.*

Addenda: Eat *raw* vegetables and fruits. Cook *only* if they *must* be cooked. Now, here are some choice mineral-rich recipes.

BEEF AND GREEN BEANS

½ pound lean, tender beef, sliced in strips	1 cup cut green beans
	1 medium green pepper, sliced
2 tablespoons sunflower seed oil	1 cup sliced celery
1 medium onion, diced	4 teaspoons bone meal flour
Pinch of sea salt	

Saute meat in hot sunflower seed oil in large skillet. Add onion, green beans, green pepper, celery. Cook for 5 minutes. Combine remaining ingredients, stir to mix thoroughly. Cook until beef is tender. Garnish with parsley and serve with hot oven rolls.

EGGPLANT-VEAL CASSEROLE

1 pound veal scallops	1 cup cubed tomatoes
2 tablespoons corn oil	½ cup diced green peppers
1 eggplant, sliced and peeled	Half teaspoon sea salt
1 cup diced onions	1 tablespoon desiccated liver

Trim off any visible fat. Heat some corn oil in skillet, then brown the meat on both sides. Place oil in a casserole. Arrange successive eggplant layers with veal, onions, tomatoes and green peppers. Season with sea salt and desiccated liver. Sprinkle with remaining corn oil. Cover casserole and bake for 75 minutes in a 350°F. oven. Remove cover during last 15 minutes.

VEGETABLE CUTLETS

2 tablespoons minced onion	¾ cup soya milk
2 tablespoons peanut oil	2 cups diced cooked vegetables
6 tablespoons bone meal flour	1 cup chopped, cooked macaroni
Pinch of kelp	

Cook onion in peanut oil until tender. Blend in bone meal flour and kelp. Gradually stir in soya milk. Boil 1 minute, stirring vigorously. Add diced cooked vegetables and the macaroni. Pour into shallow, oiled pan. Chill until firm. Cut into oblongs, 2 inches wide and 3 inches long. Roll in a cup of brewer's yeast flakes. Dip in some soya milk. Roll again in remaining yeast flakes. Saute in cooking oil for 10 minutes or until brown on both sides. Suggested vegetables to make cutlets include green beans, peas, carrots, potatoes, corn, etc.

AGAR AGAR

This is a wonderful mineral food, derived from seaweed. It is just about starch and protein free. It is a pure vegetable gelatin. When boiled, it dissolves. When cooled, it solidifies. It can be used just like gelatin in making desserts. To prepare for use, soak agar agar in hot, but not boiling water for 35 minutes, using about one quart of water for each tablespoon of the gelatin, a powerful mineral source because it is made from seaweed. Obtainable at health stores and many pharmacies.

BROWN RICE AND NUT LOAF

3 cups steamed brown rice	3 tablespoons raw nut butter
½ cup ground nut meats	4 tablespoons desiccated liver
2 teaspoons sea salt	1 tablespoon sunflower seed meal

Mix all the above ingredients until in a mold. Shape in a loaf and bake in an oiled loaf pan for 35 minutes in a 350°F. oven.

GARDEN CHICKEN

1 cup sliced celery with leaves	1 cup diced carrots and peas
2 tablespoons safflower seed oil	2 tablespoons bone meal flour
2 cups cooked diced chicken	Kelp seasoning

Cook celery in safflower seed oil for 2 minutes. Add chicken and brown slightly. Add peas and carrots and one half cup water. Cover and cook over low heat for 10 minutes. Now add remaining ingredients, stir and cook until thickened.

RICH MINERAL BROTH

The minerals in vegetable peelings should be put to use. Wash the peelings, stems and coarse outer leaves. Save in a plastic bag or jar in the refrigerator until a large amount is accumulated. Cut into small pieces. Put in large kettle. Cover with boiling water. Simmer gently for 45 minutes to draw out valuable juices. When vegetables are tender, drain. Season this liquid with kelp, a tablespoon of desiccated liver. If you prefer, add a little tomato juice or lemon juice for a zippy flavor. This is a prime source of minerals.

STUFFED SQUASH

6 medium-sized summer squashes	½ cup cottage cheese
2 cups brewer's yeast flakes	¼ cup chopped parsley
1 cup whole grain bread crumbs	2 beaten eggs
Pinch of sea salt	

Wash squashes, slice off edges. *Do not peel*. Steam until done. Halve lengthwise, remove center pulp with a spoon. Combine this pulp with all other ingredients. Fold lightly together. Fill squash shells and dot with cooking oil. Bake in an oiled shallow pan in a moderate oven for 25 minutes.

BAKED FISH O' THE SEA

2 tablespoons corn oil	¾ cup sliced celery
4 fillets of sole or flounder (about 1 pound)	2 teaspoons bone meal flour
¾ cup diced onions	¾ cup soya milk
	Pinch of kelp

Heat some oil in a baking dish. Place fillets inside. Bake in moderate oven for 10 minutes. Meanwhile, mix together all other ingredients in a kettle, except the soya milk. This is added slowly. Stir while doing so until boiling point is reached. Pour this over the fish after the aforementioned 10 minute cooking time has elapsed. Now bake for 20 more minutes or until fish is easily flaked.

WHOLE WHEAT BREAD

½ cup lukewarm water
1 yeast cake or package of dry yeast
2 cups lukewarm water
3 tablespoons buckwheat honey
1 cup soya flour
3 tablespoons vegetable shortening
½ cup bone meal flour
4 tablespoons brewer's yeast flakes
6 cups whole wheat bread flour

Add yeast to half cup lukewarm water. In large bowl, dissolve buckwheat honey in 2 cups warm water. Add softened yeast, 1 cup soya flour, 6 cups whole wheat bread flour. Stir smooth. Let this soft sponge rise until bubbly. Add remaining items, stir until dough is medium-stiff. Turn out on floured board. Knead until dough is smooth and elastic, adding flour as required, about 5 minutes. Place dough in a bowl that is warm, slightly oiled. Cover with damp cloth. Set to rise in a warm, draft-free place, until double in bulk. Knead down and let rise again, or put immediately into the pans. Preheat over to 400°F. Bake at this temperature for 10 minutes. Lower heat to 350°F. and finish baking, at least 50 minutes more. This is a powerful mineral bread and should be your staff of life.

NUT CROQUETTES

1 egg
1 cup soya milk
1 cup ground nut meats
1 cup bone meal flour
Pinch of sea salt

Add eggs to milk and beat slightly with a fork. Heat until slightly thickened. Now add dry ingredients. Mix well. Cool. Shape into croquettes. Brown over low fire in slightly oiled skillet. Serve with raw vegetable salad.

SKILLET MEAT LOAF

1½ pounds ground beef round
1 cup sunflower seed meal
1 cup diced celery
1 small diced onion

1½ teaspoons kelp
1 egg
1 cup tomato puree

½ cup tomato juice
2 tablespoons sunflower seed oil
Chopped watercress

Combine beef, sunflower seed meal, celery, onion, kelp, egg and the 1 cup tomato puree. Heat oil in medium sized skillet, tilt to coat the sides. Press meat mixture into skillet. Cover tightly and cook above *low* heat for 35 minutes until meat is cooked. Drain juices into a saucepan. Add half-cup of tomato juice. Turn meat loaf in platter. Cover with sauce. Garnish with watercress.

VEGETABLE-SHRIMP DISH

1 pound cleaned raw shrimp
1 large eggplant, peeled and
   cubed
1 medium sized onion, diced
1 minced garlic clove

¼ cup water
¼ cup minced watercress
Dash of kelp
4 slices dry whole wheat bread,
   cubed

Cook shrimp over medium heat in oiled skillet for just 2 minutes. Remove from stove. Add eggplant, onion and garlic. Cook until tender. Add all remaining ingredients except bread. Cover and simmer 15 minutes. Now add bread cubes. Cook (uncovered) for 5 minutes.

CREAMED EGGS WITH PEAS

3 tablespoons vegetable oil
1 tablespoon minced onion
½ cup mushrooms
3 tablespoons bone meal flour

2 cups soya milk
Pinch of kelp
1 tablespoon chopped pimiento
½ cup cooked peas

6 hard-boiled eggs

Put vegetable oil in top of double boiler over direct heat. Add onion and mushrooms and let simmer over low fire. Do not brown. Sprinkle bone meal flour and stir gently until blended. Add milk and blend together. Boil until cooked. Add kelp. Carefully fold in chopped pimiento, peas and sliced eggs. (Cut eggs once lengthwise, then slice.) Heat and serve in small cups.

LENTIL BURGERS

1 cup cooked lentils
3 eggs

2 cups dry bread soaked in
   mineral or spring water

¼ teaspoon celery salt

Mix well, form into burgers and saute in hot oil until crisp and brown. Serve with raw garden salad.

SOUR CREAM CAKE

4 eggs, separated
1 teaspoon lemon juice
1½ cups honey

1 cup thick sour cream
¼ teaspoon kelp
3 cups bone meal flour

Beat egg yolks until thick and lemon-colored. Add honey to cream and beat with an egg beater. Now fold in yolks and kelp, beat until fluffy light. Add bone meal flour a little at a time and fold in. Lastly, add the stiffly beaten whites. You may add raisins, nuts or other fruit if desired. Bake as a loaf at 350°F. for 40 minutes

OLIVE AND NUT SANDWICH

½ cup chopped walnuts
½ cup chopped almonds

¼ cup sunflower seed meal
½ cup chopped olives

Mix together with brewer's yeast flakes and desiccated liver granules, until a creamy consistency. Add some soya milk to make a bit more creamy. Spread on whole wheat or soya bread slices for sandwiches. Fill with slices of tomato and cucumber, if desired.

BROILED LIVER SUPREME

1 pound beef or calf's liver
2 tablespoons sunflower seed oil

1 teaspoon kelp
2 teaspoons desiccated liver powder

Slice liver about ¼ inch thick. Heat broiler. Brush broiling pan with some sunflower seed oil. Place liver on pan. Pour remaining oil over it. Broil about 5 inches from heat, about 2 minutes on each side for rare; 3 minutes for medium and 4 minutes for well done. Transfer to serving plate. Sprinkle with kelp and desiccated liver powder.

SUNSHINE CHOPS

1 cup ground sunflower seeds
¼ cup grated raw carrots
¼ cup diced celery
2 tablespoons diced chives

1 tablespoon soya oil
Pinch of kelp
1 tablespoon desiccated liver powder

½ cup tomato juice

Combine all ingredients with enough tomato juice so that chops hold a good formed shape. Put in shallow baking dish. Bake at about 325°F. until browned. Turn and brown on other side. You may broil these chops if you coat with soya or any vegetable oil.

UNCOOKED MINERAL COOKIES

3 cups mashed banana pulp
2 cups coconut meal
Slice of honey comb

1 cup nuts, sesame seeds, sunflower seeds
1 tablespoon bone meal powder

Shape into little patties and roll in ground sunflower seeds. Insert a raisin or fresh date in center of each cookie. Keep in a refrigerator until used up.

CABBAGE AND APPLE SALAD

Select tart apples. Do not skin. Dice the apples and combine with equal amounts of finely shredded raw cabbage. Mix with combined lemon juice and apple cider vinegar. Serve with lettuce.

HEALTH, FITNESS, and MEDICINE BOOKS
